Syncrude

Fostering Knowledge and Preservation

This book has been placed in the library of every school in Alberta by Syncrude Canada Ltd. in partnership with the Alberta Sport, Recreation, Parks & Wildlife Foundation. Buffalo, or bison, have a long and fascinating history in Alberta, and Syncrude is proud to play a role in furthering knowledge about the species amongst students. We dedicate this book to the many people who are helping preserve these magnificent beasts.

BUFFALO
SACRED & SACRIFICED

BUFFALO

SACRED & SACRIFICED

Grant
MacEwan

3

Buffalo – Sacred and Sacrificed

Published by Alberta Sport, Recreation, Parks & Wildlife Foundation ©1995

Printed in Canada

First Edition 1995

Alberta Sport, Recreation, Parks & Wildlife Foundation
Edmonton, Alberta

Printer
DW Friesen

Design
Studio 3 Graphics

Editor
Donna von Hauff

MacEwan, Grant, 1902-
    Buffalo: sacred and sacrificed

Includes bibliographical references.
ISBN 0-9699355-0-1

    1. American bison – History. I. Alberta Sport, Recreation, Parks and Wildlife Foundation.
II. Title

QL737.U53M255 1995   599.73'58   C95-900458-0

To Norm Gorman of Winnipeg,

Whose lifelong interest in the history of the Canadian bison and readiness to share the fruits of his research helped writers and students everywhere, this treatise is respectfully dedicated. — Grant MacEwan

Contents

Olson '94

Introduction

Canadian experience with the bison — or buffalo as most people will continue to call the species — is not a pleasant story. There is no glory in mass slaughter, regardless of the circumstances. That the conscienceless buffalo destruction of the 19th century was conducted by civilized humans against a race of the Creator's non-human children, does nothing to lessen the shame.

There was a modest but honest effort to save the race but, as if plagued by a demonic curse, almost everything attempted went wrong. Nevertheless, the fortune and misfortunes, merciless though they were at times, should be remembered as an important chapter in the histories of both Canada and the United States, with lessons for both.

That I did not give the buffalo story a higher priority and start writing it years earlier has nagged me almost as much as if I had been one of the buffalo hunters with a fast horse and a short gun in the '70s of last century — eager for the cash return of a dollar for every green hide delivered to the I.G. Baker Co. at Fort Macleod or Benton.

I have had buffalo files for much of my life and was fortunate in knowing some of the leading personalities in the buffalo story, among them Norman Luxton. It was a privilege to hear, firsthand, his accounts of the arrangements for the purchase by the Government of Canada of the only remaining big herd of privately owned bison in the world. Mr. Luxton's enthusiasm won the support of Hon. Frank Oliver who was Minister of the Interior in Sir Wilfrid Laurier's government at the time. The result was Canada's purchase of the big Michel Pablo herd of more than 700 head — nobody knew exactly how many — running on the Flathead Indian Reserve in Montana.

It was captivating to know J.A. "Dad" Gaff who had been a professional hide hunter in Kansas before coming to Canada to ranch on the south slope of the Cypress Hills, and E.J. "Bud" Cotton who was the cowboy foreman or "buffaloboy" foreman and warden on the big Wainwright Buffalo Park before its takeover for military purposes during World War II. But nothing gives me more satisfaction than to acknowledge the dedicated efforts of the late Norm Gorman of Winnipeg. I can only repeat my gratitude for the correspondence and buffalo notes that passed between us.

Norm Gorman was an eager researcher who concentrated on the buffalo transactions conducted by James McKay, Col. Sam Bedson of Stony Mountain, north of Winnipeg, Lord Strathcona of Silver Heights on Winnipeg's west side, Charles Alloway, the one-time partner of McKay, C.J. "Buffalo" Jones of Kansas and Charles Allard, friend and partner of Michel Pablo, all anxious to help in saving the buffalo race then teetering on the edge of oblivion.

After making many contributions to my files, Mr. Gorman wrote (Sept. 23, 1983) to report that he had completed his bibliography and was not going to put it in book form and publish it. He suggested that I do it. At that point I was thinking seriously about undertaking the assignment but not ready to begin. By the time my writing plans were drawn, I learned that Norm Gorman — the man who never stopped searching for newspaper items of history — had passed on. I'm glad that I can still say "Thanks."

And to my friends in libraries and archives — especially those at the Glenbow — I repeat: "Thanks for your patience. Thanks for all that you do even beyond the call of duty."

The preparation of this manuscript came as a labour of duty and love, and the task was not complete without doubt and disagreement. There was also a prolonged spell of rain making it difficult to be optimistic but, suddenly like a prayer, a rainbow appeared and I was surrounded by old and new friends who had a recipe for action. I met members of the Alberta Sport, Recreation, Parks and Wildlife Foundation including Hiske Gerding and, thereafter, things fell into place with speed and precision.

I salute this Foundation and Syncrude Canada Ltd. which gives great support to worthy outdoor causes, Alberta Treasury Branches, the Federation of Alberta Naturalists, Edmonton's YMCA, wildlife handymen Gordon Kerr, Ron Pauls and Hal Reynolds, Wes Olson and Johane Janelle for their illustrations, Rollie LaMarche, D'Arcy Levesque, Ted Hart, Wei Yew, Marilyn Cooke, Cheryl Hunt and Rudy Andersson. To each I owe a debt of thanks.

In winning praises nobody could surpass Hiske Gerding, mentioned previously, Dorothy Gray, a valued friend, and Donna von Hauff, whose editorial touch is gaining fame. I assure them all of my gratitude. — *Grant MacEwan*

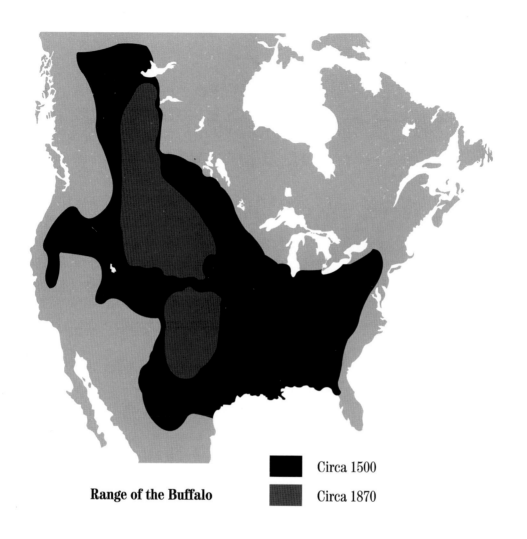

Range of the Buffalo

■	Circa 1500
▨	Circa 1870

"More than the horse to the Arab, the camel to the pilgrim in the desert, the reindeer to the Laplander, the seal to the Eskimo, or the elephant to the Hindoo, was the buffalo to the trans-Mississippi Indian. History affords no other example of where a single product of nature, whether animal or vegetable, has filled so large a place in the life of a people. The self-sustenance of the tribes of the plains would have been impossible without it, and when the buffalo disappeared these tribes fell back upon the government in hopeless dependence for the very necessities of existence."

Hiram Martin Crittenden

Chapter 1

Meet The Patriarch Of The Plains

Buffalo bulls at Banff National Park *(Whyte Museum of the Canadian Rockies)*

The aging bison bull, undisputed boss in the national park herd at Banff, stood broadside to the beams of evening light as the sun eased ever closer to the mountain horizon. He looked like the perfect buffalo model waiting for a sculptor. Every long guard hair on his powerful neck and shoulders glistened like shivers of silver while the massive brute remained perfectly motionless except for the clock-like rhythm of jaws serving the ruminant pastime of remasticating previously ingested fodder — in other words, "chewing his cud."

He had the best of claims to recognition, members of his family were North American residents for an estimated 10,000 years or more. The buffalo grazing ground extended, at one time, to fully half of the continent. It reached from the Appalachian Highlands in the east to the Rocky Mountains in the west and from northern Mexico in the south to Great Slave Lake in the Canadian north. The favoured grass was between the Mississippi River and the Rockies in the United States and between the Red River and the mountains on the Canadian side. To Canadians, the prairie bison was as distinctively western as cowboys, gophers and frozen wheat.

"Bison" may be the more correct name, but by popular usage the word "buffalo" has gained general acceptability. William T. Hornaday, a leading American authority, recognized the public preference for the word "buffalo" and the practical difficulties in changing it. He stated, "A true buffalo is an animal with no hump on its shoulders and is found only in Africa and Asia. Our animal, having a high hump, is really a bison. But inasmuch as it is known to 95 million Americans as the buffalo, it would be quite useless to attempt to bring about a universal change in the popular name." Canadians agreed with Hornaday but reserved the right to use either or both names for the big mammals.

There is only one species of the North American buffalo but there are two subspecies. The better known prairie bison or *Bison bison bison* is clearly the most valuable member of the entire wildlife family in its time, and the most abused. Its cousin, the slightly bigger wood buffalo or *Bison bison athabascae*, is most at home on the valley lands of northern rivers, mainly the Peace, Athabasca and Slave.

The old Banff park bull that seemed ready to speak or act for his race, wore a perpetual expression of defiance and unfriendliness. And if he didn't like humans, he probably had ample reasons. Park attendants said he had killed a few young bulls in his time but "never a human." They took care to add: "We never take needless chances with him or any of the mature animals. We advise all visitors to keep back from the fences. He's still a wild animal and will never accept domestication. Like all buffalo, he can be a ferocious fighter and there are no wild animals of other kinds in this country that could stand up against him. Look him over. He's built for battle — like a war tank."

Over aeons of time, this old bull's forbearers likely shared fresh meadows following the last ice age with some strange critters. The dinosaurs, we can presume, disappeared long before the first buffalo appeared. But the latter is thought to have overlapped with the huge mastodons, standing nine- or ten-feet high with tusks five-feet in length and the mammoths with 12-foot shoulders with 15-foot curved tusks. The same early buffalo would encounter native horses and camels and the ferocious sabre-tooth tigers that killed their prey by stabbing them to death with their long canine teeth. The early buffalo, however, survived and gained a dominance in both numbers and impact.

The native people, though, who relied so completely upon them for food and other essentials, killed extravagantly and often with cruelty. They clung to their convictions that the bison herds belonged exclusively to them — a gift from the Great Spirit.

Buffalo skull amid cacti and prairie grasses *(Ashdown Johnson/MacEwan Collection)*

As some western tribesmen explained it, the first buffalo herd, under the guidance of their Great Spirit or Manitou, emerged from the sea. It was a handy theory that eased the necessity of feuding about other concepts like the Genesis account of Creation and the Darwinian theory of evolution. But palaeontologists had their own ideas about the events which brought the buffalo to the North American grasslands. The migration that began in southeastern Asia — where the oldest bison bones have been found and ended on the North American prairies thousands of years and half a world away — is enough to enliven the most weary imagination.

In its ancient development, the bison was a child of the Pleistocene or Ice Age. It and the musk ox, having survived this time period, clung tenaciously to their "fur coats" which offered the best of protection against the unrelenting winter conditions. A horse or cow — caught in a blizzard without shelter — turns away from the driving gale and drifts aimlessly and dangerously. The buffalo, though, turns its storm-proof front-end to the weather to get maximum protection from its built-in shelter.

Climatic changes determined the buffalo's destiny to a large extent. We know that even a small drop in average temperature led to an accumulation of glacial ice, and that much of the northern hemisphere and nearly all of Canada was glaciated during the Ice Age. Researchers speculate that ice over the present site of Edmonton was as much as two- or three-miles deep, and in the region of today's Hudson Bay, as much as five miles. Scientists also postulate that this five miles of ice and its colossal weight may explain the depression in the earth's crust that became Hudson Bay — the Great Bay of the North.

It was inevitable in the bison story that the relatively narrow separation between Asia's Siberia and North America's Alaska would become the beast's bridge to their presence today. The enormous accumulation of ice over the land, the depletion of water from the oceans, and the exposure of ocean floors wherever the oceans were normally shallow, as over the Bering Strait, resulted in a land bridge. Man and beast walked to new surroundings, opportunities and dangers.

Even today, the Pacific Ocean water separating the two continents is less than 60-miles across and, with numerous small islands in the Aleutian chain, native people with kayaks or other small boats embarked upon many a crossing. With so much water becoming frozen in the Ice Age glaciers, this land bridge simplified intercontinental travel in both directions for humans and animals. Today's students are free to imagine the character of this two-way traffic.

Asia's Stone Age humans, ever-ready to explore for more hunting territory, would seize upon the chance to travel eastward and penetrate the new continent. While they may have been discouraged by the abundance of glacial ice, their way was not totally blocked. The big region that is now Alaska and a corridor in the Mackenzie River valley remained unglaciated and inviting to human pedestrians.

What the immigrant buffalo may have seen on the Bering "land bridge" and in the "corridor" 10,000 or 15,000 years ago is worth considering. There would be some strange and terrifying creatures moving in each direction, and a few human figures tramping eastward and southward among them. Perhaps there were horses and camels turning their backs upon their native North America, and humans and buffalo placing Asia behind them. The mastodon and mammoth, big members of the elephant family and the sabre-tooth tiger, the biggest of the cat family, were probably spectators, at least. But of all of these strange animal forms mentioned for their North American connection — the humans and the Asiatic bison — that were about to become the North American bison were the only ones destined to survive for the next 10,000 years or more on the east side of the land bridge, a tribute to the hardiness of both.

The Bering "bridge" and the unglaciated Mackenzie "corridor" were wide enough to prevent a confrontation between predators and victims. Animals like the bison had a reasonable chance of escaping to open country beyond the glacier front. The new land would appear better than what was behind them and few would choose to return.

The buffalo was the best equipped for the adopted habitat. The big quadruped, recently from Siberia, had no trouble with the climate. It shared with the musk ox the distinction of having the best front-end protection against Ice Age weather and predators. And that was not all. What animal had more skill in using a broad muzzle to "plow" through snow to reach the dried prairie grass needed for winter feed? It was Nature's gift of instinct that made the horse effective in using its front feet to move snow in order to gain the same good winter grazing.

The fur traders remembered a winter — but only one — in which the buffalo suffered from lack of feed. Nature seemed to be testing the bison to see how much they could stand. It had been a winter of heavy snow and while the melt water was still being held back by the remaining snow, the frosts returned, leaving a thick blanket of ice that neither horses nor buffalo could penetrate to reach the dried grass.

A buffalo of either sex would not likely win a beauty competition. When the Spanish leader, Coronado, and his followers saw the buffalo for the first time at the Aztec zoo in Mexico their response was, "horrible to the sight."[1] Western Indians, who relied upon the buffalo for food, shelter, clothing and even fuel, saw them as objects of sheer beauty.

They weren't handsome like a horse or deer. With a heavy and undisciplined growth of hair over the fore part of its body and almost indecent nudity over the rear part, its true comeliness was difficult to assess. It was at least as beautiful as mythology's Horn of Plenty.

White men, on their arrival in the west, were unimpressed. They saw the buffalo as dull and sulky, and of no benefit except to the Indians. Before long, however, the newcomers recognized buffalo hunts as first-class sporting events which appealed to wealthy and upper-class Britishers and others. Everyone who went for big game trophies got what he wanted, although it was costly to travel thousands of miles. After all, the head and horns from an old bull weighing 2,000 to 2,400 pounds, hanging on a European wall, would have decorative value equal to that of an African tiger. And it was easier to obtain.

Shooting a buffalo wasn't really a great feat, especially in the years of big herds. It was a strange urge which drove humans to spend time and fortune to ride out on a borrowed horse and fire a killing shot at a handsome and inoffensive animal that had only a remote chance of fighting back. The opportunity to study and gain a better understanding of this magnificent creature might have offered a greater challenge.

The buffalo could never be recommended for a family pet, but it was a prime candidate for more research than was ever conducted on its behalf. The buffalo played a leading part along with the Indian and the horse in the drama of the early west. Yes, there was competition with violence and killing, but the actors were moderately well-matched. Their performance might have gone on forever if the Europeans with their guns and desire to become rich hadn't forced themselves into the cast and brought the buffalo era to a tragic end.

People choosing to pursue the study of the buffalo would find many fascinating contradictions. The animals that appear about as placid as milk cows when seen in a park paddock can transform quickly to fighting monsters. If trim figures and light bones are conducive to speed in thoroughbred horses, the buffalo's heavy bone and cumbersome shape suggested it was a laggard, incapable of the extra speed needed for a sprint. But buffalo hunters learned that it took faster-than-average saddle horses to overtake a herd in flight. J.A. "Dad" Gaff, a hide hunter in Kansas before taking up ranching on the south slopes of Saskatchewan's Cypress Hills, said "25 per cent of the success in hunting buffalo depended upon a good gun and knowing how to use it, and the other 75 per cent was a horse race."[2]

The buffalo's speed was coupled with a surprising endurance. There were stories about a herd including calves that ran a hundred miles to escape the cruel flames of a prairie fire.[3] Further evidence of vitality and endurance was related by C.V. Alloway about his own herd, the most surprising performer being a one-day-old calf. On the morning after Governor Bedson of Stony Mountain, north of Winnipeg, bought the McKay and Alloway buffalo herd and was taking delivery of it, one of the buffalo cows dropped a calf. The herd had to be driven 22 miles from Deer Lodge on Winnipeg's west side to Stony Mountain, a trip which would test the survival instinct of the day-old calf.

The journey was completed and the calf seemed well enough but, during the night following the delivery drive, the herd broke through the fence and returned to Deer Lodge. But the herd was supposed to be at Stony Mountain and the order was given to return the herd to Stony Mountain forthwith. The calf, after walking at least 66 miles in less than 36 hours, showed no ill effects. Said Alloway: "No domestic calf could have travelled a quarter of the distance at the same age."[4]

Somebody will say: "Pretty good for critters with three-quarters of their weight on the front feet and legs, and about one-third of that in their oversized heads." While the ponderously heavy front might be a handicap in making speed, the enormous constitutional development seen in a buffalo's depth, back of its shoulders, is proof of generous thoracic development and added working space for heart and lungs.

Buffalo were not naturally belligerent to the point of looking for a fight. Unless frightened or wounded, they would rather flee than fight, but females with young calves or males with provocation could become instantly explosive. Experienced frontiersmen knew the folly of walking between a buffalo cow and her calf, or backing a bull into a corner. An aggrieved animal could be expected to charge and there was no such thing as a mild attack. A wounded animal, no longer able to run, could usually find enough strength for a close-up charge. The buffalo's aim, even when wounded, was generally accurate. The worst predicament for a rider was to be thrown into the path a wounded bull.

The frontier missionary, John McDougall, had various escapes when hunting to obtain meat supplies. On one occasion, he dismounted to walk among the dead bodies to assess the amount of meat he would have for use as fresh food and pemmican. The man of the cloth was astonished to see a big bull, thought to be dead, bound suddenly to its feet, tail held high, dashing at him. With no time to recover his horse and mount it — the frightened animal had sprinted away — McDougall was on his own. He was a good runner but not good enough to keep ahead of the angry bull. Fortunately, the beast was bleeding and becoming weaker and slower by the second. It staggered and fell before reaching the missionary and did not rise again.[5]

Buffalo horns were short and sharp, and perfectly curved for combat. Moreover, they were backed with sledgehammer thrusts. Many hunters with less familiar names were not as lucky as John McDougall, and many a horse also became a victim. Artist Paul Kane, who was in the prairie buffalo country in 1846 and '47 making sketches for later paintings, reported a clash between the bison and a band of horses that proved disastrous for the latter. The buffalo had an area offering good winter grazing and after they used their powerful heads and broad muzzles to break through the surface snow, the horses moved in. The buffalo objected to the idea of being demoted to the role of a slave to a bunch of horses and resorted to violence to get rid of the intruders. Kane reported "20 or 30"[6] horses died.

Mounted hunters, who rode too close, had the painful experience of seeing some of their best horses gored and killed. E.J. "Bud" Cotton, after riding on the Wainwright buffalo range for many years, considered himself lucky to have lost "only three saddle horses — or was it four — when riding at close range." He warned that the big animals he understood and admired were dangerously unpredictable. "They're not gentle and trustworthy like a saddle horse, or obedient like a farm dog or cuddly like an orphan lamb. They're still wild animals." He added a special warning for those who work with the buffalo. "Never, never allow yourself to come between a buffalo cow and her calf."[7]

The frontier heard many bunk-house debates about the buffalo's fighting capabilities; buffalo bulls against domestic bulls and buffalo bulls against grizzly bears. Old buffalo had the reputation of being the most difficult animal on the Canadian scene to kill, with the possible exception of the grizzly. It was known to have an extremely thick skull and a general overall toughness. James Morrow, pioneer resident and writer in southern Alberta, passed on the experience of a hunter who told of firing 18 shots — half of them musket balls — into an old buffalo bull. Yet "the poor old animal remained standing under this barrage and all the time making feeble attempts to charge. The 19th shot tumbled him over."[8]

The most spectacular Canadian stories originated out of the Cypress Hills, once known to the Blackfoot Indians as Grizzly Bear Hills. Morrow recalled a clash between a bull buffalo and a rancher's domestic bull of about the same weight. The struggle, he said, was "over in about three minutes" and the rancher's bull was "practically disembowelled."

The goriest fight of all was witnessed by Abe Farewell, a widely-known trader situated near Fort Walsh during the '70s of the last century. Apparently a grizzly had tried to make off with a buffalo calf and the mother sounded the alarm which brought an infuriated bull, presumably the herd's leader. As the bull came roaring toward the grizzly, lashing his tail in rage, the bear dropped the calf and wheeled toward the bull for a counter-attack with teeth and claws. The bear drew first blood but the buffalo struck a mighty blow that lifted the bear high in the air, and back on the buffalo's horns to be tossed again. The bear tried to run for cover but, by this time, all herd members were interested spectators or eager helpers. The cows formed a protective ring around their calves and the other bulls surrounded the grizzly. The bear, to be sure, did not escape. The young bulls trampled the last bit of life out of it and when Abe Farewell returned to examine the remains, he found that the grizzly was "literally torn to pieces."[9]

The Sarcees had their own story of how the buffalo got here. David One Spot, an 84-year-old elder from the Sarcee Reserve near Calgary, as the guest of honour and speaker at a Calgary Rotary Club luncheon on August 15, 1956, related a Sarcee story explaining how the first buffalo came to this country. Chief Jim Starlight interpreted and the legend became most popular.

"The buffalo came from a far land," said the Indian elder, "and it was like this. There were two brothers who, like some white boys, didn't get along very well. The older boy said to the younger one, 'You climb that tree and see what is in the eagle's nest.' The younger boy did what he was told to do and climbed but the older one immediately cut the tree down, and both the tree and boy fell in the river. Clinging to the tree, the younger brother floated far away to a strange land where he thought he was dying from starvation.

"By good fortune, the boy was discovered by a beautiful girl who thought he was dead. But on the chance there was still some life in the body, she took it to her home and administered life-giving steam baths. The treatment proved miraculous and the boy recovered. Then, of course, he married the girl.

"In this far-off land, the boy was to see animals that were new to him, among them the buffalo which the local people rode whenever they wished to travel. But in time the young man became lonely for his own country and persuaded his wife to return there with him. Riding two buffalo, they followed the

Blackfoot Indians hunting buffalo near Sweetgrass Hills, 1893 *(John Stanley/Glenbow Archives)*

river all summer and came finally to the part he recognized as his own. But sad news awaited him. The game animals had almost disappeared and the people were starving. To try and take his people back to the part where buffalo abounded was not likely to succeed. It would be too far. But on a still night when the moon was full, the young man's wife went to the top of the highest hill, faced the land of her birth and called, 'Buffalo! Buffalo! Buffalo!'

"The next day, huge herds of buffalo thundered in from the east. Hungry people ate buffalo meat, something they had never tasted before, and the herds that had answered the young wife's call remained to live thereafter in the country of plains and foothills. That's how the buffalo happened to be in these parts where the white man first saw them." Old David One Spot of the Sarcees said so.

1   Hornaday, William T., The Extermination of the American Bison, p. 374, Published by the Government Printing Office, Washington, 1889.
2   Gaff, J. A. "Dad", One of the many remarks attributed to "Dad" Gaff, most of which will never be authenticated.
3   Alloway, C. V., Interview with Winnipeg Tribune, Winnipeg, June 24, 1925.
4   Alloway, C. V., Interview with Winnipeg Tribune, Winnipeg, June 24, 1925.
5   McDougall, John, Saddle, Sled and Snowshoe, p. 271, Wm. Briggs, Toronto. 1896.
6   Kane, Paul, The Wanderings of an Artist, p. 396.
7   Cotton, E. J. "Bud," Notes from private conversations.
8   Morrow, James W., Early History of Southern Alberta, Lethbridge Herald, Aug. 29, 1931.
9   Morrow, James W., Early History of Southern Alberta, Lethbridge Herald, Aug. 29, 1931.

"Of all the quadrupeds that lived upon this earth, probably no other species has marshalled such innumerable hosts as those of the (North) American bison. It would have been as easy to count or evaluate the number of leaves in a forest as to calculate the number of bison living at any one given time during the history of the species prior to 1870."[10]

William T. Hornaday

Chapter 2

Big Herds From the Rio Grande To The Peace

Bison were notoriously gregarious. Like sheep and humans, they were strongly partial to their own kind in large numbers. When a buffalo appeared alone — as often happened — it might have been explained by a gunshot wound or just the animal's mistake of grazing at a careless distance from the main herd and, thereby, left behind when the main herd moved on. And, if the solitary animal was a young bull, its isolation was sometimes due to a beating from one of the older and bigger bulls, ever-ready to protect his masculine supremacy.

The Indians believed the cows — which were more active than bulls over much of the year — worked to rid themselves of the males during the spring and early summer months when they were neither needed nor wanted. As a result, the offended bulls would form their own bachelor herds. But such segregation always ended in late summer, the beginning of the breeding season. Calves were generally born in May or June, and were at once a part of the herd.

Human observers were always fascinated by the supersize herds but had difficulty in identifying a practical advantage to the animals. Certainly, herds of extreme size did nothing for the cause of better grazing. Where a herd of 50,000 or 100,000 travelled together, overgrazing was inevitable in places where the animals stopped for more that a few hours.

One possible purpose served by the supersize herd was in keeping members of the storytelling fraternity well furnished with story material. Unfortunately, stories originating in the sightings of the big herds were easy to exaggerate, leaving scholars and those interested in accurate reporting wondering how much could be believed. The herd stories were, perhaps, as reliable as the people who told them.

The importance of noting the size of the wild herds remained. Big herds were a racial characteristic, just as big flocks were typical of the passenger pigeons whose fate was as tragic as that of the bison. In contrast to most of Nature's finest treasures, one of the buffalo's distinguishing characteristics was its abundance — not its scarcity. Buffalo populations appear to have risen and fallen simultaneously in Canada and the United States because, as Canadians should have realized, they had claim upon the same herd as their American neighbours.

The first writer to enter the buffalo population game, placed the continental total prior to 1870 at 50 million, an impressive figure that nobody was qualified to challenge. It may have been, however, a disservice because the figure, with no basis in fact, was quoted again and again until it gained a good degree of acceptance. Possibly the guess was close to being accurate; more likely, it was wrong by a big margin. The author of the estimate may have advanced it in good faith, but if he had thought of safeguarding his credibility while doing something for his standing as a humorist, he might have hedged with an estimate of "50 million buffalo — plus or minus 45 million."

The Indians did not see a need for buffalo statistics but they may have had some opinions. In 1937, this writer spent several hours with an 82-year-old Assiniboine at his home in Saskatchewan's Touchwood Hills. As his tribe's expert in the construction of buffalo pounds, he enticed the animals to enter and closed the gate behind so that the cruel slaughter could begin. The old Indian drew sketches in the dry roadside sand to explain each step in construction and operation.

When asked if he would venture a guess about the total number of animals, he smiled as if to scoff at the folly of the question. After a few seconds of silence, he answered, "You could not count them all. You would run out of figures. But I will tell you. You think you have many cattle where we had buffalo. We had more buffalo on the ground than where you have cattle. If you want to know more, you count your cattle for where the buffalo ran when I was a boy."

Thinking about a practical interpretation of the Indian elder's words, reference was made to the then current cattle populations in those parts of Canada and United States that were known to have supported buffalo numbers handsomely. The total came to about 40 million. Nobody could say the Indian's reasoning wasn't plausible.

Most members of Canada's first contingent of North West Mounted Police, who trekked from Fort Dufferin in southern Manitoba to parts unknown near the Rockies, had never seen a prairie bison. They didn't believe the stories about the fantastically big herds that were "too big to be counted." But Irish-born Constable E.H. Maunsell, who became a prominent Alberta rancher, wrote about what he saw.

Three-hundred-and-eighteen officers and men, 310 horses, 142 oxen and enough wagons, carts, guns and supplies, which made the cavalcade more than two-miles long on the trail, departed from Fort Dufferin on July 8, 1874. Seventy-six days and almost 900 miles later, the force was somewhere south of the future site of Medicine Hat, cold, tired, lousy and lost. Without the numerous buffalo shot for meat along the way, the travellers could have added, "and hungry too."

When they made camp beside the west Butte of the Sweetgrass Hills, the weather turned ugly with snow and cold. It was at this point that the Commissioners issued the famous and merciful order directing every officer and man to surrender one blanket per person for the relief of their suffering horses. After one night at that location, members of the force awakened to a complete change of scenery, from snow-white to buffalo-brown. The Commissioners, who intended to start over the trail to Fort Benton, found themselves completely surrounded and imprisoned by the herd.

Maunsell recalled the scene as one "that none of us would ever forget." He wrote: "Far to the west, perhaps over a hundred miles away were the Rocky Mountains glistening in fresh snow. To the south were the three Buttes, apparently only a short walk but in reality about 12 miles... To the east was a sight which no eye will ever see again. The snowstorm had evidently reminded the buffalo that it was time to go south. We were on a height and as far as the eye could see to the east, there was a mass of buffalo slowly drifting, their dark bodies slowly moving in relief against the snow-covered ground."[11]

One of Maunsell's fellow travellers speculated that there were "a million head." Another group of Mounted Police riding eastward from Fort Macleod to Fort Qu'Appelle reported that they were within good viewing distance of buffalo continuously.

Nobody admitted a love for bison but until killing became a business, most people found it easy to admire the big shaggy creatures. John McDougall, with many years of residence in the prairie west, hunted them with a gun when meat was needed but never ceased to respect them for their adaptability and endurance. He met them under varied and strange circumstances and could tell of narrow escapes from the attacks of wounded bulls. Especially worthy of admiration, said McDougall, was the adult instinct, particularly found with mature bulls, to rush to the protection of young animals in trouble.

Many times he had watched when a bear or wolf appeared and the buffalo "organization" — like a well-trained fire brigade — gathered the calves together. The cluster of young ones was then circled by the cows, their heads and horns pointing toward the predator, their bodies forming a wall between the calves and the threatening killers. The bulls positioned themselves in front of the cows. Those who had witnessed the "organized defence" in action described it as beautiful to watch.

It was never intended that the stories about record buffalo herds would become competitive. Population estimates of extremely big herds were little more than guesses and were far from reliable unless backed by counts. But the estimates were somebody's fun and useful as conversation pieces. Rev. John McDougall would have been the first to agree. He had his own story about the big herd he saw from his watching position on Spy Hill on Calgary's north side in 1875.[12]

It was the year in which the Mounted Police built Fort Calgary. It was probably mid-summer when McDougall stood on the hill and saw the herd reaching almost to the horizon and wondered how many animals were present. But in suggesting the figure of half-a-million, he did have the semblance of a basis. Earlier in the season he had visited Montana and was in the Sun River Valley when the big spring round-up of cattle was in progress. Standing on a high cliff, he had looked down on the herd being rounded up. The roundup captain told him that there were 500,000 cattle by actual count. Later on Spy Hill when viewing the biggest herd in his memory, McDougall recalled the Montana experience and tried to remember the image. It wasn't difficult for McDougall to convince himself that the view of the buffalo herd was no less impressive than the view of half-a-million Montana cattle.

The most widely heralded big herd on the continent was the one seen and reported by Richard Irving Dodge, a lieutenant-colonel in the United States Services. He was a southerner with a good and sympathetic understanding of the wild herd that appeared now and then in unbelievable numbers along the Arkansas River. There the hide hunters made an early beginning and Dodge was a protesting viewer. He shot occasionally to obtain meat for his table but made it clear that he had never killed for financial gain or entertainment.

His encounter with the huge herd of which he wrote, was in May, 1871. He wrote, "in a light wagon from Old Fort Zara to Fort Larned, on the Arkansas, for thirty-four miles. At least twenty-five miles of this distance was through one immense herd, composed of countless smaller herds... on their journey north. The whole country appeared one mass of buffalo... My situation was by no means pleasant."[13]

The international buffalo authority, Hornaday, wrote: "It is safe to say that no man ever saw in one day a greater panorama of wild life than that unrolled before Colonel R.I. Dodge in May 1871." By Hornaday's calculations, it was probably part of the great southern herd "of about three-and-one-half million animals."[14]

People who sang hopefully for "a home where the buffalo roam," should have known where the roaming took place, and understood that there was more than one big herd. Huge herds could add to the pressure on grass resources and posed the danger of overgrazing. The prairie buffalo seemed to understand and practised "rotational grazing" by means of their annual, rotational tours or migrations. The wood buffalo, clinging to their own habitat in northern river valleys, did not migrate or did it on an insignificant scale.

The prairie-dwelling animals seemed to know at all times where they wanted to go and followed the traditional migration pattern, approximately but not rigidly, year after year. The travel routes were sufficiently understood by native people and others, or they thought they knew where to find the best hunting at any given season of the year. Native people were generally right but occasionally erred, and a "feast or famine" lifestyle was ever present in buffalo country.

The two biggest continental herds, the south and the north, were effectively separated by the Missouri River. The northern herd, commonly called the Canadian, appeared to have another major division. There were buffalo which favoured the brushwood country west of the Pembina as a wintering ground and those which instinctively gravitated to the grass in today's east central Alberta.

It was the Pembina-West herd, wintering on Dakota grass, that saved the Selkirk settlers from starvation during their first two winters in the country. And it was the central eastern Alberta herd upon which the 100 to 150 residents of Fort Edmonton depended on for their meat and pemmican. The Pembina-West herd appeared to migrate across the Regina Plains, making a big clockwise circle and passing south of Fort Edmonton on its way back to Pembina-West.

Professor A.S. Morton, who spoke with documented evidence on matters of western Canadian history, had his own views about the second of the two major herds in the Canadian west. This was the herd that was believed to winter between the north and south branches of the Saskatchewan River and travel southeast in the spring, circling clockwise to pass south of present-day Regina, west toward today's Medicine Hat and back toward the good winter grazing between the rivers. It wasn't as simple as it sounds, however, because the buffalo were smart enough to change directions now and then in order to find the best grazing.

10   Hornaday, William T., Annual Report of the United States National Museum, Smithsonian Institute, Para II, p. 373, 1887.
11   Maunsell, E.H., With The North West Mounted Police Force, Scarlet and Gold, Second edition, NWMP Veterans Assoc., Vancouver, BC, 1920.
12   McDougall, John, On The Western Trails In The Seventies, p. 207, Wm. Briggs, Toronto. 1911.

"The dying struggles of so many huge and powerful animals crowded together, created a revolting and terrible scene, dreadful from the excess of its cruelty and waste of life, but with occasional displays of wonderful brute strength and rage; while man in his savage, untutored, and heathen state shows both in deed and expression how little he is superior to the noble beasts he so wantonly and cruelly destroys."

Henry Y. Hind[15]

Chapter 3

Bow-and-Arrow Hunting Was Too Slow

H.G. Wells, author of the universally popular *Outline of History*, informed his readers that Neolithic Man, wandering around Europe and Asia 10,000 or 20,000 years ago, held his stone axe as his most useful tool or weapon. Next in order of importance was his recent acquisition, the bow-and-arrow combination, an invention that brought him to new heights of inventive pride. This new hunting weapon was sure to prove more challenging and more effective than the long wooden spear with a chipped stone point securely lashed to it, or a throwing dart possessing a similar stone tip. If an assessment could be made of the human family's various weapons for hunting and fighting, it would have shown the bow-and-arrow in the foremost position for the longest time.

The immigrants found game in abundance — big animals offering easy targets, gigantic mastodons in small and declining numbers and buffalo. With good weapons, hunting for meat was easy. But the bow-and-arrow hunters on the North American range encountered problems they hadn't considered. These buffalo critters, especially the old bulls, had thicker and tougher skins than any newcomer hunter would have expected, requiring phenomenal force to effect penetration. The hunters also experienced trouble in finding the kinds of trees and wood they wanted for making bows and arrows. Almost certainly, they were looking for a coniferous tree with unusual strength and elasticity in its wood, a native of the Far East and known later as the "yew tree." But the hunters weren't going to find it in the buffalo country. What they did find were some good substitutes that now have familiar names.

Prairie Indians of recent times cannot explain when the ultimate choices of wood for bows and arrows were expressed. However, they are confident that hardwood was not used extensively for the very practical reason that it wasn't to be found nearby, and the poplars were rejected for lack of strength and toughness in their wood. However, it is said that the Bow River took its name in recognition of the red willow and black choke cherry cut in its valley for bows and the Saskatoon wood selected for arrow shafts. Nobody said they were the best of all native woods for the hunter's purposes, but from the difficulties of distance to stronger kinds, they emerged as the "best available" for the Blackfoot, Sarcees and Stoneys.

The Crees and Assinboines, who ranged farther into the southeast, favoured bur oak, prairie ash and white elm, all favoured with strength and resilience. By splitting a heavy piece, a worker obtained the weight he wanted along with the strength and elasticity so greatly desired in a powerful bow. Some of the native people in the late years of buffalo hunting accepted red willow or cherrywood for arrow shafts but searched for something stronger for their bows. There wasn't much wrong with the power of bows and arrows made in the cherrywood and red willow country which a hunter could propel through the body of a mature buffalo bull — in one side and out on the other — and still have enough force to penetrate and kill a second buffalo running alongside. It wasn't something that happened often but Blackfoot hunters insisted that one of their tribesmen did it.

The family life on what has been described as north America's oldest buffalo range, revolved entirely around the unending hunting activities and endless recovery and preparation of the edible parts. Tribesman in the east and south of the continent cultivated enough beans, squash, pumpkins and Indian corn to vary the otherwise meat diet, and forced an omnivorous food classification upon themselves. But diets in the west were strictly carnivorous.

Adult males were fully occupied with the hunt. Mothers and wives looked after the tepees, gathered fuel for the fireplaces, carried water and made buffalo meat ready for eating. Girls helped mothers and, using pieces of charcoal, sketched outlines of buffalo on dry hides, whitened buffalo skulls, shoulder blades and stones. For boys, miniature bows-and-arrows were their first playthings. If a boy had an artistic instinct, he might try sketching buffalo on dry skins and then attack the picture with his miniature bow-and-arrows. And at a tender age, he followed his father who trailed game day after day, thus embarking upon the only educational exercises he was likely to experience. Everything revolved around the hunters and the buffalo. If bedtime stories existed for these youngsters, they too would have been about buffalo, perhaps about a good little buffalo that obeyed his mother and didn't get lost and a bad little buffalo who disobeyed and wandered alone into the woods and was lost for a week.

There are those in every generation, however, who look for newer, easier and faster ways of accomplishing their purpose. The buffalo frontier was ready for its first mass slaughter. The buffalo jump was a simple device, effective but cruel. Nobody will succeed in dating the first planned kill but it is thought to be 6,000 years ago, the age of Alberta's ancient Head-Smashed-In Jump. But just as more explicit dates and details about the first mass slaughter are lacking, so is the precise reasoning that condoned or encouraged the needless cruelty and waste on such a large scale, other than the jumps were exciting and made food gathering easy.

Organizing for the jump was complex and the choice of site called for great care. Once chosen, the same site might be used for hundreds of years. The essential requirement was a level location that allowed the hunters to guide and then stampede a herd across a course which terminated abruptly at an almost invisible brink. The animals had no time to turn and, thus, no alternative to plunging over a cliff to their death or crippling injury some 20- or 40-feet below. Bows-and-arrows were then used to kill the injured. Women and children moved in to dress carcasses and remove such meat and tasty bits as were wanted or needed, and then the feast began. No buffalo in the pit could escape.

The Province of Alberta identified at least 150 buffalo jump sites, principally in the southwest where foothills and plains meet. Head- Smashed-In was clearly the favourite. Unfortunately, vandals and overly eager collectors did much damage to the site before its archaeological treasures were adequately protected. Many of the valuable arrowheads and related artifacts were whisked across the border to the United States before the plundering was halted.

Only after the site was documented by researchers did its historical significance appear. Serious study began in 1965 and was followed a couple of years later by the deeding of the land to the provincial government and the construction of an enclosing fence. Authorized digging proceeded and proved most revealing. The accumulations of bones and other animal waste from the killings had raised the floor of the pit below the cliff by 11 metres or 36 feet!

Nobody even ventured to guess the probable millions upon millions of buffalo that plunged 10 metres or more to meet instant or lingering death. The

Head Smashed-In-Buffalo Jump, west of Fort Macleod, 1912 *(E.S. Gardiner/Glenbow Archives)*

accumulation of animal matter of all kinds was a veritable treasure trove of arrowheads and other stone artifacts that spoke more loudly than words. While there may have been some loss of treasures before the site was properly supervised, Head-Smashed-In is the oldest and best preserved bison jump in north America.[16]

This site was one of Canada's first nominations for international recognition as a "World Heritage Site," sponsored by the United Nations Educational, Scientific and Cultural Organization (UNESCO) and among the first approved. This provincial showpiece and world-class centre — about a dozen miles west of Fort Macleod — draws tourists from all over the world. Tourists have been heard to comment, "It's great but it's too bad that the poor old buffalo that were treated so shamefully didn't survive to get a bigger bit of the glory."

The most common question arising from the Head-Smashed-In showpiece concerned the origin of the name. It wasn't much wonder. The explanation, as offered by the Government of Alberta, makes the name quite intriguing. "About 150 years ago, according to legend, a young brave wanted to witness the plunge of countless buffalo as his people drove them to their deaths over the sandstone cliffs. Standing under the shelter of a ledge, like a man behind a waterfall, he watched the great beasts cascade past him. But the hunt was unusually good that day, and as the bodies mounted, he became trapped between the animals and the cliff. When his people came to do the butchering, they found him with his skull crushed by weight of the buffalo. Thus, they named the place Head-Smashed-In."[17]

Mass slaughter of the prairie buffalo must have been a hideous sight to behold. Between the buffalo jump and the buffalo pound, there wasn't much to tempt a spectator's choice. The jump was the more spectacular, but where the land was uniformly level and a sharp precipice offering a drop of eight or ten metres was difficult to find, a herd that could be trapped in a large enclosure or pound offered the best chance for a successful meat harvest.

Prairie Indians had individuals who were acknowledged specialists in pound construction and operation. The outstanding Cree leader, Chief Poundmaker, got his name from his father whose special skills were recognized. In like manner, the 82-year-old Assiniboine, with whom this writer had a long roadside visit in 1937, made it clear that the construction of buffalo pounds had been one of his two specialties, the other was in enticing the suspicious herds into the pounds. His secret in mesmerizing and drawing them inside the corral-like fence was a small bell, the tingle from which the buffalo could not resist. He admitted that on some occasions he had been loaned to nearby Cree bands to share the magic of his bell.

Most prairie pounds, related the Assinboine, were oval or circular, between 100 and 150 feet in diameter, and partially hidden from view. If logs were

Cliff killsite and lower trail at Head Smashed-In Buffalo Jump *(Alberta Multiculturalism/Interpretive Collections)*

available and permanency desired, wood was used in construction. But where logs were scarce, the fence was made from branches laced together with green willow. The rule was one gate only. It was positioned at the approach end. A heavy log was placed as a minor obstacle on the ground at the entrance, and the soil was excavated to a depth of a foot or more on the corral side, thereby making the jump into the corral easier than the jump out.

Most importantly, explained the elder Assiniboine, was the placement of the two long rows of posts extending for at least a mile from the corral entrance to the mouth of the "funnel." If the two most remote posts were a mile apart and a mile from the pound, the "funnel" would conform to a perfect triangle with each side one mile in length. Buffalo skins or pieces of leather clothing were then hung on the posts of the two lines to discourage the buffalo being driven toward the pound from departing from the course laid out for them. Braves hid behind the two lines, ready to rise and wave something like a robe if the frantic herd threatened to change direction and dash for freedom. As the herd approached the pound gate, more and more men and boys left their hiding posts and chased the buffalo toward the only opening they could see — the opening of the corral. Jumping through the gate, the animals followed the fence and the entrance was quickly blocked with logs and the slaughter began.

There was no order or formality. Anybody with a bow-and-arrow or gun to discharge could take aim as often as he or she liked. The carcasses piled up in total disarray. After the slaughter, the women and bigger children commenced the tedious tasks of skinning, dressing, stretching hides, separating lean meat for drying and pemmican, recovering especially choice parts of the carcass for their own families and preparing for a tribal feast later in the day.

Dr. James Hector, who was second in command of the Palliser Expedition appointed by the Imperial Government early in 1857 and, Henry Hind, appointed by the Canadian government to report on the prospects for farming and immigration, were both in the west later in that year and witnessed buffalo pound slaughters. Neither liked what he saw but both being good writers, left valuable accounts.

Dr. Hector kept pioneer farm hours. On the morning of December 26, 1857, he was travelling west from Fort Pitt at 4:30 a.m. when he was alerted by the sound of "bawling and screaming." When he investigated, he discovered Indians conducting a buffalo pound slaughter. They had succeeded in driving a large band of buffalo into the pound during the night and had commenced the slaughter at first light. "The scene," wrote Hector, "was more repulsive than pleasant."

The pound had more than a hundred buffalo of all ages in a mad state of confusion when Hector arrived. Some were already dead, others were in death struggles and settling in piles on the pound floor which was already layered with rotting body parts from earlier slaughters. But, as the visitor observed, this event had taken on a distinctively competitive twist, almost like an athletic contest. The contestants drove an arrow into the hump or side of a mature cow or bull as it galloped past on the inside of the fence and then attempted to recover the arrow by jumping into the enclosure on a later encirclement, seizing the protruding arrow and pulling it out.

Hind noted, if one of the enraged bulls or cows saw what was going on, the person playing the game had to be both nimble and lucky to get out of the ring alive. The young male braves, however, never deserted their passion to prove their bravery. With dangers near and success important — the Manitou was likely to be watching. This may explain what Dr. Hector saw under the pound entrance; a collection of "bridles, powder horns, tobacco, beads and the like," for the Great Spirit, "only to be stolen by the first scamp in the camp who could manage the theft adroitly ... "[18]

Henry Y. Hind was the English geologist who believed the South Saskatchewan River could be diverted into the Qu'Appelle Valley, thus providing a possible steamboat service between Fort Garry and the mouth of the Elbow River where Calgary was to arise. He disliked buffalo slaughters too, but he was determined to see everything the friendly Crees had to show him. Perhaps it was a coincidence that he was near today's Eyebrow, southeast of Elbow, Saskatchewan, when a buffalo drive and pound slaughter was being conducted.

Approaching the Indian encampment on a summer morning in 1858, Hind sent a message to Chief Mis-tick-oos — known also as "Short-Stick" — that he wished to visit. The Chief was courteous but thoughtful and replied that the visitor should delay his arrival by one hour to let his people complete the task of moving the buffalo pound fence and operation to a new site. The old location had become so filled and fouled with decaying buffalo bodies and parts that few could endure its intensity. Hind, who had never been nearer than a mile from the old and offending site, agreed. He was interested in seeing the old and abandoned location but, after what he had heard from the Chief, he made his study from a distance of about half-a-mile.

At the specified hour, the Chief came to meet Prof. Hind and informed him that the herd was coming into view. Hind could see the animals leaping into the enclosure and circling to find an outlet. The gate was blocked closed with logs and the tribesmen began popping up just inches apart around the new pound fence, opening fire with bows-and-arrows, guns of primitive design and even pointed wooden poles. What followed was sheer Pandemonium, a place which in Greek mythology was the "abode of demons." Hind described dead and dying buffalo — over 200 of them — tossed in every conceivable position. "Some lay on their backs," Hind wrote with disgust, "with eyes staring from their heads and tongues thrust out through clotted gore. Others were impaled on the horns of the old and strong bulls. Others were lying with broken backs, two or three deep. One little calf hung suspended on the horns of a bull which had impaled it on the wild race around the pound."[19]

By no stretch of imagination can the story of pound slaughter be made to sound pleasant. But it is a part of our history and history can be expected to tell all, yet yield useful messages and lessons. One question was often asked; why were the young and vigorous animals with their full breeding lives ahead of them not turned back to the wild state? John McDougall, who spent many years on the frontier and was on good terms with the native people, offered this comment: "Not one buffalo is allowed to escape. The young and the poor must die with the strong and the fat for it is believed that if they were spared, they would tell the rest (of the buffalo) and make it impossible to bring any more buffalo into a pound."[20]

13   Dodge, Richard Irving, Lt.-Col., The Plains of the Great West, p. 120, G.W. Putman's Sons, New York, 1877.
14   Hornaday, William T., The American Natural History, p. 9, of Vol. II, Charles Scribner's Son's, New York, 1914.
15   Hind, Henry Y., Narrative Of The Canadian Red River Exploring Expedition of 1857 an Assiniboine and Saskatchewan Expedition of 1858, Vol. 1, p. 359, Longman, Green, Longman and Roberts, London, 1860.
16   Harper, Tim, Canada's Marvels In Worldwide Hall Of Fame, Calgary Herald, Feb. 25, 1984.
17   Culture and Multiculturalism, Government of Alberta, Head-Smashed-In-Buffalo-Jump, no date.
18   Hector, Dr. James, The Journals, Detailed Reports and Observations by Captain John Palliser, Presented to both Houses of Parliament, London, May 19, 1863.
19   Hind, Henry Y., Narrative Of The Canadian Red River Exploring Expedition of 1857 and Of The Assiniboine and Saskatchewan Exploring expedition of 1858, Vol. 1, p. 358, Longman, Green, Longman and Roberts, London, 1860.
20   McDougall, Rev. John, Saddle, Sled and Snowshoe, p. 271, William Briggs, Toronto, 1896.

"I have great hopes that the buffalo may be domesticated in a better and more effective manner ... by taking out a large body of men on horseback to the plains and when you find a herd of (buffalo) cows, spread your men into an extended line and drive the herd before you gently without alarming them unnecessarily and follow them day after day till you bring them to the plains near the settlement where a few men must be employed to watch them constantly to prevent their straying away and prevent their being hunted and disturbed. By degrees they will grow less wild, especially if in winter they are supplied with hay and may probably admit to a cross (with) a European bull."[21]

Earl of Selkirk

Chapter 4

A Brief Boom In Buffalo Wool

The first of the Selkirk settlers arrived at the forks of the Red and Assiniboine Rivers in the autumn of 1812. They were tired after spending 61 days crossing the Atlantic and after the long canoe trip from York Factory to Red River. The party numbering 70 men, women and children leaving Scotland, arrived at Red River with 71 souls, Mrs. McLean having given birth to a daughter during the voyage.

With this contingent of settlers came a flock of 21 Spanish Merino sheep, thoughtfully provided by Lord Selkirk. It was hoped that the animals would flourish and give the settlers a foundation for a profitable international trade. But the sheep "with the golden fleece" failed to live up to expectations due to mismanagement and predators.

Resourceful people were asking if there was an acceptable substitute for sheep wool, or if there was a practical means of stocking Red River farms with cattle and sheep. While Lord Selkirk may have been the first to enquire about the use of musk-ox and buffalo hair in spinning programs, it was John Pritchard, who advanced a working plan for the Red River Buffalo Wool Company. "We wouldn't have to kill more buffalo," he said, "if we just collected the hides and hair from the animals the hunters destroy." He knew the animal had two coats, a fine weatherproof undercoat and an outer coat of long and coarse fibres. Andrew Colvile, Lord Selkirk's brother-in-law and executor of his estate, authorized, on May 25, 1820 — less than seven weeks after the Earl's death — a grant of 100 acres at Point Douglas to John Pritchard for the Buffalo Wool Company.

While death spared Lord Selkirk the controversy that followed the Buffalo Wool scheme, he held firm in his interest in partial or total domestication of the animal. When his 1814 proposal to win the confidence of a big herd by gentle restraint and regular feeding of hay close to the settlement failed to materialize, Selkirk had another plan that was too late to be tested under his instructions. It consisted of trying to break the migration pattern by loosely holding the herd north of Portage le Prairie and gradually moving their winter feeding site nearer to Point Douglas. He reasoned that if the wild things rejected the attempt to domesticate, the meat supplies would be available at a shorter distance for the settlers.

The interest in giving the buffalo a bigger place in the colony was revived when William Laidlaw, hired by Selkirk, became manager of the experimental farm in 1818. That year, when the wild herd came unusually close to the settlement, Laidlaw went out with horses and dogs to capture some calves. He returned with five or six but only one survived. By midsummer, however, the young heifer was following the man who fed her "like a dog." More settlers were going on expeditions to capture buffalo calves and more met with success. By 1821, Alexander Macdonell wrote Andrew Colvile that, in his opinion, these buffalo heifers would prove to be "good milkers as well as good workers and if this be so, they are the best stock for the settlement, being the most hardy and already adapted to the climate."[22]

Optimism can be dangerous and so it was in the case of John Pritchard. His enthusiasm led him to send to Mr. Colvile, the Hudson's Bay Company's chief executive officer in London, one buffalo heifer and one young bull. The shipment went via York Factory, crated, but nobody said "gift-wrapped." It arrived in London in good order but not without embarrassment that brought little to the cause of buffalo wool.

Pritchard raised enough local capital to complete the warehouse and get started at the essential work of separating the fine undercoat from the long and coarse outercoat. He appealed to settlers and hunters to bring buffalo skins with fur to him for which he would pay one shilling, a sixpence per pound for hair or wool and six shillings each for hides. A good skin, he found, would furnish six or seven pounds of the coat fibres, of which two or three pounds of fine quality material appeared suitable for export as wool. The balance, being of lower quality, could be used, presumably, for coarse cloth, blankets and mattresses. There was still a lower grade that Pritchard considered suitable for the making of rope.

By June of 1821, Pritchard had 700 buffalo hides, 300 pounds of what he called "fine wool" and 1,000 pounds of the coarser product. But he urgently needed some return from his expenditures, and he needed a serious judgement about the marketable- worth of his "buffalo wool" to convince skeptics like George Simpson, Governor of the Hudson's Bay Company in Rupert's Land, whose criticism of Pritchard was deadly. "Pritchard and his Buffalo Wool Company make a great noise. He is a wild visionary, a speculative creature without a particle of solidarity and but a moderate share of judgement. If that business were properly managed, I have no doubt of it turning out well."[23]

The statement told about as much about Simpson as about Pritchard who, apart from being overly optimistic, was a good citizen. His error, however, was a big one because many locals had invested their small savings in the venture. The mistake arose from the failure to recognize the differences between wool and hair. Wool fibre is distinctive by its serrated or zigzag character. Hair fibres can be twisted together to make a yarn but, without the serrations, it lacks the interlocking quality and strength of a woollen yarn.

Sheep, however, produce wool and buffalo, although enjoying excellent weather-proof coats, grow hair. The British woollen millers were never very hopeful about the potential of buffalo wool but, at the request of Andre Colvile and out of respect for Lord Selkirk's widow, who wanted to help the settlers at Red River, they tried to work with the buffalo wool and they did produce some coarse garments. Lady Selkirk's loyalty to the Red River Settlement which was founded by her late husband was admirable. She not only coaxed the British millers to try again, but humbled herself by wearing some of the heavy and drab shawls, sweaters, jackets and stockings made from Red River buffalo hair. She hoped that her London society friends might follow her example and begin a new trend in British fashions.

The distressing news reached Red River in March, 1824, when Colvile reported to Pritchard, saying: "I am sorry to say that the result of the sale of last year's importation of wool is not at all encouraging... I fear the wool will not answer your expectations. Success will depend on what you can make of it by converting it to cloth which you can sell in the settlement. If you can show to the satisfaction of Governor Simpson and the Council that you can make a profitable concern of the leather and cloth business out of which you can extinguish your debt, I have no doubt they will be disposed to assist."[24] Some Red River residents lost their savings, others were misled about the promise of prosperity and a few settlers abandoned their little farms to accept the inflated wages offered by the Company's cheerful manager, John Pritchard. The Buffalo Wool Company, however, gave the Red River settlement its first taste of prosperity, an experience with specialized industry and an economic boom.

One of those who did not deviate from earlier duties was William Laidlaw, the manager of the experimental farm, who was interested in domesticating buffalo. He was the essence of stability and resourcefulness. When Indians stole most of his work horses at the experimental farm where he was trying to advance his acreage of cultivated land, he made a better plow and hitched it to an improvised team consisting of two horses, one milk cow, and the buffalo heifer that had been captured as a calf.

And while the rest of the community was being carried away by the prospect of a buffalo wool enterprise, William Laidlaw was establishing what almost certainly was Canada's first buffalo park. It wouldn't be a big range but it would be an experimental centre for all activities related to the domestication of buffalo and all studies focusing on hybridization of cattle and buffalo.

"Buffalo hunting here, like bear-hunting in India, has become a popular and favourite amusement among all classes; and Red River, in consequence, has been brought into some degree of notice, by the presence of strangers from foreign countries. We are now occasionally visited by men of science as well as men of pleasure. The war road of the savage and the solitary haunt of the bear, have of late been resorted to by the florist, the botanist and the geologist; nor is it uncommon now-a-days to see Officers of the Guards, Knights, Baronets, and some of the higher nobility of England and other countries, coursing their steeds over the boundless plains, and enjoying the pleasures of the chase among the half-breeds and savages of the country. Distinction of rank is, of course, out of the question; and, at the close of the adventurous day, all squat down in merry mood together, enjoying the social freedom of equality round Nature's table, and the noble treat of a fresh buffalo-steak served up in the style of the country — that is to say, roasted on a forked stick before the fire; a keen appetite their only sauce, cold water their only beverage."[25]

Alexander Ross

Chapter 5

Aristocrats From Abroad Came For A "Shoot"

Instead of going on a safari in Africa, many Britishers chose buffalo hunting in Rupert's Land. Trophies were easier to obtain and much less costly. And what could look more imposing on an Old Country wall than the massive head of a prairie bison bull. When the new hunters arrived at Fort Garry — with small arsenals of hunting weapons, warm clothing fashioned for Arctic wear, stocks of fine wine, bulging wallets, meerschaum pipes and monocles — the local residents were ready to take the English money. All visitors hoped to engage the most skilful guide in the country, James McKay, a 300-pound Scottish halfbreed, born at Fort Edmonton and raised for most of his life at Fort Garry. Hiring him as a guide was tantamount to buying the best life insurance for a hunting trip, partly because he was on friendly terms with all tribes and partly because he possessed the muscle power of an additional horse, handy when wagons loaded with hunting gear and supplies became stuck in mud bogs.

Many of the returning British hunters became well known at Fort Garry. Men like Col. Cooper and Capt. Thynne of the Grenadier Guards, Lord Dunsmore and Capt. Cooper of the Fusiliers, Capt. John Palliser who became a leading figure in shaping the agricultural destiny of the new west, Lord Milton and Dr. Cheadle who came as a team, and the Earl of Southesk all had a hankering for hunting buffalo.

There were, in a sense, two John Pallisers. The one whose expeditions and studies of soil, climate and opportunities for western settlement conducted in 1857, '58 and '59 furnished the first scientific directives for prairie agriculture. His memory was kept alive by Palliser Pass, Palliser River, Palliser Triangle, Palliser Hotel, Palliser Constituency, Palliser Wheat Growers Association, Palliser Mountains and Palliser Report. But there was the earlier John Palliser who spent 1847 and '48 on one prolonged buffalo hunt, mainly in the region of the Missouri River, south of the International Boundary. The two Palliser images were explainable only by the fact that he was more mature in one case than the other, even though it was the same red-headed Irish engineer and bachelor.

He made his mistakes — even in his assessment of the potential of the new west — but nothing, including the error of a lengthy buffalo hunting spree when he didn't need the meat, was enough to rob him of the glory he deserved for his resource studies. Regardless of what the critics may have said about his hunting, he demonstrated a pronounced fondness for wildlife, as the hours of his departure from the buffalo range would suggest. His concluding act was to load onto a Missouri River boat some of the "friends" he made during his visit: two buffalo calves, one buffalo cow, several deer, one young black bear and one first cross-Husky dog known as "Ismah", all destined to travel together to Ireland.

The Earl of Southesk in 1859 and '60, along with a substantial party, spent seven months on the prairies and in the mountains enjoying a long and prodigal "shoot." One of the highlights of the seven months was obviously being on the prairies when, with the best of guns and plenty of ammunition, "the countryside as far as the eye could see was black with herds of buffalo." That he and his party had no hope of consuming or in any way using more than an infinitesimal part of what was killed was not a worry. To his credit, the Earl used his pen extensively and wrote descriptively of buffalo and other scenes: "They were on a dry prairie," he wrote, "slightly undulated in character, here and there hilly and bounded by higher ranges in the west and toward the north. Immense herds were stringing across the whole face of the country. The deep rolling voice of the mighty multitude came gradually on the air like the booming of a distant ocean."[26]

The following year, Lord Milton and Dr. Cheadle assigned themselves the task of finding the North West Passage by land while enjoying the buffalo hunts without stint. Their success in finding the big herds was much greater than finding the illusive passage. Like most overseas hunting parties, they did something for the Fort Garry and Red River economy, but it wasn't great or lasting unless dollar values could be attached for the entertainment they provided.

It was, however, the Indians who may have delivered the most stinging rebuke to overseas hunters. The warning, issued from a band of Cree and Assiniboine people who were at war with the Blackfoot at the time, forced the Englishmen to listen, demurely. The visitors were members of Lord Dunsmore's hunting party including officers from the Imperial Army who accepted the castigation without debate.

They had expected to find big herds and easy hunting along the Qu'Appelle and South Saskatchewan Rivers but at Fort Ellice they were informed of a large war party, 950 tepees in all. The Cree and Assiniboine allies were out to teach the Blackfoot a lesson or two. When the hunters met up with the Indians, the tribesmen, who did nothing to hide their anger, did most of the talking. They made no secret of the fact that they had robbed earlier white hunters, leaving them without weapons or horses. The Assiniboine chief, Red Stone by name, identified himself but remained silent, leaving it to his foremost brave to do the speaking.

The Indian speaker, as everybody soon realized, was a polished orator. "You palefaces," he said, "must be very rich when you can travel so far to hunt on our land without even asking our permission. We think you can't object if we remove something from your pockets because when enjoying yourselves, you are reducing our buffalo and leaving us poorer. Sometimes, we have trouble in feeding our families and yet you think you can come here and shoot down our buffalo. You would take food out of the mouths of my children, just for your pleasure. It is now our determination to rob or shoot all intruders in the future."

The speaker's anger grew as he considered the outrage of strangers shooting animals for no more than entertainment. "What would you think," he asked, with his gun pointed at the British army men, "if we went to your country and began shooting your cattle and tramping down your crops because we found it fun? Wouldn't you feel like scolding us or shooting back? I'm speaking for my Chief and warning you; don't come again thinking you'll be lucky and get away with your badness. Don't forget to tell the other people who live where you come from that we will speak with our guns next time. There must be an end to the bad manners and destruction you bring."[27]

There was no rebuttal or debate. The confused hunters rode quietly away. It should have been a good lesson but the invasions of hunters from afar did not end — not while buffalo remained. Some of the "invasions" proved strangely complex. The year 1881 found the name of another of England's favourite sons — John Douglas Sutherland Campbell, better known as the Marquis of Lorne, Governor General of Canada — being bandied about on the buffalo range. The distinguished Britisher was a Scot born in London and married to Princess Louise, the daughter of Queen Victoria.

It was his fourth year as the Queen's representative in Canada and he was anxious to improve his understanding of the Canadian west. He requested a tour by horse-drawn wagon from the end of the railroad at Portage la Prairie to the foothills and mountains. The vice-regal party was to leave Winnipeg on the first of August, travel to Portage la Prairie by rail, then to Battleford by wagon and on to Calgary and Fort Macleod by the same means. It was reported that a buffalo hunt would be organized along the route for the edification and entertainment of His Excellency. There was a muffled protest that at this time in history when the wild species was teetering on the brink of extinction, any public demonstration of further slaughter would be in very bad taste. The message seemed to reach the tour planners and nothing more was heard about the proposed kill.

The official party left Battleford on the morning of September 1, and was at Sounding Lake by the evening of the 3rd. So far, the travellers hadn't seen a single buffalo. Presumably, the bison had vanished. But they hadn't and on the 7th, when the party was at the Red Deer River and about to ford, somebody shouted, "Look! Buffalo!" Somewhere near today's Drumheller, a herd of 10 buffalo appeared. The Governor General's party was caught up at once with excitement. If there was a conservationist in the party, his voice was lost in the demand for a "run." That the 10 buffalo in sight might be the only ones surviving, didn't seem to matter. The only voice or voices that could have and should have declared against a kill, did not respond and there was a hurried preparation of the best horses and best guns. In those darkest of hours in buffalo history, members of the vice-regal party rode out to further reduce the population. A short time later, they returned in triumph having killed three of the 10 rare animals and, to mark the victory, there was a celebration and feast with fresh buffalo steaks served as the "piece de resistance."

The names of the Governor's servants and friends who participated in the "shoot" on that sad day in September, 1881, may have been withheld — just as the exact part the Governor General had in authorizing the hunt was never very clear — but there was public protest about the event. While hunting laws were still almost nonexistent and nobody was charged, it was agreed that the Governor General was responsible for his servants and the others who travelled with him. Otherwise, the distinguished diplomat, writer and poet enjoyed a highly successful tour. Dear to thousands of Canadian hearts are the words of the hymn, "Unto the Hills Around Do I Lift Up My Longing Eyes" — said to have been written at Banff by the Governor General who became the 9th Duke of Argyll.[28]

22 Macdonell, Alexander, Letter to Andrew Colvile, 1821, no other date.
23 Simpson, George, Letter to Andrew Colvile, Sept. 3, 1821, Selkirk Papers.
24 Colvile, Andrew, Letter to John Pritchard, March 11, 1824.
25 Ross, Alexander, The Red River Settlement, p. 241, Smith, Elder and Co. London, 1856.
26 Southesk, James Carnegie, 9th Earl of, Saskatchewan and the Rocky Mountains, James Campbell and Sons, Toronto, 1875.
27 The Nor'-Wester, Fort Garry, Hunting Tour In The Western Prairies, Oct. 9, 1862.
28 Saskatchewan Herald, Battleford, Oct. 17, 1881.

"... Assiniboia was supplied by Nature in unusual abundance with the necessities for human existence. In 1813 more than 35 tons of pemmican were prepared there for the North West and Hudson's Bay Companies' trade in furs. At the same time the buffalo furnished for half a century the staple article of food for the Red River Settlement and for many years, the fisheries of the territories afforded a supply of provisions second only to the proceeds of the buffalo hunt. The prolific harvests of the prairie were not subject to the task of forest clearing which filled the early settlement of Nova Scotia or Ontario with unrecorded toil and privation."[29]

Chester Martin

Chapter 6

The Big Buffalo Hunt — Red River Style

Lord Selkirk's long-suffering colonists, who located on narrow riverlot farms where the city of Winnipeg arose, did not hesitate to declare that, without the buffalo meat supplies delivered regularly from the plains, they would have starved in their first winters in the country. The well-organized Red River hunt, however, was not a Selkirk Settlement invention. It was probably an Indian device which, for the Canadian natives, began in the 18th century with horses they stole from their southern neighbours. The new hunting pattern was quickly adopted by the Métis whose fathers and grandfathers had been voyageurs. With horses to help them, the Métis and half-breeds wanted no other occupation than running buffalo.

The first of the Selkirk settlers — 70 of them under the leadership of the jovial Irishman, Owen Keveny — arrived at the mouth of the Assiniboine on the Red River on October 27, 1812. They were informed that this was the area from which they would choose their riverlot farms but, because winter was near and no food reserves had been secured, "not even a bag of pemmican," the settlers would be escorted to Pembina, about 60 miles south. There the settlers found a small number of log cabins and the makings for more and, best of all, they were much closer to a favourite wintering ground for buffalo.

Miles Macdonell, who was Lord Selkirk's "right-hand man," had talked to a St. Lawrence River Frenchman, Jean Baptiste Lagimodiere. He persuaded him to winter near the buffalo and to hunt and forward the meat to Pembina by toboggan. The plan worked well. By supplementing the meat with fish taken from the Red River, high-protein rations were unfailing. Miles Macdonell was so satisfied with the result that he ordered a similar arrangement for the settlers' second winter.

As the settlers began to grow some grain, vegetables and potatoes, they were less dependant upon the buffalo. But with few cattle and no sheep or pigs, their interest in the wild herds diminished only measurably. One of the troubles in the early years was that settlers did not have fast enough horses to overtake a fleeing buffalo, and they lacked experience in hunting from horseback. And the

Métis — who might have furnished the best of instructions about hunting on horses — were not on friendly terms with the settlers. The conflict reached a climax on June 19, 1816, the sorrowful day of the Battle of Seven Oaks when 20 of the settlers and one of the Métis were killed.

For the next few years there was no hope of achieving cooperation between the two. The settlers who suffered so greatly in the Battle of Seven Oaks entertained a bitter hatred, especially for the Métis leader, Cuthbert Grant. But, after one and then two years, the "detestable fellow" was being seen in a different light and the settlers expressed the view that to know him better might be to trust him more. "Perhaps we need Cuthbert Grant and his soldiers more than we've realized." They were ready to reassess this man who led his people in buffalo hunts and against the Sioux — known as "the tigers of the plains." It was a challenging thought that without the people of mixed blood, the Selkirk Settlement would be completely vulnerable to the Sioux Indians.

A proposal was taken to the settlement leaders and churchmen that steps should be taken to consolidate the Métis scattered along the river at a central point close to the settlement where the settlers might assist the Métis in the event of a Sioux attack. More realistically, the plan called for the Métis to act as a protective bulwark for the settlement. Cuthbert Grant was favourably inclined to the idea and it took shape. He was given a tract of land 16 miles west of Fort Garry as a new hub or core for his people and what had been known as White Horse Plains on the Assiniboine River, took the name of Grantown.

When Grant's people became neighbours of the settlement a new respect began to show. The annual or biannual buffalo hunts — upon which Grant's people depended for much of their food — appeared increasingly attractive to the settlers. In 1820, just four years after the Battle of Seven Oaks, 520 carts, many the property of the Selkirk people, left on a joint hunt under the command of Cuthbert Grant. It was a great success and for the next 20 years, the Red River enterprise became bigger every year.

The biggest organized buffalo hunt in the world and the best in organization was the one that originated beside the "Red River of the North" and in most years encroached upon Dakota Territory. Friends of the event complained that they had never found the appropriate name for the event which they said combined the most notable characteristics of a harvest festival, a military manoeuvre under a three-star field marshal, an Indian potlach and a gold rush to the Yukon. When the date of a forthcoming Red River hunt was announced, three "streams" of hunters with families prepared for the trek to the point of assembly, a short distance upstream from Fort Pembina. They travelled, generally, in a relaxed and happy mood.

The biggest group, after 1820, consisted mainly of Selkirk settlers. They started at Fort Garry and travelled 10 miles west on the north side of the Assiniboine to cross the latter at the ford known as "the Passage" and take the trail almost due south to the Pembina Hills and the meeting place in the Pembina Valley. The second "stream" made up of seasoned Métis hunters from White Horse Plains, travelled east to the same ford on the Assiniboine and south to the Pembina Valley rendezvous. And the third group, composed of Métis still living at Fort Pembina, were already close to the meeting place.

As soon as all groups were present in the valley, the camp crier announced the customary organization meeting with free seats on the valley grass. The first order of business called for the election by vote of the leader or president of the hunt. For the Métis, that elected leader would hold office until the next hunt which might be a year away. It was then for the leader or president or chief captain to call for the election of ten field captains who would be expected to serve their chief as members of a cabinet would support their prime minister. To complete the organization, each of the ten field captains then named ten "soldiers" or minor officers to work under their respective field captains, primarily in keeping order.

Nevertheless, the most skilful buffalo hunters on the continent proved to be much better makers of history than recorders. No one knows exactly when the Red River buffalo hunts began or who was the first elected chief captain — but the general opinion is that the hunts started before the coming of the Selkirk settlers and that Cuthbert Grant may have been the first leader. One point is accepted, that Chief Captain Grant continued as long as he wanted to stay and was followed by Jean Baptiste Wilkie, an English halfbreed who was raised among the French. He, too, remained in the high office for many years.

John Hawkes, author of *Saskatchewan and Its People*, after drawing extensively upon the Red River historian, Alexander Ross, writes that the Red River hunt camp of 1840 "occupied as much ground as a modern city and was all in a circle." He reports: "When the roll was called in the camp on the third evening, it numbered 1630 souls. The rules and regulations were read, the officials were installed, and all matters settled without a scratch of a pen."[30]

Ross was any eye-witness at the Red River hunts on various occasions and wrote assiduously about the event of 1840, the biggest up to that time. The Fort Garry hunters — with whom he travelled — left Fort Garry on June 15 and camped three days later in the beautiful Pembina Valley where the hunters from a wide area gathered. Two meetings were held, one for the roll-call and election of the chief captain, and the second for announcement and approval of the rules by which camping and hunting would be conducted. Neither took more than a few minutes because buffalo hunters saw no glory in oratory.

At the second meeting, the full slate of officers were presented and approved and the chief captain probably announced populations for everything counted during the first meeting, including horses, oxen and dogs. The roll-call and various other statistical counts revealed 1630 souls, 1210 Red River carts, no fewer that 400 hunters and 542 dogs acting as if they hadn't had a "square meal" since the buffalo hunt of 12 months earlier. Of the dogs, Ross said: "Sufficient in themselves to consume no small numbers of animals per day, like their masters, they dearly relish a bit of buffalo meat."

The rules to govern the 1840 Red River Buffalo Hunt contained nothing very new. But inasmuch as rules were never adopted for more than one year at a time, or until the expiry of the chief captain's one-year term, they demanded frequent attention to ensure that nobody breaking them could plead ignorance. It was like "a traffic by-law for buffalo hunters" — warnings that everyone could understand, but written by buffalo hunters rather than lawyers.

1. No buffalo to be run on the Sabbath Day.
2. No party to fork off, lag behind or go before, without permission.
3. No person or party to run buffalo before the general order.
4. Every captain with his men, in turn, to patrol the camp and keep guard.
5. For the first trespass against these laws, the offender's saddle and bridle to be cut up.
6. For the second offence, the coat to be taken off the offender's back and be cut up.
7. For the third offence, the offender to be flogged.
8. Any person convicted of theft, even to the value of a sinue, to be brought to the camp and the crier to call out his or her name three times, adding the word 'thief' each time.[31]

On July 3rd, 18 days and 250 miles from Fort Garry, Ross and his fellow hunters were deep in the grassland that would someday belong to the State of North Dakota, gazing at the first big herd of bison they had encountered and plotting their attack. Early next morning, while Captain Wilkie held his spyglass to an eye and studied the distant herd and the rough ground, 400 excited hunters mounted 400 nervous horses. At 8 o'clock, the Captain gave the order and the whole cavalcade advanced toward the buffalo, first at a slow trot, then a little faster, and still a little faster. The buffalo were still more than a mile away and totally unaware of their danger. Not until the horsemen were within four- or five-hundred yards and travelling at a fast gallop, did the bulls paw the ground, curve their tails and flee. Ross recorded, "In less time than we have taken with this description, a thousand carcasses strew the plains."

"On this occasion the surface was rocky and full of badger holes. Twenty-three horses and riders were at one moment all sprawling on the ground; one horse, gored by a bull, was killed on the spot, two more disabled by the fall. One rider broke his shoulder blade; another burst his gun and lost three of his fingers by the accident; and a third was struck on the knee by an exhausted ball. These accidents will not be thought overly numerous, considering the result, for in the evening no less than 1375 tongues were brought into camp. . . The rider of a good horse seldom fires till within three- or four- yards of his object and never misses. And what is admirable in point of training, the moment the shot is fired, the steed springs to one side to avoid stumbling over the animal... When the runners leave the camp, the carts are prepared to follow to bring in the meat. . . "[32]

Alexander Ross was not one to pass up a good story, especially a buffalo story that illustrates how close frontier people lived to danger; "A friend of the writer's about this time went to enjoy a few weeks sport on the plains, and often repeated, with a comic and serious air, a scene which took place in his own presence. Some of the hunters who were accompanying him were conveying their families across a large plain, intersected here and there with clumps of wood. When in the act of rounding one of those woody islands, a herd of buffalo suddenly burst into view causing two dogs who were drawing a sled on which a child and some luggage were being conveyed, to set off at full speed in pursuit, leaving the father and mother in a state of despair for the safety of their only child. The dogs soon reached the heels of the buffalo and all were mixed pell-mell together, the dogs running, the sled swinging to and fro, and the buffalo kicking. At length a bull gored one of the dogs and his head getting entangled in the harness, went off at the gallop, carrying the dog on his horns, the other suspended by the traces, and the sled and child whirling behind him. The enraged animal ran a good half-mile before he shook himself clear of the encumbrance although pursued by a large party, by whom many shots were fired at him without effect. The state of the parents' feelings may be imagined; yet to their utter astonishment, although both dogs were killed, the child escaped unhurt."[33]

29   Martin, Chester, Lord Selkirk's Work In Canada, p. 188, Oxford University Press, Toronto, 1916.
30   Hawkes, John, The Story Of Saskatchewan And Its People, Vol. 1, p. 59, S.J.J. Clarke, Publisher, Regina, 1924
31   Ross, Alexander, The Red River Settlement, p. 249, Smith, Elder and Co., London, 1856
32   Ross, Alexander, The Red River Settlement, p. 257, Smith, Elder and Co., London, 1856.
33   Ross, Alexander, The Red River Settlement, p. 247, Smith, Elder and Co., London, 1856.

"(Pemmican) is the travelling provision in the fur land. . . There is no risk of spoiling if given reasonable care. . . It is one of the most perfect forms of condensed food known and is excelled by no other provision in satisfying qualities. . . Halfbreeds and Indians will eat four pounds of it in a single day. It is estimated that on an average, the carcasses of two buffalo are required to make one bag (or 100 pounds) of pemmican."[34]

H.M. Robinson

Chapter 7

All For The Love Of Pemmican

Speaking in a low-pitched monotone, the Assiniboine elder with shoulder-length hair and a deep scar on his forehead, had two messages, both related to the buffalo. He couldn't recall the buffalo days but he remembered the helplessness felt by his parents when the buffalo did not return. As long as his father lived, he had sorrowed about the loss but did not lose faith that someday the bison make a glorious return out of the sky or out of the earth.

The Assiniboine had two messages, neither of them startlingly new. The first was a restatement with added conviction that the buffalo were, to begin with, a special concession from a merciful Great Spirit to the prairie tribes, a wide-ranging gift of goodness that would include unfailing pemmican food, clothing, shelter, fuel and even useful objects from the buffalo body, some of which remained unnamed. When the buffalo vanished, everything so dear to the native hearts vanished too.

The other message had a newness about it. The old man had a dream transmitting a warning from the Great Spirit. It was a warning that the greedy fellows flocking into this country from beyond the eastern ocean, could not be trusted with the Great Spirit's natural treasures after the newcomers discovered they were saleable. The killing, burning or depleting would not stop. They would show no conscience in destroying buffalo, birds, fish, soil fertility, fur-bearing animals and even good scenery if there was money to be had. Indians, said the old Assiniboine, would never be guilty of killing the last bird of a race, or the last buffalo, or cutting the last trees in a forest, or selling the last oil from a well. What's the hurry to get that money in the bank and leave Nature's wonderful storehouse poor and sick?

Pemmican simply symbolized the long list of good things that came with the buffalo and some of which that were lost with the buffalo, explained the old man. Things that might have supported the Indian's chosen way of life, forever. It's not surprising that the aboriginal people felt aggrieved, and experienced hopeful dreams of the buffalo's return. Its record as a supplier of human needs was never equalled. Pemmican was but one of the many food substances and necessities for which the Indian people had a permanent debt to the buffalo. There were the tidbits like tongue, bone marrow, hump or boss, tenderloin and liver that never lost their appeal. But most mature Indians — particularly noticeable among the Cree women — agreed it was quite wrong to kill buffalo for their tongues alone and then waste the balance.

The old Assiniboine became defensive, saying that his people were naturally thrifty and shouldn't be blamed for the extravagance and mistakes of a few who were wasteful. Indians didn't waste anything on stylish clothes, he said. Their leather clothes and moccasins were warm and they were worn for years. "Don't forget that our tepees were our homes and they were made from buffalo skins too. And did you ever see rawhide Indian canoes, often called 'bullboats.' They saved many white men from drowning. Thank the buffalo for them too. There's a lot more to be told. We made candles from buffalo tallow. We made knives and scrapers and things from buffalo bones. We stuck handles to buffalo shoulder blades and got hoes for hoeing the ground. When the Indians needed bottles but had no glass, they used buffalo bladders. Handy, wouldn't you agree? And let me tell you about the big bags we needed for carrying and storing pemmican. We wanted bags big enough to hold 100 pounds and the mature buffalo's first stomach was just the right size. In case you don't know, I will tell you that the buffalo, like the milk cow or ox, has four stomachs or sections to one stomach, all different in size and shape. The first one is the paunch. It's the biggest one and its great size made it just right for storing pemmican. When the Great Spirit was making the buffalo, he thought of everything."

"Bet you didn't know this," the Assiniboine continued, "much of the leather used in making tires for Red River cart wheels, enough to wrap the rims of every wheel, came from the same buffalo that gave us the meat for pemmican. There was no available iron for metal tires and the cart wheels needed something to prevent them from collapsing. So what did those pemmican-eaters do? They just cut the wet rawhide into strips and wrapped it around the rims of the wheels, tight, and left it to dry. As the strips dried they shrank and tightened and became as hard as iron and the cart had good tires. If a tire became weakened by wear, it was easy to cut the old one off and rewrap the rim and wait for the new tire to dry. Instead of carrying 'a spare tire,' the cart driver carried a supply of the wet rawhide that he called 'babiche.' Good arrangement, eh?"

There were many more uses for buffalo hides and "spare parts" from a carcass. Indians made their own saddles and bridles from buffalo skins and glue from buffalo hoofs. Buffalo brains were rubbed into the drying skins to help in tanning. The old Indian then said he was telling all this to make the point that of all the contributions made by the buffalo, the most important, by far, was the gift of food. The mixture of lean meat and melted fat and possibly some ripe berries was packed away for later use, making the native people feel as rich and secure as if they had the white man's money in the bank. The Indian elder had an afterthought. He had, he apologized, almost forgotten to mention the buffalo's role in furnishing campfire fuel for a cold evening where there was no wood. Prairie travellers in buffalo country discovered long ago that dry "buffalo chips," or dry buffalo dung served the purpose very well.

There was more work in recovering the annual or biannual pemmican harvest than met the eye. The division of work was much the same for Indians, Métis and whites. The men did the hunting and the boasting, and the women and old men – who were no longer interested in the rough and tumble of the chase – dressed, skinned and removed the lean meat in strips and hung it on branches or cart wheels for drying in the sun. In due course, the dried strips were ground by pounding them between stones, mixed with melted fat, about three parts of dried meat to one part of fat, and some ripe saskatoon or raspberries were added if the season permitted. The finished product was then packed into buffalo stomach bags, each sewn closed with a buffalo-bone needle and sinue.

The "nutritional panacea" — as some enthusiasts have chosen to label it — seemed capable of carrying its own guarantee against spoilage until the next big hunt. Even though it was made without salt, salt wasn't usually available in buffalo country, natives and traders who ate it insisted that it was their favourite food. It offered maximum convenience by being ever-ready, ever-satisfying and ever-tasty without the need for dishes. Humans on heavy meat diets didn't require much salt and were better without it. Meat-eating members of the cat family do not go looking for salt. Deer, buffalo and other vegetarians, however, having a constant need for salt not found in their regular diets, are ever-ready to travel great distances to salt licks.

Human food tastes are known to differ widely. Most pemmican-eaters have been loyally enthusiastic although there was no reason why all should react in exactly the same way to pemmican. Nor is it impossible that humour could explain some of the peculiarities in human taste. H.M. Robinson, whose name appears earlier on these pages, wrote extensively about buffalo meat and pemmican. Perhaps he was more honest than most writers, or maybe he intended to bring smiles of scepticism to readers. After stating without hint of doubt on his own part that pemmican is the most perfectly balanced food, he added, as if making a concession to his conscience, that when flavoured with berries and sugar, pemmican is "nearly good."[35]

Pemmican preservation as practised long ago had another advantage. Being at a time of simple household techniques, long before the adoption of kitchen refrigerators and basement freezers, and even before the use of glass sealers and tin cans for canning, the inventive pemmican-makers didn't appear to be suffering in the least.

Thus, the final act in field operations consisted of loading the precious pemmican — a sure safeguard against starvation — into the Red River carts, those frontier contraptions which proved that horse or ox-drawn vehicles could be made strong even in the total absence of nails, bolts and other metal fasteners, and axle grease. In most cases, the carts moved on dry and screaming axles and were pulled by single oxen hitched in shafts with the aid of one-ox yokes. Nine hundred to a thousand pounds, or nine to 10 big bags of pemmican, was the usual load for a cart and a single ox. The buffalo hunt was not generally declared at an end until the hunters' carts were carrying at least three-quarters of that amount.

The native hunters could claim the credit for making pemmican popular without, in any way, restricting the time-honoured methods. There were no secrets about the operations. Consequently, the same basic fare was adopted by natives of all tribes in buffalo country, traders, western voyageurs and many of the first settlers. Ultimately, it was the fur-traders' reliance on pemmican that brought hostility and war to Rupert's Land in 1814 and 1816, inviting the conclusion that there is still more pemmican in western history or more history in pemmican than readers expect to find.

The competition between the two huge fur-trading companies, the Hudson's Bay Company and the North West Company, was bitter at the best of times. It was worse, though, after the former appeared to support Lord Selkirk's farm settlement at the confluence of the Red and Assiniboine Rivers. Almost at once, the Montreal or North West Company and the settlers were in conflict over the available pemmican, which was not enough to meet the traders' needs for rations for voyageurs moving furs and the settlers' needs for survival.

Let nobody suppose that pemmican wasn't considered worthy of a fight. The conflict became ugly when, on January 8, 1814, Miles Macdonell, who was Lord Selkirk's resident governor, issued a public proclamation forbidding the removal of pemmican or any other food product from Lord Selkirk's territory known as Assiniboia. The North West Company men were furious. They had purchased large supplies and stood ready to deliver the pemmican to the big canoe brigades going east to Fort William and west to Fort Edmonton. The canoemen couldn't toil through their daylight-to-darkness shifts without good food, and there was nothing in prospect if they failed to get the pemmican bought for them by their company. The Nor'-Westers had no intention of submitting to Macdonell's whim or to see their own crews and men grounded. In May, 1814, Macdonell's authority was put to the test.

Much of the Nor'-Westers' supplies were in storage at posts high on the Assiniboine River. Macdonell guessed accurately that the Nor'-Westers would try to sneak a big shipment down and into the Red River valley to the big brigades by darkness. The Nor'-Wester's shipment got as far as Fort Souris on the Assiniboine River where the valuable supplies were placed in hiding. Macdonell's men discovered the hiding place and a monster seizure was planned just as if it were a big bank robbery. Macdonell sent his sheriff, John Spencer, and several armed men. On May 27, 1814, Spencer and his men knocked at the fort gate and when there was no response, he ordered his men to use their axes to cut through it.

John Pritchard, the man in charge of the post, refused to surrender the stores. But Spencer had the strength and the guns, and his men moved the supplies to Macdonell's boats — 479 bags of pemmican or about 25 tons, 93 kegs of grease and a quantity of unprocessed meat. Pritchard was arrested for resisting a legal order and the huge haul of pemmican was moved to Fort Douglas on the Red River. It looked like the biggest pemmican seizure in history. Indeed, history may show it as a preliminary to the tragic Battle of Seven Oaks on June 19, 1816, sometimes called the Battle of the Pemmican.

34   Robinson, H.M., The Great Fur Land, p. 117, 162, 164, Sampson Low, Marston, Searle and Co., London, 1879.
35   Robinson, H.M., The Great Fur Land, p. 164, Sampson Low, Marston, Searle and Co., London, 1879.

*"The hunters and frontiersmen who accomplished their
destruction have handed down to us a contemptuous opinion of the size,
character and general appearance of our bison. And how could it be otherwise
than that a man who would find it in his heart to murder a majestic bull
bison for a hide worth only a dollar, should form a one-dollar estimate of the
grandest ruminant that ever trod the earth? Men who butcher African
elephants for their ivory, also entertain a similar estimate of their victims."[36]*

William T. Hornaday

Chapter 8

The Profligate Hide Hunters

Buffalo country attracted hunters from every level of society, especially in the '70s of the last century. There were the pemmican hunters with legitimate purposes and the least wasteful of killing practices. There were the "pot hunters" who didn't hesitate to kill a three-quarter-ton bison cow or a one-ton bull for a few morsels of tongue or tenderloin. And there were the hide-hunters who dominated the '70s with new and powerful guns but no improvement in conscience. They killed lavishly for the one or two-dollars per mature hide that American tanners were prepared to pay.

The advent of the Union Pacific Railway in 1869 brought thousands of people to the southwest, most of whom desired "easy money." Some tried any job that required the use of a saddle horse and gun. When a hunt was planned, two skinners were required for every person assigned to shoot, and their job was far from enviable. The man with the gun was generally self-employed but skinners were wage-earners. The employer was the only one who stayed clean; skinners were required to remove the hides from the carcasses, and stretch and stake each skin on the ground for a partial drying. They constantly handled hides made clammy and odorous from blood and visceral fluids. The smell of death, it was told, seemed to hang in the air on the "firing range." Men, who wondered if they would ever be clean again, must have wondered why they were there.

J.A. Allen, who wrote *History of the American Bison* in 1877, described the living conditions in the hide hunters' camps in the southwestern United States. He wrote that the mealtime tin cup for each man consisted merely ". . .of a battered fruit-can. Each man's hunting knife not only does duty in butchering the buffalo, but is the sole implement used in despatching his food, supplying the places of spoon and fork as well as knife. The bill of fare consists of strong coffee, often without milk or sugar, 'yeast-powder bread,' and buffalo meat fried in buffalo tallow. When the meal is cooked, the party encircles the skillet, dips bread in the fat and eats the bread with his fingers. . . They sleep generally in the open air, in winter as well as summer, subjected to every inclemency of the weather. As may well be imagined, a buffalo hunter at the end of the season, is by no means prepossessing in his appearance, being, in addition to his filthy aspect, a paradise for hordes of nameless parasites. They are yet a rollicking set, and occasionally include "men of intelligence" who formerly possessed an ordinary degree of refinement.[37]

Allen was perhaps thinking of the most famous buffalo hunter of them all, "Buffalo Bill" Cody. This Iowa-born boy made his mark on the more westerly frontier and may have been a showman as much as he was a buffalo hunter. He could also claim the world's record on the strength of having shot and killed 4,280 buffalo in one year. While he was criticized for excessive killing for the sake of records and vanity —it was at this point in his life that he gained the moniker, Buffalo Bill — he did keep the Union Pacific workers supplied with buffalo meat. Cody became known as a master handler of horses, lariats and guns and, in later years, he organized his own Wild West Show and toured both North America and Europe.

The most widely heralded buffalo shooting competition of all time brought Cody and a similarly noted hunter, William Comstock from Kansas, together, and attracted the gaze of the sporting world. It was agreed that the two men would shoot from horses and the man who totalled the largest number of kills between 8 a.m. and 4 p.m. on the appointed day would become the world champion. The contest was planned for east of Sheridan, Wyoming, where organizers expected to find herds in sufficient numbers to keep the contestants busy all day. Guests and officials travelled from as far as St. Louis by special trains.

When an acceptable herd was spotted, the two mounted men approached from the rear and divided it, Cody in pursuit of one side and Comstock, the other. Each man was followed by his official judge and referee who made a formal count of kills. At the end of the first run, the score was 38 kills for Cody and 23 for Comstock. With no new herd in sight, an intermission was called and champagne served, but before the recess ended a small herd came into sight. The two men mounted and rode away for the second run, the score from which brought Cody's total to 56 and Comstock's to 37. There was still another run and, at the conclusion, Buffalo Bill was declared the champion with 69 kills for the day. Comstock acknowledged defeat with a score of 46.

Buffalo Bill Cody, with his captivating characteristics, remained a controversial figure as author C.M. MacInnes reveals *In The Shadow Of The Rockies*. "The notorious Buffalo Bill, whose claim to immortality seems to be a singularly negative one, is said to have killed four-thousand-two-hundred-and-eighty [buffalo] in eighteen months and forty-eight in fifty minutes." Some

American frontiersmen believed that the more buffalo they killed, the sooner the hated Indians would disappear, and so zest was added to the holocaust.[38] There appears to have been support by the administrations of both the U.S. Congress and the Canadian House of Commons for the mass slaughter of buffalo. It was seen as a step in preventing their Indians from leaving the reserves to satisfy their intense hunger. However, Canadians of the present time would almost certainly stand firmly with author MacInnes in denying hero worship to the champion buffalo killer.

Americans found Buffalo Bill to be a source of first-class entertainment and helpful in preserving their lore and local history. Canadians, apart from any feelings of revulsion from thoughts of mass slaughter, may have looked with some envy upon the American buffalo hunters, while overlooking their own. It would probably come as a surprise to Canadians that they had gained, by immigration, one of the leading buffalo hunters from the State of Kansas. His arrival to cattle ranch in the Cypress Hills was too late for buffalo hunting on the Canadian side but, as a contemporary and friend of Buffalo Bill Cody and Wild Bill Hickok, he brought a wealth of colour and showed how closely the Canadian and American frontiers were related.

J.A. Gaff, known as "Dad Gaff," became a conspicuous part of the western frontier. Born in Indiana in 1850, he was on the buffalo range in Kansas in 1868, entering the buffalo business in a small and modest manner, about the only way a young hunter could get started before the trade in hides and robes gained an identity. In truth, he started with tongues. He would ride out on the range in the early morning, having acquired a horse, a 12-pound Sharps buffalo gun and a stock of ammunition, shoot some eight or nine buffalo, remove only their tongues and place them in his saddlebag. At the end of the day, he sold them to a dealer for 25 or 50 cents each for shipment to a city market. Gaff thought he was making "big money" but when the market changed to favour hides, he became one of the early hide hunters in Kansas. He told of killing 80 buffalo in one day and 5 200 — almost a thousand more than Cody's alleged record — in one year.

Gaff, who was known as a good neighbour in the ranching community on the south slope of the Cypress Hills, didn't boast about the magnitude of his killing. It was just another fact of frontier history, like carrying a revolver in one's belt was also part of it. He knew all about those hand guns, "they could be damned disagreeable yet a wise man would no more leave home without his six-shooter than walk down the street of Maple Creek without his pants."

He said that during the peak years of the hide business in Kansas, the skinned and rotting carcasses were so numerous on the plains that a person stepping from one dead body to another could walk for 25 miles without placing a foot on the ground, and that no story was so good that it couldn't be made better with a little inflation. He admitted, "It was a hell of a waste and a hell of a way to treat good animals."

Dad Gaff, by a strange coincidence, became in his later years, the proprietor and operator of the village hotel in Saskatchewan's southwest corner. He had found himself in Govanlock after a late night and felt that it would be unwise to drive back to his ranch. He called at the village hotel where the welcome was not cordial. The owner said he didn't have a room. The rancher suspected discrimination and said: "Come on, now. Do I have to buy your hotel to get a room?" The owner took offence and answered, "You couldn't buy this hotel and you know it." Gaff asked, "What's your price?" The owner named a figure and Gaff produced a cheque book, wrote out the price in full and said, "Now you clear out or I'll have you arrested for loitering. I'll choose my own room for tonight." He lived there until his death in 1941.

The hide hunters who overran the southern ranges were working north of the Missouri River and on the Canadian side three years later, with the same devastating results. Outwardly, there was life in the buffalo-related businesses. Green hides, slippery, slimy, smelly things for which the hunters were pleased to accept one or two dollars each and the eastern tanners were eager to receive, numbered among Western Canada's leading exports. At least a dozen trading posts in the west made it known that green hides were accepted for reshipment to St. Paul, Minnesota, or to the I.G. Baker Company at Fort Macleod or Fort Benton. The volume of gun and ammunition sales was higher than ever; it sounded like a "Good Times" report.

The bad news came. The buffalo population which had been in slow decline for several decades had, since the advent of the hide hunters, accelerated. The absence of precise population statistics for buffalo is a handicap with which scholars will have to live. Figures comparable to population numbers for the nation's cattle and horses were not published, but some scattered figures for buffalo hides marketed in the years under review are quite indicative. The fact that the figures are from different sources will be seen as a weakness, but still well worth noting. They are supposed to show the number of buffalo hides marketed from Fort Macleod in each of four years:

Hides marketed by I.G. Baker Co., Fort Macleod

1874	250,000
1877	30,000
1878	12,797
1879	5,764[39]

To the above figures for the years 1877, '78 and '79, the editor appended the observation: "From these figures it will be seen how rapidly extermination is overtaking the buffalo and how terrible must be the suffering among the Indians who have to rely upon them for food." The bison was not yet extinct, but it was not too soon for tears. These great, noble North Americans — which had withstood 10,000 years of droughts, floods, natural enemies, famine, disease, extremes of winter cold and summer heat, blizzards, fires and a lot more — had been humbled by new guns against which they did not have a chance, and distant governments that allowed it to happen so as to ease their own problem in keeping the Indians on the new reserves.

36 Hornaday, William T., The Extermination Of The American Bison, Vol. II, p. 393, Government Printing Office, Washington, 1889.
37 Allen, Joel Asaph, History of the American Bison, p. 582, Government Printing Office, Washington, 1877.
38 MacInnes, C.M., In The Shadow Of The Rockies, p. 143, Rivingtons, London, 1930.
39 The figures for 1877, '78 and '79 are from the Saskatchewan Herald, Battleford, Sept. 8, 1879. The figure for 1874 is probably from the Saskatchewan Herald also but that hasn't been confirmed.

"We all see that the day is coming when the buffalo will all be killed and we shall have nothing more to live on and then you will come into our camp and see the poor Blackfoot starving. I know that the heart of the white soldier will be sorry for us and they will tell the Great Mother who will not let her children starve. We are getting shut in; the Crees are coming into our country from the north and the Whites from the south and east and they will all destroy our means of living; but still, although we plainly see these days coming, we will not join the Sioux against the Whites but will depend upon you (the Mounted Police) to help us."[40]

Chief Crowfoot

Chapter 9

The First Legislation To Protect Proved A Failure

Whence came the first and clearest plea for the protection of the bison? It wasn't from the lords of the fur trade or the parliamentarians in Ottawa or Winnipeg, or the happy hunters who enjoyed the sport of killing or found it profitable. Nor was it from the church missionaries who were more concerned about inter-denominational competition. It came from a relatively little-known Cree Indian chief who was never a self-seeker of attention, never rated as a great leader like Chief Crowfoot or a former warrior like Chief Piapot or a famous artist like Allen Sapp. Chief Sweet Grass was just a modest tribesman who was opposed to mass slaughter. If prairie tribes planned wisely, he reasoned, their people would never be hungry and never have to resort to the wastefulness and cruelty of driving herds over a precipice, or killing hundreds of the big animals in a pound.

In 1876, when the hide hunters were overrunning the prairie country, Sweet Grass stood alone with his belief that white and native hunters were making greedy mistakes. It was also the year in which the Government of Canada hoped to gain Indian support for a treaty with the Plains Crees, and because their country was so extensive, government officials were willing to conduct the negotiations at two points rather than one — the first at Fort Carlton in the eastern part of the region and the other at Fort Pitt in the west, both served by the North Saskatchewan River.

Earlier western treaties had been negotiated and signed at the rate of one per year after 1871. There was, however, a special urgency about adding the Cree nation. The Honourable Alexander Morris, Lieutenant-Governor of Manitoba and the Northwest Territories, served as Chief Commissioner. The two other commissioners were James McKay, the Scottish halfbreed born at Fort Edmonton, and W.J. Christie, a long-time servant of the Hudson's Bay Company.

In the course of the Fort Carlton sessions, Chief Beardy, notorious for his trickery, emerged as the trouble-maker, making the reliable Chief Mist-ah-Wah-Sis more appreciated than ever. The declining buffalo herds, though, did not get much attention until the commissioners went to Fort Pitt. There, the quiet little man, Chief Sweet Grass, instead of obeying the Chief Commissioner's instructions to restrict discussion to the proposed treaty, ignored everything he considered of less importance than saving the buffalo.

"The Great King, our Father," he said, "is looking upon us this day. He regards all people as equal. He has mercy on the whole earth. He has opened a new world for us. I have pity for all those who must depend on the buffalo. I want this, my brother (the Lieutenant-Governor) to commence to act for me, that the buffalo may be protected. It is for that reason that I give you my hand. If spared, I shall commence at once to clear a small piece of land for myself and others of my kinsmen. We will commence, hand-in-hand, to protect the buffalo. . . Use your utmost to help me to save the buffalo for our children."[41] Among the spectators and listeners was the great dissenter, Chief Big Bear, and Sweet Grass did not let the moment pass without turning to his fellow Cree and calling upon him for his support: "Think of our children and all who come after us," he said.

Sweet Grass did well in winning friends for his cause. The Chipewyan Chief came forward to say: "Sweet Grass has spoken for all of us. What he says, we all say now." And the Lieutenant-Governor, who was present as the presiding officer and had reason to be angry at Sweet Grass for taking up so much negotiating time for his personal mission, showed no displeasure and smiled broadly as if he might be a convert to the idea. He admitted that he was "much pleased with the conduct of the Battle River Crees and would report such to the Queen's Councillors."

Morris was followed by Lieutenant-Governor David Laird but Sweet Grass' plea was reported. The first Order of Business when the new governor faced the Territorial Council at the 1877 meeting was an Ordinance For The Protection Of The Buffalo." Chief Sweet Grass would have been elated, but tragedy intervened. The popular little chief, who most likely inspired the Ordinance, lost his life in an accidental shooting on the reserve, just weeks after the signing of Treaty Number Six at Fort Pitt.

The 1877 meeting of the Territorial Council was the first to be conducted at Fort Livingstone, overlooking the Swan River in today's northeastern Saskatchewan. The unpopular structure in an out-of-the-way part of the Territories had been built as the headquarters for the North West Mounted Police, but it was used only briefly by the Force. It became the Hon. David Laird's legislative home for the 1877 Session before moving to the new territorial capital for the 1878 Session. The Council of '77 consisted of, in addition to Lieutenant-Governor Laird, Mounted Police Commissioner James F. Macleod, and Magistrates Matthew Ryan and Hugh Richardson, and Amadee E. Forget, Clerk of the Council.

The Lieutenant-Governor read The Speech From The Throne in which he said: "You will be invited to consider what steps ought to be taken to protect the buffalo from wanton destruction. The extinction of this animal in which many Indians and others largely rely for support, should, if possible, be prevented, at least until stock raising can be introduced to take the place which the buffalo has supplied for many generations. Whereas it is expedient to provide for the protection of buffalo: Be it therefore enacted by the Lieutenant-Governor of the North West Territories, by and with the advice and consent of the Council thereof, as follows:

1. No pound, pit or like enclosure or contrivance shall, at any time, be formed or used in the North West Territories for the capture of buffalo; nor shall it be lawful to destroy buffalo by running them into rivers or lakes, or over steep banks or precipices.

2. It shall be unlawful at any season, to hunt or kill buffalo for the mere motive of amusement, or wanton destruction, or solely to secure their tongues, choice cuts or peltries; and the proof in any case, that less than one-half of the flesh of a buffalo has been used or removed shall be sufficient evidence of the violation of this section.

3. It shall be unlawful to kill buffalo of either sex under two years of age, or to have the dead bodies or the peltries, or any other part of the bodies of such young buffalo in possession.

4. On and after the fifteenth day of November, one thousand eight hundred and seventy-seven, and in every year thereafter, the period between the fifteenth day of November and the fourteenth day of the following August, inclusive, shall be a closed season for female buffalo, or to have in possession the dead bodies or the peltries, or any other part of the bodies of female buffalo killed in the said closed season: Provided, that nothing contained in this section shall extend or apply to Indians or non-Treaty Indians, between the fifteenth day of November and the fourteenth day of the following February, inclusive.

5. Nothwithstanding anything contained in this ordinance, it shall be lawful for any traveller or other person in circumstances of pressing necessity to kill buffalo to satisfy his immediate wants.

6. In order to convict any person of unlawfully killing buffalo, it shall be sufficient to prove that such person was one of a party accessory to such killing, and taking the life of each and every buffalo unlawfully killed shall be deemed a distinct and separate offence.

7. Every person convicted of an offence against one of the foregoing provisions of this ordinance shall be liable, for each and every offence, to

a fine not exceeding one hundred dollars, with costs of prosecution, and in default of payment to be imprisoned for a term not exceeding three months.

8. When any offence is committed against this ordinance, it shall be the duty of any sheriff, policeman, constable or sub-constable, or other peace officer, upon view thereof or upon the information of any two persons, who shall declare their names and place of abode, to forthwith arrest such offender by the authority of this ordinance, and without further warrant to bring him before a Judge, Stipendary Magistrate, or Justice of the Peace to be dealt with according to the law.

9. Every offence against any of the sections of this ordinance may be prosecuted, in a summary manner, before any Judge, Stipendary Magistrate, or Justice of the Peace.

10. One half of any pecuniary penalty recovered under this ordinance shall be paid to the informer.

11. This ordinance shall come into force on the first day of June in the present year, one- thousand-eight-hundred-and-seventy-seven."[42]

It was a first-class effort and Sweet Grass would have been happy, although it is doubtful if the ordinance was ever tested in a court of law. Shocking as it must have seemed to true conservationists, if there were any, the Council of the Northwest Territories, meeting for the first time at Battleford in 1878, was asked to reconsider The Ordinance for the Protection of the Buffalo, passed in the previous year. With a minimum of explanation, the new Bill entitled "An Ordinance to Repeal the Ordinance for the Protection of the Buffalo," was introduced on July 29, 1878. The rescinding ordinance passed quickly through the various stages until it achieved its purpose on August 2, 1878, when the official record announced to the world that "The Ordinance number five of 1877, entitled 'An Ordinance For The Protection Of The Buffalo' Is Hereby Repealed." The contentious bylaw lasted all of one year.

It was sad but true and the slaughter continued. Sinister deeds were taking place at the International Boundary which a big part of the remaining herds normally crossed at least twice a year. American forces were known to be turning back the migrating herds so that their Indians could kill and eat while the Canadian Indians went hungry. Canadian Indians — seeing the buffalo turned back and prevented from entering Canada — pursued hunts and made trouble while the Canadian authorities concluded that the sooner the buffalo were destroyed, the sooner their Indians would accept reservation life.[43]

40   Chief Crowfoot, as told to North West Mounted Police Commissioner, James F. Macleod, Commissioner's Annual Report to the Secretary of State, 1877.
41   Morris, Lt.-Gov. Alexander, The Treaties of Canada With The Indians, p. 236 - 244, Belfords, Clarke and Co., Toronto, 1880.
42   Journal Of The Council Of The North West Territories, Session of 1877, Printed by the Government of the North West Territories, Regina, 1886.
43   Steele, Col. S.B., Forty Years In Canada, p. 146, Hubert Jenkins, Ltd., London 1914.

"From time immemorial, this child of the plains had lived on the buffalo. To rob him of this animal was to deprive him of his livelihood. To him the buffalo was the staff of life, the very condition of his continued existence. When, then, the white man began to come in numbers, when the buffalo were hunted for their robes, when these beasts were slaughtered in thousands in all parts of the west, the outlook became serious for the Red Man. Improvident as he was, he did not realize the inroads upon his capital, his greatest source of well-being. He joined in the great drives, the terrible slaughter, the wholesale destruction. He could not believe that there would be any end to the innumerable herds that were as numerous as the sands of the sea. But though a white man could ride through an unbroken line of these great bovines for 25 miles, though Sir George Simpson saw herds that reached as far as human eye could see in all directions, the poor Indian was to learn that such horrid wanton slaughter by white men and red men, could have but one ending."[44]

Archibald Oswald MacRae

Chapter 10

Who Shot The Last One?

From 1877, the year of the signing of Blackfoot Treaty No. 7, the big herds were seen no more. After another three years, even a small "bunch" was "a rare sighting" and by 1884, the prairie race had, for all practical purposes, disappeared. Still there were stragglers and small clusters that seemed to come out of hiding to greatly excite the hunters, especially those who dreamed of shooting "the last one," even though there was a growing number of conservation-minded citizens who were finding the competitive interest in the "last kill" quite revolting. "Why kill the last one at all?" they were asking. "Why would anybody want the distinction of shooting the last of any race, especially if the person already had about as much meat in his icehouse and smokehouse and curing crocks as he could handle?"

Be that as it may, the rumour of a sighting of a solitary buffalo or small group of the nervous survivors produced a flurry of excitement among hunters eager for the pursuit. They spouted handy excuses about being "short of fresh meat," or "too hard up to buy butcher shop meat," knowing very well that the expense of travel, of ammunition and of lost time from a wage-earning job would totally preclude the possibility of obtaining a bargain in buffalo beef from the hunt.

Most reports about the killing of the last free-ranging prairie buffalo are difficult to authenticate. It is a well-tested theory that when events of historic significance are not dated and in some way confirmed soon after happening, chances are they will never be entirely satisfactory to the working historian. It is fairly clear, however, that with each succeeding year after 1882, the number of buffalo killed seemed to drop by about 50 per cent. The number indicated by hides handled and other bits of information for 1883 suggested about half as many buffalo killed as in 1882 and the number for 1885 about half of what it was in '84. The count for 1888, as far as one can judge, was considerably less than half of what it was in 1887.

Kerry Wood, lifelong student of natural history, recognized the problem and after repeating the question, "Who killed the last wild buffalo on the unfenced lands of the west?" answered, "Here we have the makings of a grand argument because almost every region had its own 'authentic' — but unwritten — buffalo record. In Alberta, it was believed that a starving band of Cree Indians found and killed a small group of buffalo cows and calves on the banks of the Red Deer River, near the present site of Trochu, during 1888."[45] That account gained some credence when the Calgary Tribune of June 20 printed information from the mayor of Calgary that a halfbreed, Sanderson by name, shot two buffalo bulls in the same general area, on the same river, in the same year.[46] It was, however, a case of stretching the facts.

It is possible, nevertheless, that it was the same Red Deer River kill to which Kerry Wood alluded, that western historian George Shepherd referred to when he commented: "When the Mounted Police came to our western plains in 1874, the buffalo were still here but vanishing rapidly. The last recorded killing in western Canada was a gaunt old bull in the Red Deer Valley in 1888. By that time competent observers estimated that of the millions of buffalo once roaming our prairies, there remained less than one hundred living on the face of the earth, and this is close enough to total extinction."[47]

W. Henry McKay of Medicine Hat, in writing a piece about his father, Samuel McKay, for the Calgary-based magazine, *Canadian Cattlemen*, brought new light to the search for the last killing shots fired at the prairie buffalo. Pursuing a small herd of 11 head, McKay shot two bulls and said he could have taken more. Moreover, it was another killing in that year, 1888, which appears increasingly to mark the finale of buffalo hunting on the Canadian plains. The place of the shooting, McKay's son believed, was southwest, a few miles, from the Village of Cereal, in east central Alberta.

Anybody reading the account, as written by Henry McKay, would be impressed by the supporting detail. "I was only six years of age at the time," he wrote, "but I remember well when (my father) returned to Medicine Hat with the two buffalo heads. Mr. R.C. Porter of Medicine Hat could substantiate this as he was there at the time, also Thomas Hargrave, the Many Islands Lake rancher."

Another person who could bear witness, according to Henry McKay was Alex Gardipee. He had the sole responsibility for the care of the milk cow taken along to feed the buffalo calves if any were left as orphans after the shooting. The milk cow was not needed, however, because no calves were seen. McKay, it seems, sold the two heads for $50 each and said he could have sold many more.[48]

John Peter Turner — who was for the longest time the official voice of North West Mounted Police history — made a useful contribution to the discussions about the last members of the wild herd to become victims of hunters' guns. "One of the last links with the early west was forever severed in July (1888),"

Turner wrote in *Volume II* of his excellent record. "While stationed on detachment duty at the Sixty-Mile Bush on the Battleford-Swift Current Trail, Constables J.D. Nicholson and William McNair learned from a freighter . . . of a small herd of buffalo frequenting the Badlands near Tramping Lake, southeast of Eagle Hills. . . The two constables decided to locate the animals, if possible, but found travelling so difficult among the alkali lowlands bordering Tramping Lake, they were obliged to give up the search. On their return, they met James Clinkskill of Battleford, one of the newly elected members of the Legislature, who had two hid quarters of fresh buffalo meat on his buckboard. He had procured it from some halfbreeds who killed five of the animals near Tramping Lake. One of the quarters was turned over to the two constables and, thus, closed the record of the last wild buffalo on the Canadian plains."[49]

The fact is that nobody knows positively who shot the last buffalo. Nor does it matter much any more. It was, to be sure, a bullet that signalled the end of a frontier chapter, a sad, bloody, tragic chapter that weakened human qualifications for a role in supervising environmental matters, local or global. On this point, however, humans did not agree. No polls were taken to determine public opinion. No doubt, there was a larger body of silent support for the wholesale slaughter policy, especially among people in "high places" in Ottawa and Washington, more than any one was prepared to admit.

At Fort Benton, Montana, an editor with more zeal than benevolence, declared that there was too much of "this maudlin, idle sentimentality" about saving the buffalo. "We propose to change our tone and earnestly recommend the slaughtering of buffalo. Of course, a herd of them should be kept in the national park as an addition to its attractions and curiosities but, barring the presence of such a herd, we would be glad to announce today, that there is not a buffalo within a thousand miles of this territory. For as long as buffalo roam over any part of it, whether on or off reservations, cattle-killing and horse-stealing Indians will continue to plague our settlers. The buffalo is the dirty vagabond of his genus and his special mission in the northwest has been, for years, the promotion of vagabondism among the Indians. . . Kill or chase away the buffalo and it may yet be possible to reach the Red Man's intelligence, for whatever Indian agents and missionaries may claim, his brain is situated in his stomach."[50]

Probably, many readers agreed; possibly more shook their heads, saying, "Sad, if true." Surely, as time has passed, more and more citizens are responding by asking — when will man learn that he cannot go on forever imposing his greed and cruelty upon the earth's sensitive biosphere?

"Soon even the Indian realized that the animal which had provided his food, clothing and practically all his needs — the most superb creature of its kind — was confronted by extinction. And with the realization there came regrets; he bemoaned the enormity of the loss, a loss which he had helped to consummate so swiftly.

Believing that there were still many buffalo in the south, the Crees of the Canadian plains cried to the Manitou to send the 'musketayo mustoosh' back to its former haunts. In a frenzy of faith the worried red man supplicated the gods by propping buffalo skulls upright, the faces of which were painted with the magic of vermilion and turned towards the north. While these and other offerings were being made in propitiation, it happened by strange coincidence, that at widely separated points more practical influences were at work.

Upon these influences rested the only ray of hope that shone through the gloom of waste. There remained a mere chance that a blot so irrevocable as the extinction of the buffalo would not besmirch the colonization efforts of civilized mankind."[51]

John Peter Turner

Chapter 11

A Ray Of Hope For Buffalo Return

It was a narrow escape and not many Canadians realized how close their planet came to losing the plains strain of the North American bison, completely and permanently. Without the resourcefulness of the Scottish halfbreed, James McKay, the Irish immigrant, Charles Alloway and the Montana Indian, Sam Walking Coyote, the subspecies might now be numbered with the dinosaur, passenger pigeon and great auk.

As partners in freighting in the age of Red River carts and their ox slaves, sending hundreds of carts as far south as St. Paul and as far west as Fort Edmonton, 500 miles of deeply rutted trails, McKay and Alloway knew each other well. They were, however, more or less strangers to the Indian and would have given the impression of having nothing in common with him except a hankering to do something about the diminishing buffalo. The three were distinctive personalities. The Indian, whose family lived in western Montana, was serving a self-imposed exile for tepee discord in the summer of 1873. Sam's father had the reputation of throwing marrow bones, with unerring aim, at anybody with whom he did not agree, and his mother-in-law always carried a switch when she had a message for Sam.

For his summer headquarters, Pend d'Oreille Indian Sam pitched his tepee on the south side of the Milk River, probably near today's Coutts. He was an expert hunter and never hungered but he did become weary of life as a bachelor. He was tired of boiling his own buffalo meat. He decided to go home, hoping, of course, that he would be pardoned by his easily-angered family members. Wisely, he concluded that reconciliation would be easier to gain if he was seen returning with a gift. But in the absence of stores and trading posts, selecting gifts for volatile relations and in-laws wasn't easy.

As it happened, six orphaned buffalo calves from cows Sam and other hunters killed were hanging around the camp looking hungry and dejected. He gathered tender bits of vegetation and placed them out with fresh water to encourage the calves to stay. He was considering trying to take the six calves back home with him for use as gifts. The calves were noticeably nervous at first and progress was slow but he continued to find feed with extra succulence and palatability and the calves gained confidence. Still, there were troubles. There were mountains to be crossed and two calves died. But the remaining four motherless calves — two bulls and two females made it all the way. The old anger on the part of Sam's family melted moderately but the mother-in-law showed no interest in young buffalo.

Sam decided to retain the ownership and "turned the calves over temporarily to the care of the priests at the Mission of St. Ignatius, near the Flathead Reserve." Sam was then free to go on his carefree way. Buffalo calves were not a saleable commodity anyway and Sam may have forgotten in short order that he owned them.[52] But whether Sam was conscious or not of possible sale values, his four calves matured and became regular breeders. Notwithstanding a few deaths along the way, Sam's herd in 1883 stood at 13 head and they were suddenly saleable at prices of which the owner had never dreamed. Suddenly, he had a new interest in his herd and when Michel Pablo and Charles Allard offered $2500 for 10 of the animals, Sam shouted "Sold."

The cash in his pockets was a new experience for Sam. He was suspicious of cheques and when Pablo was about to settle for the 10 buffalo he bought, Sam wanted the full sum of $2500 in currency or gold. An eyewitness described the scene: Sam accepted the payment and made 25 piles on the ground, each supposed to contain $100. A fox ran by when the count was in progress and Sam, Pablo and Allard, sprang to their feet, seized their guns and pursued, leaving the 25 piles of gold or whatever on the grass. The fox was too fast and by good luck, the cash was neither taken nor disturbed.

"Bud" Cotton who worked for many years at the National Buffalo Park at Wainwright wrote a brief but sad concluding note about Sam Walking Coyote's days after he received payment for his 10 buffalo. "Walking Coyote immediately hit [headed] for town and after a few brief weeks of city life, was found dead under the Missoula bridge. Thus passed away one of the founders of our present buffalo herds."[53] Sam Walking Coyote may have acted upon an impulse and without a carefully drawn purpose for the buffalo calves other than appeasement of his family. But he displayed imagination and skill, and deserves credit for the buffalo recovery which began in the Milk River Valley

The rehabilitation scene shifted next to Manitoba where an observer might have seen the halfbreed, James McKay, driving a team of fast horses about the countryside, filling the double seat of the buggy with his 350 pounds "on the hoof." If his friend and partner in the recovery of buffalo calves, Charles Alloway, was accompanying, he needed a separate buggy. They travelled deep into buffalo country with Métis hunting parties to recover calves left as pathetic orphans, candidates for starvation. Perhaps the McKay and Alloway purpose was not entirely new to Manitoba. Wasn't it from Fort Douglas on the Red River, the centre of the colony, that settlers travelled to capture orphan buffalo calves, hoping they could be raised in captivity and then used like oxen in farm operations?

Lord Selkirk's idea was, in light of the serious shortage of oxen and milk cows, a very good one. But domestication was more difficult than anybody expected and success was minimal. From his home in Scotland, Selkirk passed the proposal to Miles Macdonell, Governor of the Colony, when the settlers were still in their first year of residence: "It would be an interesting experiment," he wrote, "to know whether a cross between our cattle and the buffalo will succeed. I am curious to hear what success you have in attempting to domesticate the latter."[54] Macdonell's reply, written from Fort Douglas, informed his Lordship: "I have been quite unsuccessful in rearing buffalo calves. Several were caught and brought to Fort Daer last spring but they died for want of milk. I hope to have better success another year."[55]

McKay, whose father was a Scot in the service of the Hudson's Bay Co. and whose mother was a native woman, saw hundreds of orphan calves facing probable starvation. With that in mind, McKay and Alloway ordered a milk cow to be brought from Prince Albert, tied it behind their cart and proceeded toward a likely hunting ground near Battleford. It was a wise provision even though teaching or persuading a calf to drink was often as much of a challenge as finding the milk supply. But the two Winnipeg men were lucky, and with a cooperative cow and calves driven by starvation, success was had. The cow distinguished herself by raising all three bison calves.

James McKay's success in capturing and raising buffalo calves was just one of many reasons why Fort Garry's foremost handy man in the '70s of last century deserves praise. He was a government appointee and interpreter for no less than five treaties and, at times, the only person in the country who had the confidence of both Indians and non-Indians. McKay was an original member of the Manitoba Executive Council and remained on it until it was abolished. Then he sat as the elected Member of the Legislature for the Constituency of Lake Winnipeg and became the Minister of Agriculture. McKay was, perhaps, the most influential person in early Manitoba. Conservation and diplomacy came easy to this superman of size and strength.

Manitobans of his generation delighted in relating the events of 1877 when Governor General Lord Dufferin and Lady Dufferin paid an official visit to Manitoba. Both Lord and Lady Dufferin admitted their captivation for McKay and

Stony Mountain proved unforgettable for the visitors. The official party left Fort Garry in horse-drawn carriages and it planned that the Governor General would, at a certain point near the "Mountain," leave the carriage and ride the rest of the way in a Red River cart, hitched to a tandem team of 30 oxen. Thus His Excellency would be driven to meet Col. Samuel Bedson who, like McKay, was destined to make buffalo history in Manitoba.

Lady Dufferin, however, didn't want to be excluded from riding behind the 30 oxen, but there was resistance to changing the plan. She caught the attention of "her friend," James McKay and signalled for him. Understanding her wishes exactly, he placed his powerful arm around the Lady's waist, gently lifted her into the Red River cart and backed away. Some people were shocked but the Lady apparently loved it. In her memoirs, she wrote: "We were very sorry to say farewell to Mr. McKay, whose substantial figure in his well-known buggy, was one of the last things we saw as we steamed away."[56]

There was no doubt about McKay's popularity in early Manitoba or about the importance of his conservation gesture in laying the foundation for one of the first captive herds of prairie buffalo. There is, however, some doubt about the accuracy of certain buffalo records that bear his name. The year of delivery of the first McKay—Alloway calves at McKay's Deer Lodge has become a confused issue. Mr. Alloway, in an interview conducted by the Winnipeg Tribune on June 24, 1925, said: "It was away back in 1873 . . . that [The] Hon. James McKay and [I] decided to send Patadoux Ducharme, a French halfbreed hunter to get a domestic cow in Prince Albert. We were linked up with a brigade of halfbreeds killing for pemmican. We came upon the buffalo southwest of Battleford on the Battle River. That spring we got three good calves, two bulls and a heifer, after their mothers were killed. We took all summer to get them in. We kept them at Deer Lodge and they did well. The same cow raised three. By the spring of 1878, our herd had grown from five calves to 13."[57]

However, there is a *Manitoba Free Press* entry from October 12, 1876 informing that: "Five buffalo calves brought in from the plains by the Hon. James McKay are now the occupants of a paddock adjoining that gentleman's residence at Silver Heights. Three more are on their way to join the first arrivals."[58] The press report of the 1876 hunt did not mention Mr. Alloway's name although his interview with the Winnipeg Tribune indicated that he still considered himself a full partner in the buffalo herd.

Mrs. Margaret Rowand McKay, daughter of Chief Factor John Rowand of Fort Edmonton and wife of James McKay, died early in 1879 and her husband late in the same year. McKay had been sick for much of his last year. His funeral was said to have been the biggest that Winnipeg had ever experienced; people attending said in emotional whispers: "Manitoba will never be the same again."

An auction sale was held to liquidate Mr. McKay's extensive chattels. The sale was announced for January 20, 1880 and concluded late on its third day. There was special interest in the fine furnishings from Deer Lodge, the McKay home, the string of thoroughbred race horses and the little herd of buffalo, perhaps the only privately owned herd in Canada at a time when it was still possible to see wild specimens or even small herds on parts of the plains. Charles Alloway, who held a partner's interest in the bison, might have been ready to buy the McKay share and take the animals away as his exclusive property, but he had no place at which to keep them, and he and his brother, William, and a third party had recently started a private banking business, Alloway and Champion. It wasn't a proper time to be thinking of further investment in buffalo.

The editor of the Winnipeg Tribune believed that 1500 people were present at the sale. Not many of them were there to buy buffalo but many were present to see them in captivity. The same editor was anxious that nobody in attendance would overlook the rarity of the occasion. "The great novelty of yesterday's proceedings," he wrote, "was the sale of the herd of buffalo. We won't be positive but we are half inclined to think that this is the first time ever that buffalo have been brought under the (auctioneer's) hammer."[59]

Genuine buyers at an auction sale are always far outnumbered by spectators and seekers of entertainment. Nonetheless, the late James McKay would have been greatly pleased to know how many potential buyers were present from a distance, even from as far away as Scotland. Apparently, there were at least three parties bidding on the entire herd as a "package," two of them being the Scots: "Messrs. James Walker and Alex Halden of Fifeshire, Scotland."[60]

It would also have been gratifying to Mr. McKay if he could have known that the successful bidder for the herd was a friend and neighbour for some years, an animal lover and a gentleman. Samuel L. Bedson, warden of the Stony Mountain federal penitentiary, who had his own farm in the area, paid $1000 for the 13 moderately young buffalo. But penitentiary wardens were not paid extravagantly and Col. Bedson was obliged to borrow the money from Donald Smith, later the Lord Strathcona, and also a neighbour of McKay.

The influence of the McKay—Alloway efforts in the restoration of the prairie buffalo for park and other captive herds were in no way less far reaching and useful than Sam Walking Coyote's contribution. All three men are owed a debt of thanks by Canadians.

"The buffalo which but a few years ago swarmed over nearly every portion of the country that is now divided into Manitoba and the North West Territories, is now a thing of the past and it is a matter for regret that the Dominion Government should have allowed almost the last survivors to be bought by a United States speculator and removed from Manitoba. Since the herds became extinct on the prairies, the late Lt.-Col. Bedson had, for some years, a small herd at Stony Mountain near Winnipeg. He secured the nucleus of his herd (in 1880) from the executors of the late Hon. James McKay of Deer Lodge, near Winnipeg, and by careful management, this herd . . . increased to about 90. Two years ago, the herd was sold to a Mr. Jones of Kansas, U.S.A., who removed them to that state. It is stated that he will exhibit them at the World's Columbian Exposition in Chicago . . . The only surviving specimens of the buffalo of the plains, now in Canada, are a few at Sir Donald Smith's farm at Silver Heights, near Winnipeg."[61]

The Western World

Chapter 12

Bedson's Buffalo Become International

Samuel Lawrence Bedson, with his birthplace in England, said he was born in a soldier's uniform. In keeping with family tradition, he was, in 1885, a 43-year-old officer with the rank of quartermaster sergeant, marching west under the command of Col. Garnet Wolsley, for the suppression of the Red River Insurrection, and seeing western Canada for the first time. When his battalion was disbanded in the next year, he was appointed warden of the recently created provincial jail being set up at Lower Fort Garry where his battalion had been quartered. He was in Manitoba to stay and forge an essential link in the chain of events that would do much to rescue the prairie buffalo from threatened oblivion by helping to create a North American "stockpile" of breeding animals that would, ultimately, be brought back in triumph to buffalo country in Canada.

In pursuing a purpose, Nature can be devious. In Bedson's first year in Manitoba, the Government of Canada acknowledged the need for a penitentiary for the area and asked Bedson to conduct a study and recommend a site. His advice to build on Stony Mountain was accepted and construction began in 1874, at about which time Bedson was appointed warden of the institution. He became one of the best known and popular citizens in Manitoba. His personality and his involvement with buffalo, needless to say, contributed more to his popularity than an association with a penitentiary.

Settlers in the district, less than 20 miles north of Winnipeg, watched with interest as the "pen" was built, describing it as "the castle," a term which, in the light of its appearance on the commanding eminence, was not inappropriate. It ensured that the warden received the added appellation of nursery rhyme fame, "The King of the Castle." Years later, when Bedson was referred to as "The King of the Castle", one of his admirers interjected saying, "Call him what you like but don't forget that in all likelihood, Canada would not have had Wainwright Buffalo Park and the best collection of park buffalo in the world if it hadn't been for Col. Bedson in the years after 1880."

The penitentiary was still incomplete when Governor General and Lady Dufferin paid an official visit in August, 1877 and it was still two-and-one-half years before Bedson had his herd of buffalo but it was significant that the two key men in directing the vice-regal reception and entertainment — Col. Bedson and Hon. James McKay — were the two who deserved the highest praise in the Manitoba struggle to save the buffalo. The same two men took much pride in their farms, especially in their horses and then in their buffalo. As Norm Gorman, who researched the Bedson characteristics with special care, pointed out, the Colonel had a sympathetic feeling for all animals. "He was no hunter," Gorman wrote. "He would rather catch and tame a coyote or a bear than shoot it." Well remembered was his team of young moose orphans which he and his stockman, Joe Daniels, hitched to a toboggan for a cross-country winter tour.

Starting with 13 head, Bedson's herd grew rapidly, leading somebody to observe — probably as intended humour — that the high rate of increase in the Bedson herd was an indication that the owner had to be a most efficient operator or possess some of the traits of a successful horse rustler. But the suggestion of theft had to be intended as a joke because there was no other herd of buffalo in the country from which to steal and Benson had never been suspected of stealing anything, not even an opinion or a kiss. His success, however, might have been explained, in part, by his well-known feeling of kindness for animals, wild or domesticated. He was known to carry an orphan moose home rather than desert it to starvation. His barnyard had known some strange tenants, and visitors who made the mistake of wandering around the Bedson yard after dark knew exactly what it was like to stumble over a tethered bear or a half-grown buffalo bull.

James McKay died in December, 1879, and an auction sale of his farm and household effects, including 13 buffalo, was announced for January 20, 1880. Warden Bedson entertained a secret desire to buy a small breeding foundation of the species but was sure he could not pay for more than four or five head. And he was discouraged to learn that there were buyers for the animals from as far away as Scotland.

The sale started at noon on January 20 and ended late on January 22, and the buffalo that were expected to be offered individually were presented as a herd. Bedson was sure the plan would eliminate him as a buyer, but he had visited Sir Donald Smith and secured a loan for up to a thousand dollars. When the bidding ended, probably nobody was more surprised than Bedson to find himself the owner of the last surviving herd of prairie buffalo in Canada for the unbelievable total of one thousand dollars. He was happy with the purchase but now he was worried about how he would get them home to Stony Mountain.

He told himself it could be done. He would have two of his own hired workers on good horses and borrow two riders from the McKay farm who were familiar with the buffalo. The plans for the morning drive, though, were complicated by the night-time birth of a bison calf. Bedson felt the cow and calf should remain behind but one of the cowboys believed that the calf could survive the 21-mile walk. As related earlier, the calf passed its first test with distinction. But after walking over the wintry trail from Deer Lodge to Stony Mountain and bedding down in the snow beside its mother at the end of the day, the little fellow followed the 13 older buffalo which broke out of their new paddock during the night and returned to Deer Lodge.

The cowboys agreed that the buffalo did not appear to be overly tired and favored an immediate repetition of the drive. Before nightfall, the buffalo were again at Stony Mountain and more securely enclosed. And the calf of 48-hours — seen taking a reviving swig of mother's milk — was none the worse from its walk of at least 63 miles in 36 hours. Bedson was impressed by the obvious stamina that he hoped to see incorporated in the genetic constitution of a hybrid strain or breed emerging from Canada's domestic cattle and the buffalo.

Bedson's buffalo were picturesque and exciting if not always congenial and cooperative. He must have realized that with a paddock full of buffalo and a penitentiary full of prisoners, there would be no dull moments for him. As time passed, he discovered that the species was more amenable to domestication than he and many others had expected. Increasingly, his bison were being allowed to roam about the community although some neighbors said they were a nuisance. Joe Daniels, the cowboy in charge, was satisfied most of the time to let the animals choose their directions but "keep in touch with them" and know where they were at all times. Bedson was convinced that animals allowed to wander away at will, were more likely to wander back to the barnyard that offered hay, water and salt.

It may have been a natural springtime urge that induced five of Bedson's buffalo to stray westward farther than usual in April, 1889, and encounter trouble with hunters. Bedson had sold the herd almost a year earlier but only part of it had been delivered. Regardless of who would bear the loss, Bedson was upset about it and public indignation was intense.

The five animals had been missing for a few days before Bedson sent one of his experienced men to find them. Following clues, Sam McCormack rode toward Portage la Prairie and at High Bluff he learned that the five animals were there until a family of traditional hunters surrendered to the temptation to pursue and shoot. Three of the five were killed and a fourth was wounded. McCormack, at that point, turned his attention to the recovery of the hides and heads, and the giving of all possible assistance to the police working on the case. The shooting of four buffalo was seen as a heavy loss and there was nothing of benefit from the affair except a clear call from the press and public for laws that "will punish severely anyone destroying one of these now almost extinct animals."[62]

Bedson did not become tired of the buffalo but larger numbers and circumstances were producing more problems. From the 13 original head the herd had grown to 85 head of breeding animals and enough hybrids to make a total of 118, nine years later. The increasing density of farm settlement was forcing a retreat from the practice of allowing his animals to run more or less at large and, finally, the warden was about to retire shortly and keeping the herd would be difficult if not impossible. There would be no problem in finding a buyer and, so, he cut out enough buffalo and hybrids to be given to Sir Donald Smith to liquidate his debt of $1,000 used to buy the buffalo, and then sold the remainder to C.J. "Buffalo" Jones of Garden City, Kansas, USA — 83 head for a total reported to be between $15,000 and $50,000 — the lower figure considered most plausible.

The animals in the Jones purchase were to be shipped from the Winnipeg Stockyard, roughly half in late 1888 and the balance in '89. Nobody seemed to anticipate the difficulties in bringing the herds into the stockyard at Winnipeg and loading them on freight cars. "Buffalo" Jones sent some of his best cowboys to Manitoba to assist in the movement and loading, but it is doubtful if the American rodeo performers among them had ever seen anything more spectacular or hazardous than what awaited them at the loading chutes in Winnipeg.

The first task was to gather all the Bedson buffalo, including the ones that enjoyed the freedom to roam, and deliver them inside the massive stone walls, five feet high and a foot and one-half in thickness, that surrounded the stable-yard at Stony Mountain. It was a wall to halt an army tank even though it didn't impress Bedson's buffalo.

The buffalo had seen the barnyard setting many times before and with memories of good hay, they had no hesitation in entering the open gate again. But when the heavy gate was closed behind them, their wild superstition was instantly fired. With the old "boss bull" taking the lead, the herd began to mill or circle, looking for a way of escape. It looked like the start of a stampede, certainly no place for human loiterers, observers immediately climbed to the top of the fence. But one man, wiser in the ways of buffalo, left the fence to find a safer observation point, farther away. He did it just as the old bull who seemed to be in command led "the buffalo brigade" in a charge that opened the wall and allowed every member of the herd to follow, on the run to the grassland beyond.

The wall was patched up with loose stones and when the herd was again rounded up in the morning, the six riders who were to direct the drive to the Winnipeg Stockyard, about 15 miles across country, made a quick division and cut out 33 head for the Winnipeg delivery. With luck, they would be at the stockyard in five or six hours and have the buffalo loaded and billed to "Buffalo" Jones by sundown.

No doubt the cowboys were glad to be on their way before the buffalo wrecked more Stony Mountain property. They were walking and running quietly, like homestead country oxen. But as the herd approached the entrance to the stockyard, and another gate, the "boss bull" gave a warning. Thirty-three short buffalo tails went up like banners at a political convention and the herd broke into a gallop, straight for Stony Mountain. It took an hour but the herd was finally turned and travelling again toward the stockyard. Common sense told the riders that the buffalo would be getting tired and ready to forget their silly caprice. But the buffalo were not familiar with that reasoning and when the gate was opened, there was another coordinated dash.

The riders decided to pause for lunch, let the horses cool off and the buffalo graze for a while. "We'll try again at one o'clock," the cowboy foreman announced, and so it was. Men and horses were tired, buffalo and horses wanted water and buffalo needed time to consume a stomachful of dry Manitoba grass, still pretty good stuff when frozen. At one o'clock, cowboys and horses were again in motion, pressing the contrary brutes toward the entrance. Each time they tried the result was the same until late in the afternoon when a wall of human spectators so blurred the outline of the gate that the buffalo were inside without appearing to be aware of it and the big gate was finally closed.

Next morning, December 14, men on horses and men on foot tried to force the 33 unyielding critters into the loading chutes leading upward to the freight cars. But as might have been expected by this time, the buffalo were having nothing to do with the little compartments with gates, and more hours were spent and lost coaxing, threatening, goading and trying trickery. Then the unexpected happened.

A *Winnipeg Free Press* reporter gave the credit for the success to the old buffalo bull, who presumably decided that the buffalo resistance had gone far enough. Cowboy frustration was reaching its limit when, in the words of the reporter, "a tremendous old bull which had been making trouble all day by breaking away and hooking the younger cattle, undertook to run the show himself and where the men failed, he succeeded. He got behind the herd and began making it exceedingly lively for the buffalo ahead, prodding them, bellowing at them, and driving the laggards forward with vigorous prods of his horns. The old fellow was trying in the manner which buffalo have followed from time immemorial to work up a stampede.

"When his dream of a stampede wasn't materializing, he would try something else. Tossing his head scornfully, he wheeled about and ran back into the compartment he had just left, jumped into the next one, clearing a fence ten feet high. Not liking the looks of the new quarters he jumped back again and then struck out wildly for Stony Mountain. He cleared every obstacle until he reached the board fence which bound the west side of the stockyards. This paling is fourteen-feet high but he jumped at it, struck it near the top, went through it with a crash, and struck out for home across the prairies, a very much disturbed and agitated buffalo."[63]

The display of buffalo determination won admiration. According to a Winnipeg resident who had been watching, every time the buffalo broke away from the mounted riders, there were at least a few cheers from spectators who wished all the animals could remain in Manitoba. The train carrying the buffalo was to stop for feeding and watering of the animals at Grand Forks, St. Paul and Minneapolis. At each point, city crowds of adults and school children came to enjoy, study and mourn the shattered remnant of a once-mighty race. One of the town's newspaper editors wrote appreciatively, "Two carloads of live buffalo en route from Winnipeg to Kansas via the M. and M., unloading to feed at this point and a concourse of spectators were present to look on. One little calf was the sole juvenile of the party and he seemed lost in the crowd of adult buffalo. These creatures were the property of Major Bedson, warden of the penitentiary of Stony Mountain, Manitoba, and are the lone representatives of the nearly extinct race . . ."[64]

The calf that drew so much admiration at Grand Forks was one of the victims of the rough journey by freight. Several buffalo were trampled to death on the trip and the calf would be the most likely to suffer. It is easy to speculate and say the cars were overcrowded. But the journey was completed and to prove that the wild brutes were not becoming more gentle, the hazards and losses were just as high when the second shipment was made to "Buffalo" Jones' ranch a year later. Indeed, the most frightening experience was in the second year's shipment when 13 of the wildest buffalo escaped right in an occupied section of Kansas City and were completely out of control. It was said that pandemonium prevailed for a few hours but, miraculously, the demonic big beasts were all captured in the wooded area beside the Missouri River and there were no injuries.

It is a wonder that Bedson, working closely with the bison for a decade, escaped serious injury. The stories about his narrow escapes were numerous. One told many times by his daughter, Menotah, had a Christmas afternoon setting. Guests were showing about as much interest in a buffalo-powered sleigh ride as in the promise of roast turkey. The fun-loving Colonel ordered that a certain two-year-old bull be harnessed and hitched to a toboggan. Everybody present wanted a reserved seat on the toboggan. The harnessed buffalo was brought out, restrained by half a dozen prisoners on stable duty, by holding back on a stout rope around the bull's neck.

The guests probably made the bull nervous and his patience was wearing thin. Riders were seated when the bull, without warning, leaped forward, upsetting the toboggan and scattering the attendants holding the rope. The angered animal headed for an open gate and was soon out of sight. Mr. Bedson thought the bull would return to its stable shelter when darkness came. There was no point in pursuing until there was some indication of the direction chosen. Nothing more was seen of toboggan or bull for many days.

Months passed without a clue but spring brought a letter from north Dakota, enquiring if a stray buffalo with a heavy rope knotted around his neck might belong in Manitoba. A Bedson employee was sent to Dakota where he readily identified the bull with a rope around his neck that had left home in a huff on Christmas day. He was now a famous bull and Mr. Bedson wondered if the animal was worth the high cost of bringing him back. What the owner decided is not clear.

Another adventure story featured Bedson's buffalo bull, Blizzard, a story enriched by the pen of an unnamed Manitoba Daily Free Press reporter. Let the reporter tell the story.

Bedson's Birthday

"Mr. S.D. Bedson, the genial Warden of the Government resort at Stony Mountain, celebrated his golden birthday on the 13th. Any ordinary man under the pressure of a hard winter, would have contented himself on such an occasion with a quiet little family party at home, supplemented by the usual plum pudding and a jorum of punch. But Mr. Bedson is not an ordinary man. His wild, untamed spirit could not break the commonplace orthodox method of commemorating such an important event. He determined, if he were going to have a celebration at all, that it should be one which everybody participating therein should remember for some time.

"Mr. Bedson is the proprietor of a herd of genuine buffalo — the greatest aggregation, in fact, of buffalo flesh ever combined under one management in the world. Some of the animals are comparatively docile but some of the old stagers are patriarchal in their dignity, and don't care to be trifled with. Mr. Bedson, after thinking the matter over, determined to have a buffalo sleigh ride. He would bend one of these rugged monarchs of the plain to his purpose — he would career over the illimitable prairie behind a steed whose unbroken spirit knew no yoke — a steed such as mortal man had never driven before. He would do this, and in doing this he would be original.

"On the afternoon of the 13th Mr. Bedson sallied forth, and selected a lively old bull rejoicing in the name of 'Blizzard' — an amiable looking animal with a dark bay eye and a voice like a bellowing Hector. After some little trouble he managed to enclose 'Blizzard' in an ox harness, and then attach him to an ordinary sled. For reasons that are obvious, Mr. Bedson did not care to use his best cutter on this occasion, even though it was his birthday. 'Blizzard' did not appear to understand the new wrinkle to which he was being subjected, and an ominous twinkle in his eye, betokened that the blood of his ancestors, which had never brooked servitude before, was beginning to simmer. The other members of the herd also manifested decided signs of dissatisfaction at the unusual proceedings and looked considerably annoyed.

"When all was ready, Mr. and Mrs. Bedson, together with several other ladies and gentlemen took their places in the sleigh, and prepared for a delightful and novel drive. Mr. Bedson was driving and politely suggested to 'Blizzard' that it was time to start. But 'Blizzard' evidently thought differently — he wasn't quite ready. Then 'Old Joe' (one of Mr. Bedson's helpers) began to expostulate, but as his remarks produced no effect, Mr. Secretan chipped in, and taking hold of one horn while Joe struggled with the other, they endeavoured to induce a forward movement on the part of 'Blizzard.' This was becoming a little too familiar. The animal seemed to think so too. He hesitated a moment, collected himself together, took a long breath, and just as Mr. Burrows was reaching out to twist his tail, he shot forward like a catapult, taking the sleigh and passengers with him. Joe and 'Sec' were thunderstruck, and made a desperate rush to get out of the way, but the bull was too quick for them. He gave a shake of his head that sent 'Joe' head over heels into a snow bank, and then gave 'Sec' a lift that sent him some ten feet into space, and he alighted about a dozen yards off in a snow drift, on the opposite side of Joe. Then 'Blizzard' sped on like a whirlwind. Joe at once commenced to pray and 'Sec' had just started on 'Now I lay me,' when they discovered that the danger was over, and suspended the services till a more fitting occasion. Old 'Blizzard' was now on his metal and he rushed over the prairie with an alacrity that caused Mr. Nursey's hair to stand on end, and induced serious reflections over his past life. Mr. Bedson hollered 'Whoa, Blizzard — whoa boy,' while Darby Taylor with remarkable coolness, deliberately fell over the tailboard, his momentum enabling him to plow a broad furrow along the trail for a rod or two, at the end of which he sat looking at the fleeting panorama with a expression of bewilderment on his face that absolutely begged description. Mr. Burrows was the next to drop overboard in a soft drift, but 'Blizzard' and the balance of the outfit took a lively spin over the prairies and finally came back to the starting point without further accident. Mr. Nursey said it was the most invigorating trip he has ever taken since the good old days when he used to take his airings on the back of Norquay's immortal mule.

"This is the first time a buffalo has ever been driven to harness in this country. It is quite possible that it will be the last. The time made has not been accurately determined, but it is generally believed that the record will equal anything ever attempted on the Stonewall (rail) Branch."[65]

After the sale to "Buffalo" Jones and the delivery, Mr. Bedson was down to one aging buffalo bull and the Winnipeg press noted: "But one buffalo remains out at Stony Mountain of the fine herd that recently roamed the plains in that locality and he is old, lame and evidently lonesome."[66] His friends probably said that if the old bull is lonely, so is Sam Bedson. He didn't want to sell his buffalo herd but the warden was still a man with broad interests, including lifelong loyalties to his early military years. When rebellion broke on the south Saskatchewan River in 1885, he quickly offered his services and General Middleton asked him to accept the post of Chief Transport Officer. He accepted and saw service on the trails and on the *Steamship Northcote* when it came under fire near Batoche.

"Buffalo" Jones, being a showman and dealer, saw that members of Bedson's former herd visited many lands. Some were taken to the World's Fair at Paris, some to the World's Fair at Chicago and others were sold to remote parts of the world.

What would prove of lasting interest to Canadians was the sale of the herd to Allard and Pablo of western Montana. After Allard's death in 1896, his share of buffalo was taken over by Pablo who came to have the biggest herd in the world and with whom the Government of Canada negotiated to buy and bring back to Canada in 1907. It is easy to believe that most of the herd purchased by the Government of Canada at that time, traced in one line or another to Bedson stock.

"The cutting off of the northward spring migrations (of the buffalo) deprived Sitting Bull of practically all his normal supplies. It also gravely embarrassed the Canadians, and especially the newly formed North West Mounted Police, who had the task of keeping order in the territory. It seems certain, then, that an appalling slaughter of buffalo took place below the 49th parallel in 1878—'79, simply for the purpose of starving Sitting Bull. . . Buffalo were apparently killed off without any concern as to their use, either for hides or for meat. It was all very reprehensible.

"But lest we perceive not the beam in our own eye from watching the mote in our neighbor's, we should also give heed to the Canadian side of the case. The famous Red River buffalo hunts went on annually from about the second decade of the nineteenth century to the final disappearance of the buffalo in the '80s. The slaughter was great, and in some cases apparently wanton. . . Professor Henry Hind estimates that the number of buffalo killed by the Red River settlers between 1820 and 1840 was not less than 652,000."[67]

Henry Bayne MacDonald

Chapter 13

The Man Named Pablo

Gone were the pemmican years, the organized buffalo hunts by settlers and hide hunters, and the massive herds that imparted a blackish hue upon portions of the prairie landscape. The mainstream of Canadian buffalo history that once gushed vigorously across the plains dwindled to a point close to disappearance. But it didn't quite disappear because there remained bubbling trickles from unsuspected new "springs" born in the dreams of men like James McKay, Charles Alloway and Samuel Bedson of Manitoba, the enthusiasm of "Buffalo" Jones of Kansas City and revival of interest and purpose in the minuscule "stream" generated by Sam Walking Coyote's fluke possession of several orphan buffalo calves intended to buy indulgence from an irate mother-in-law. Nevertheless, the "streams" were there, giving support to the poet's words: "Back to their springs, like the rain, shall fill them full of refreshment: That which the fountain sends forth returns again to the fountain."[68]

Captive buffalo were moving back to their "headwaters" in northwestern Montana where a man named Pablo ranched near the small town named Pablo. It was on the east side of the Flathead Indian Reserve and the south end of Flathead Lake that Michel Pablo already had grazing rights and dreamed of adding buffalo to his existing livestock. He was a frontiersman of the first order, big and muscular and jovial, and he could classify as a halfbreed but differed from most members of the race by possessing no Anglo-Saxon blood. His mother was a full-blood Blackfoot and his father a Mexican who migrated to Montana and lived on the Blackfoot Reserve after his marriage. Michel, was born at Fort Benton about 1845 or '46.[69]

Michel became an orphan when his father died first and his mother soon after. Before graduating from his teen years, he came to the Jocko or Flathead Reserve as an interpreter. There he met and became a close and lasting friend and then a business partner in the breeding of buffalo on the Flathead Reserve with Charles A. Allard.

Pablo met and married a native girl from the reserve, whose father was a halfbreed resident and whose mother was a full-blood Pend d'Oreille Indian.

Michel was extremely popular on the reserve and was adopted by the Federation of Kootenies, Pend d'Oreilles and Flatheads, following which he took up ranching. He built a fine ranch home on the reservation property and his enterprise prospered.

As a member of the tribe, Pablo immediately enjoyed various new benefits, including a share of money paid by the Northern Pacific Railway as compensation for reservation land taken for right-of-way. No doubt, much of such money was used or squandered for celebrations but not in Pablo's case. As he explained, every cent of such money was invested in a beginner's herd of breeding cattle; in this instance, a herd of eight breeding heifers that ultimately paid good dividends. In the meantime, his wife was employed as a cook at the Indian Agency and her earnings resulted in still more cattle.[70]

Pablo was doing well and so was his friend Allard. Both were good horsemen, both were students of Nature and admirers with Lord Byron of Nature's "Universal throne, her woods, her wilds, her waters . . ." If there had been rodeos in their early years, both men would have been candidates for competition. Allard, being more of a showman than Pablo, was often invited to display his roping and riding skills in public.

Some writers believed that Allard was the first to propose the purchase of the little herd by the partners, and moving it to the Pablo pasture on the reservation. In any case, Pablo favored the idea and Sam Walking Coyote was surprised to hear that his buffalo were so saleable. He accepted the Allard-Pablo offer of $250 each for the ten head. It was then that the two purchasers moved to meet the inexperienced Indian's whim by measuring out 25 piles of gold — each worth a hundred dollars. The two buyers were pleased with their investment and let it be known that they were ready to consider further purchases. For the seller, things were likewise good but not for long. The 25 gold piles were short-lived and Sam faced a sad and early end.

Pablo became the more eager of the partners and asked Allard if he knew of any other buffalo owners who might be interested in selling. Allard thought at once of that tall lean owner with the Vandyke beard and the face and figure of the American's Uncle Sam, Charles Jesse Jones or "Buffalo Jones." There was a rumor that he might be getting out of the buffalo business. It didn't happen fast enough to accommodate Pablo's fervent desire, but it did happen in 1893. The Flathead partners bought what was described as a "remnant" of the Jones herd, then at Omaha, Nebraska, 26 buffalo of pure breeding and 18 hybrids — 44 head in all.

By the terms of the sale, Jones would deliver at Butte, Montana, by the only practical means at the time, meaning an unmarked route through much rough country. The pessimists had much to say but to the surprise of most spectators, the drive was made successfully, thereby establishing an unofficial world record for distance with buffalo.[71]

It was a drive of roughly 900 miles by the cross-country route with a further drive of between 100 and 150 miles from Butte to the Flathead Reserve. With this most recent addition, Allard and Pablo had at least 36 buffalo of pure breeding and the hybrids as well.

And the fabulous Jones, it should be noted, was still far from retirement or withdrawal from his self-appointed roles of adventurer and "stunt man" in the buffalo fraternity. He was frequently in western Canada — occasionally on the trail of the musk-oxen in the far north and almost constantly in the news — and in 1906 he made a buffalo drive of about 1,000 miles from the Goodnight Ranch in Texas to a point in northern Arizona.[72] Friends said it was typical of the man. The episode began when the ranch proprietor lost interest in his buffalo, kept mainly for hunting festivals. Jones happened to be present on a day when the owner was in a reckless mood and told Jones he could have all the buffalo he could round up and drive away for a payment of $10. Days later, according to the story, Jones was seen leaving the ranch with half a hundred animals or more, heading for Flagstaff, Arizona. The drive took almost a year but, once again, Jones made good.

The same story told of Jones leaving his new herd in the care of one of his men and going to the eastern United States, on business — not to return. Only after some long years did the faithful caretaker go to court to receive an order giving him the ownership of the herd in lieu of the time he spent waiting for Jones to return.

But Jones had to be remembered as a man with great skill in handling buffalo, calves in particular, and raising them on domestic cows' milk. After becoming a national dealer in buffalo, he found he could not breed enough of the bison to meet the demand so turned his attention to catching young calves and raising them on domestic cows or cows' milk. He probably knew that he was exaggerating when he said that buffalo milk was much richer than Jersey milk but he had no complaint about the good growth made by his kidnapped buffalo calves on domestic cows' milk. His only mistake in the year of the biggest calf recovery, he admitted, was in not taking enough domestic cows to the hunt. He took 20 cows and should have taken 40, he said.

Some of the domestic cows rejected all advances by the foreign babies but the majority were quick to form motherly attachments, and as for the calves, hunger made them very eager. Jones cited one experience of exceptional interest in the search for mutual compatibility. The men roped a certain old red cow with a near-buffalo color and a warlike disposition and hobbled her, then picked out the youngest calf which was making an adult-size display of battle, "butting and fighting viciously. The cow turned her head and promptly kicked so hard she broke the hobble and sent the calf into a somersault. But when the cow was again made secure, the calf was returned for a second trial. This time the reception was completely reversed and after a few moments, cow and calf seemed to have discovered a perfect loyalty. Within an hour, the curly little rascal was lying close to his new mother, chuck full of milk and as happy as a clam. The calf was never wild after that and the cow found an affection for all the buffalo calves and would allow two of them to suckle her at once, although she would drive off a domestic calf."

One calf, Jones related, demonstrated a definite preference for milk from a beer bottle with rubber nipple. Another wanted its milk from a certain white bucket and certainly not from a pail of another color. These accounts were from notes made in 1888 in which season Jones and his men captured and converted 37 buffalo calves that were added to the herd. It was a record performance and in that year, it was a last chance.

The cost of the recovery program was $1,825, which Jones considered a good investment, "besides the consolation of performing a duty toward preserving a great race and at the same time atoning for wickedness of former years in slaying so many of the noble animals."[73]

All the while, the Flathead scene was changing too. Charles Allard died in 1896, by which time, the Allard and Pablo herd contained 300 buffalo — half of which belonged to Pablo and the other half would revert to the Allard estate to be divided equally between Allard's widow, daughters and two sons.

Mrs. Allard sold her share of the animals to Charles Conrad of Kalispell who, some years later, sold almost a hundred head to the Government of Canada and saw them shipped to the big park at Wainwright. The Allard daughters and brother, Joseph, sold their buffalo to Judge Woodrow of Missoula. The animals were resold, a short time later, to the famous 101 Ranch.[74]

During the course of these developments, Michel Pablo was making some sales from his share of the big herd. But growth from natural increases far surpassed the sales and, a few years later, when the Government of Canada was prepared to buy and recover a substantial part of the surviving world herd of the plains bison, Michel Pablo was the one and only owner who could fill the order, and at a time when — some say miraculously — Pablo found it necessary to sell. What followed constituted one of the most exciting chapters in the history of wild life conservation in Canada — or in the world.

44 MacRae, Archibald Oswald, History of the Province of Alberta, p. 259, The Western Canadian History Company, 1912.
45 Wood, Kerry, The Last Buffalo, Farm And Ranch Review, Calgary, Sept., 1975.
46 Shelton, A.E., was Mayor of Calgary in 1888.
47 Shepherd, George, Saskatoon Star Phoenix and reprinted in Calgary, Alberta on March 19, 1951.
48 McKay, W. Henry, Last Buffalo? Canadian Cattlemen, p. 22, June, 1948.
49 Turner, J.P., The North West Mounted Police, Vol. II, p. 399, Ling's Printer, Ottawa.
50 Benton Record, Montana, Dec. 29, 1881.
51 Turner, John Peter, The Tragedy of the Buffalo, RCMP Quarterly, Vol. 10, No. 1, July 1942, Ottawa.
52 Turner, John Peter, The Tragedy Of The Buffalo, RCMP Quarterly, Vol. 10, p. 16, July 1942.
53 Cotton, E.J. "Bud", The Bone Pile Butte, Canadian Cattlemen, Calgary, p. 57, Sept. Issue, 1948.
54 Lord Selkirk, Letter to Miles Macdonell, 1813, Selkirk Papers.
55 Miles Macdonell, Letter to Lord Selkirk, July 17, 1813, Selkirk Papers.
56 Lady Dufferin, My Canadian Journal, 1872-1878, D. Appleton and Co., 1891.
57 Alloway, Charles, Interview, Winnipeg Tribune, June 24, 1925.
58 Daily Free Press, Winnipeg, Oct. 12, 1876.
59 Winnipeg Tribune, Jan. 21, 1880.
60 Winnipeg Tribune, Jan. 21, 1880.
61 The Western World, Winnipeg, p. 276, Dec., 1891.
62 Manitoba Daily Free Press, Winnipeg, April 19, 1889.
63 Manitoba Daily Free Press, Winnipeg, Dec. 18, 1888.
64 Grand Forkes Plaindealer, as copied by the Manitoba Daily Free Press, Dec. 18, 1888.
65 Manitoba Daily Free Press, Winnipeg, Feb. 17, 1883.
66 Manitoba Daily Free Press, Winnipeg, Sept. 12, 1890.
67 MacDonald, Henry Bayne, The Killing of the Buffalo, The Beaver, Dec., 1935, The Hudson's Bay Co., Winnipeg, 1935.
68 Longfellow, Henry Wadsworth.
69 Coder, George, Research notes on Pablo and Charles Allard. Glenbow Archives, Calgary.
70 Ibid.
71 Luxton, Norman, The Last Of The Buffalo, published by Tom Jones, Cincinnati, 1909.
72 Hyatt, Robert M., The World's Strangest Cattle Drive. The Western Horseman, Oct., 1951.
73 Jones, C.J. "Buffalo," Biography compiled by Col. Henry Inman, Forty Years of Adventure Crane and Co., Iopeka, Kansas, 1899.
74 Luxton, Norman, The Last of the Buffalo, Tom Appes, Cincinnati, 1909.

"If you wish to get some idea of the difficulty of loading buffalo into stock cars, accept the opinion of a man familiar with the job: 'Take the most ornery range steer that ever stood on hoofs, multiply his meanness by 10, his stubbornness by 15, his strength by 40 and his endurance by 50 and then add the products.'

"It was a frequent occurrence during the loading to have the walls of a corral which were constructed of fir plank two inches thick and eight inches wide, spiked upon piles driven into the ground four and a half feet apart, smashed as though they were pine boards."[75]

D.J. Benham

Chapter 14

The Wildest Roundup In Human History

For a weather-beaten old cowboy, Michel Pablo, the news reported from Washington brought no cheer. He wished that people in the capital would attend to government affairs and leave the cow and buffalo business to him and his neighbors. It was rumored that the big Flathead Reserve on which the Pablo herd of buffalo had grown from a total of 10 head in 1884 to something more than 400 head 21 years later was about to be opened for home-steading and settlement, and that grazing and ranching might be terminated on short notice. If this happened, there would be no alternative but to sell the herd, and who would want such a large and ill-tempered bunch of critters.

Pablo's friends said the government ought to, in the name of conservation, relocate the herd or buy it outright at a fair valuation and use it to stock a national buffalo park. But even before Pablo began to think about a course of action, a mystery dealer appeared at his door and offered him $25 per head for the entire herd. Pablo feigned a laugh to hide his anger. He realized that he could make at least that much by slaughtering the animals and selling the meat. He answered his visitor with a polite, "No thank you," but the man apparently returned, offering $50 per head. Again Pablo refused.

It was suspected that the visitor was an undercover agent for Washington authorities. Nevertheless, the stranger came again and this time with the proposal for only Pablo's ears. If he, the visitor, could get a cash bonus of $10,000 for himself, he believed he could "wangle" the sale of the herd at $75 per head for Pablo. The agent, however, was talking to the wrong man. Pablo was a humble fellow, one who would never compromise his insistence upon honest trading.

Americans who were anxious to keep the big herd on American soil went to the office of the President of the United States. It was widely known that Theodore Roosevelt was an ardent conservationist and sure to be an advocate of any reasonable plan to keep the big herd together on American soil. The President's response was supportive. He forwarded his recommendation to Congress with a request for support of a "National Buffalo Park" project. But its Members were in an economy mood and approval was denied.

The first Canadian proposal for the purchase of the big Pablo herd, with most of its "taproots" deep in Canada's prairie soil, didn't escape without similar threats of obliteration. Most eastern parliamentarians saw the bison as just one more wild prairie critter. Sir Wilfrid Laurier was said to have merely shaken his head when the recommendation to purchase the Pablo herd was first advanced. Negotiations for the purchase of Pablo's herd began in 1906 and were conducted by a mere "two or three" inconspicuous Canadians. They may have been unassuming, but they were vocal conservationists able to conduct official business without waste of words.

When asked to identify the most influential Canadian figures in securing the return of the great buffalo treasure, Norman Luxton of Banff gave full credit to Alexander Ayotte, who grew up in the French Canadian community of St. Jean Baptiste, on the Red River, about 45 miles south of Winnipeg and a servant of the Dominion Department of Immigration, in Manitoba when the buffalo question was becoming a burning issue. Together with Ayotte, Mr. Luxton also named Howard Douglas, a pioneer western newspaperman before his appointment as Superintendent of the Banff National Park, and Hon. Frank Oliver, the first newspaper publisher in Alberta, who hauled a printing press from Winnipeg to Fort Edmonton by Red River cart in 1880. Oliver sat as a Member of the House of Commons for 21 years and as Minister of the Interior between 1905 and 1911 — the time period when the Pablo herd was being purchased and delivered to their Alberta home parks. And with less modesty, Norman Luxton — who was born in Manitoba in 1876 when it was still possible "to shoot a buffalo for dinner" — might have added his own name to the distinguished list.

Douglas and Ayotte were adamant that Canada should not fail to acquire the big herd. Both men worked diligently but quietly in the "hush! hush!" atmosphere of their own design to generate interest in the "right quarters." Douglas won and held the complete confidence of the highly respected Norman Luxton, and the latter held the ear of the Hon. Frank Oliver who had become the west's most vocal advocate. The little clique of buffalo-lovers became a team.

Early in 1906, Douglas made another visit to the Flathead Reserve to see the buffalo again and establish a complete understanding with Michel Pablo. He learned much about the habits of Pablo's wild but attractive brutes in addition to the probable costs if they were bought and moved to Canada. There was also the unpleasant reactions, including violence, that could be expected when the local and surrounding population learned that the last big body of the native animals, they had come to believe belonged to them, was about to leave the country. Pablo was aware of the possible animosity and said, as if to absolve himself, "We gave our American people a chance to make our buffalo secure on this side of the boundary and when they missed it, they can't blame anybody but themselves."

The rumors of a sale, like hot embers in a dry peat bog, smoldered and smoked for months and then in early 1907 the story broke like flames of fire. An option had been obtained by the Government of Canada and followed soon thereafter by an agreement of sale, duly signed. When the deal was finally a matter of record, many citizens were shocked by the realization that they were about to lose one of their most distinctive area attractions. Many wanted the U.S. government to intervene, to call out the army if necessary but stop the sale. Some talked of taking the law into their own hands, starting with a raid on the loading corrals and chutes at Ravalli, on the Missoula side of the reserve.

Most protesters agreed that they did not mind embarrassing the Canadians, but they did not want to hurt the highly respected Pablo. Any damage at the corrals, sufficient to release the buffalo being held there and allow them to dash back to their ranges, would present a serious delay and heavy loss for Pablo, which was not their purpose.

Despite the sporadic flurries of protest, the Flathead Reserve neighbors must have been greatly impressed and more than a little proud on learning that their friend, Michel Pablo, had on February 25, 1907, sold his great herd of buffalo to none other than "His Majesty, King Edward the Seventh, represented by the Minister of the Interior of Canada." Everybody on the Reserve wanted to see the proof. The legal document made the King of Great Britain and Ireland look very much like another buffalo rancher and left its message in these words:

"Whereas the Vendor is the owner of a herd of buffalo now in his corrals on the Flathead Reserve in the said State of Montana, numbering not less than three hundred and not more than four hundred head, and has agreed with the Minister for the absolute sale to him of the said buffalo at and for the price or sum of two hundred dollars per head upon and according to the terms and conditions hereinafter mentioned:

"Now Therefore THIS Indenture Witnesseth As Follows:

"In pursuance of the said agreement and in consideration of the sum of two hundred dollars per head of buffalo to be paid by the Minister to the Vendor as hereinafter mentioned, the Vendor doth bargain, sell and assign unto His Majesty, His successors and assignees all the herd of buffalo numbering not less than three hundred nor more than four hundred head, now in possession of and being the property of the Vendor and which are now upon his premises and in his corrals on the Flathead Reserve in the said State of Montana, together with all the rights, title, interest, property, claim and demand whatsoever of the Vendor of, in and to the same.

"The Vendor shall deliver the said herd of buffalo and every of them, and unload the same from the cars at the city of Edmonton in the Province of Alberta in the Dominion of Canada, free and clear of all charges for shipping, freight, transportation and other charges and expenses whatsoever, except customs duties — which duties shall be borne by the Minister.

"The Vendor hereby guarantees that the said herd of buffalo and every of them are all thoroughbred and that he will deliver the animals at Edmonton as aforesaid in the best possible condition, free from injury, and not crippled in any manner, such delivery to be made of the bulls and the younger buffalo in the month of May, 1907, and of the cows and calves not before the month of July 1907, and not later than the month of August, 1907.

"The Minister hereby agrees to pay or cause to be paid to the Vendor the sum of two hundred dollars per head for each and every buffalo unloaded and delivered at Edmonton as aforesaid in good condition, free from injury and not crippled in any manner.

"As a guarantee of the said payment and the fulfilment of the provisions of this Indenture, the Minister shall deposit with the First National Bank of Missoula in the said State of Montana, on or before the 2nd day of March, 1907, the sum of ten thousand dollars to be paid over to the Vendor on the final delivery by him at Edmonton of the herd of buffalo as hereinbefore provided for; upon the receipt by the Bank of the certificate hereinafter mentioned, and as a portion of the total consideration of the sale of said buffalo at the price of two hundred dollars per head.

"As a further guarantee for the payment of the balance of purchase money required by this Indenture and before any shipment of buffalo is made from Ravalli Station on the line of the Northern Pacific Railway — which shall be understood to be the place of shipment — the Minister will deposit with the First National Bank of Missoula aforesaid such moneys in excess of the said sum of ten thousand dollars as shall be required to pay in full for all the buffalo to be shipped when the number thereof is ascertained to the satisfaction of the Minister as nearly as may be, and in case the deposit of money required by this paragraph is not duly made, the Vendor shall be at liberty to treat this Indenture as fulfilled on his part and shall be entitled to receive from the Bank the sum of ten thousand dollars as forfeited by the Minister.

"Upon the receipt by said Bank of a certificate signed by the Minister or his duly authorized agent certifying to the number of buffalo delivered at Edmonton in fulfilment of the terms and according to the conditions of this Indenture, there shall be paid out by said Bank to the Vendor such of the moneys so deposited by way of guarantee aforesaid as shall be required to pay for said buffalo so delivered at the rate of two hundred dollars per head and the balance of all such moneys shall be held by the Bank for the use of and shall be returned to the Minister.

"In addition to the price of two hundred dollars per head hereinbefore agreed to be paid for said buffalo and in consideration of the shipment, transportation, delivery and unloading of the same at Edmonton, as aforesaid, the Minister will pay or cause to be paid unto the Vendor at Edmonton the sum of eighteen thousand dollars of lawful money of Canada. If however it shall be proven to the satisfaction of the Minister that any of the animals so delivered are not thoroughbred, the Vendor shall not be paid any price therefore, and such share of expense as might have been incurred by the shipment shall be deducted.

"The Vendor doth hereby for himself, his heirs, executors and administrators, covenant with His Majesty and His successors that the Vendor is now rightfully and absolutely possessed of and entitled to the said herd of buffalo and every of them and has now in himself good right to sell and assign the same unto His Majesty and His successors in manner aforesaid and according to the intent and meaning of these present.

"And that His Majesty and His successors upon the due fulfilment on his part of the terms of this Indenture shall and may from time to time, and at all times thereafter peaceably and quietly have, hold, and possess and enjoy the said hereby assigned herd of buffalo and every of them to and for his and their own use and benefit without any manner of hinderance, interruption, molestation, claim or demand whatsoever, of, from or by the Vendor, or any other person or persons whomsoever."[76]

When springtime, 1907, came to the hundred square miles of the Flathead Reserve, at least half of Michel Pablo's buffalo cows had calves, all yellow-brown teddy-bear in color which warned humans to keep back a safe distance. Cows were more dangerous than bulls during calving season. Pablo knew he had a big roundup job on his hands. He had 35 of the best working cowboys in the business and each one had a good horse and two spares. But when contemplating the explosive temperament of his buffalo and the craggy topography of his range, he wished he had 50 cowboys and 150 horses. He realized that he would be lucky if he could collect all the buffalo on his range in two general roundups before the end of summer. Nothing quite like this had ever been done before. He was older than most of his riders but he understood the buffalo disposition. He relied heavily upon the son and namesake of his former partner, Charles Allard. The senior Allard was known to "deliver anything with hair on it to the inside of a corral and bolt the gate." Charlie Jr. was thought to be as good a man.

Each morning during the roundup, the crew would start the day's drive, hopefully with one of the many segregated herds. They worked it toward Pablo's ranch and Ravalli where the heavy stockyard corrals were reinforced with two-by-

Charles Allard and his cowboys during buffalo roundup prior to shipment of the herd to Canada, 1906-1908
(Glenbow Archives)

six or two-by-eight inch fir planking of the best quality. The Ravalli corrals had held buffalo before but never the numbers expected in 1907. Setbacks, accidents and days of total failure were expected together with bull fights and frontal attacks on humans but Pablo believed there was an angel who made the protection of men working with buffalo its special responsibility.

A certain amount of sorting and segregating was being done throughout the time of the roundup. It would be a mistake, for example, to place cows, calves and old and cantankerous bulls in the same car because of the danger of injury to the calves. Thus, the cows and calves were being held back from the spring contingent to be shipped in the autumn. The necessary separations and holdings for days and nights in the open were monotonous, even depressing. Nobody wanted the assignment. A night stampede was one of the hazards, quite enough to make a cowboy wish he had never left the farm. It didn't take much to start a midnight dash — as one of the men on night duty did so effectively with nothing more than a spell of sneezing.

A disproportionately high number of old bulls were included in the spring shipment of 1907 and many of them had grown belligerent with age. Always ready for a fight, they were also the first to sense an opportunity for a dash to freedom, with the remainder of the herd following. There were constant fights among them for herd supremacy but nobody could fail to admire their haste in coming to the protection of the cows and calves. These "self-appointed" guardians would fight any foe, regardless of the odds, while the cows sought shelter behind them and the calves behind the cows.

Pablo and his men breathed relief when the old bulls — big, shaggy, crusty and courageous — were loaded onto the freight cars at Ravalli. Getting them there, though, was not easy. In some instances these paragons of determination and cussedness were not loaded until they were literally dragged up the loading chutes and into the cars by sheer force, compounded by block and tackle. Spectators who believed they had witnessed the ultimate in resistance found that at journey's end in Alberta the same bulls, each weighing a ton, stubbornly refused to leave the car and had to be roped and again dragged out by the block and tackle technique.

The first shipment of Pablo buffalo going to Canada consisted of 200 head in 17 freight-cars, loaded at Ravalli in May, 1907. Howard Douglas and Alexander Ayotte, the principal planners for the Canadian government, hoped the new buffalo range at Wainwright would be ready to receive the animals but, when that proved impossible, 16 square miles of natural parkland in the Beaver Hills prepared as a refuge for a herd of native elk, was used. The 17 carloads of buffalo were rebilled from Edmonton to the Village of Lamont, situated just a short run from the northeast corner of Elk Island National Park and, thus, this park became the Pablo bisons' first Canadian home.

From Flathead Reserve to Elk Island National Park was a journey of about 800 miles but — if speed meant anything — the buffalo never travelled better. On both the Northern Pacific and the Canadian Pacific Railways the buffalo cars were accorded the luxury service of a passenger schedule, similar to the speed of the famous "silk trains" that, in crossing Canada, travelled as near to non stop as was possible.

That first shipment of buffalo to Canada gave Pablo and his cowboys and their horses a minimum of trouble. But nobody could say as much about the second shipment for which the roundup was to have started in early August. There was no obvious reason for the difference but the second aggregation proved to be trouble right up to the moment when the doors were closed and bolted on the last car. Instead of starting the roundup in August, Pablo ordered that it be delayed one month, mainly to share more equitably the limited supply of good cowboys and well-trained horses. If he believed he needed more of both, he was right. The shortage of both, no doubt, explained why the second roundup was fraught with trouble.

It certainly wasn't a pleasant outing for the horsemen who came close to exhaustion and were in their saddles until so stiffened that they couldn't get out. Nor was it any better for the horses, some of which became useless for further saddle service. And the reward, in terms of buffalo corralled, barely compensated for the effort. Much of the trouble stemmed from the inadequate number of horses and riders.

A first-hand account of the second roundup, that began on September 10, 1907, was provided by D.J. Benham. The correspondent for Winnipeg's *Manitoba Free Press* travelled to Montana with the Pablo gang. He saw the shortage of cowboys as a problem and wrote: "He," meaning Mr. Pablo, "could muster only seven (men) beside himself on the first day. They rode the range all that day without finding a hero. On the following day, good fortune smiled and they ran a bunch of 66 into the corrals at the Pablo ranch, without much difficulty. Next morning found the riders early on the range with fresh mounts and flushed by the success of the previous day. No such good luck awaited them, however. For hours they searched the ravines and the badlands along the Pend d'Oreille River without finding a hoof. Then suddenly a great herd of nearly 125 head was sighted and Mr. Pablo marshalled his little band for the attack. Horses were rested, saddle cinches were tightened and they galloped away."[77]

At this point, the Manitoba correspondent was to learn one lesson well, the sheer unpredictability of buffalo and the folly of trying to lead, guide or direct them contrary to their desires. In the hours that followed, the cowboys were sometimes in pursuit, sometimes being pursued. When they rode too close to a fleeing bull, "a vicious charge" resulted and the rider had to extend his horse to the limit to escape the horns of the monster. Old cows whose calves displayed distress from the fierce pursuit were the most defiant when their progress was blocked.

The correspondent wrote: "Goaded to desperation, the herd began to scatter like chaff before a wind, rushing behind and before the riders, away to liberty in the mountains, miles beyond the Pend d'Oreille River, until finally only 30 head remained, within the cordon of riders. By splendid riding, almost reckless in its daring, these were driven to the very wings of the corral. Here they made a final mad rush for liberty and the jaded horses were unable to cope with the situation or to respond to the spur. Thus, every buffalo escaped, the thirty head taking almost as many different directions back to their range, while the exhausted horses and their weary riders were laid up for recuperation."

The total failure of this drive convinced Mr. Pablo to discontinue the roundup until he was able to obtain a bigger crew of cowboys and cow horses. Four days later he had enlisted 23 cowboys but, sad to say, the buffalo were as ornery as ever. Benham — seeing one herd after another break away from the roundup crew — wrote: "This was the most nerve-wracking and cruel day's work of the entire roundup and for hours after the last buffalo had disappeared horses and riders came straggling in exhausted. The animal, with heads drooping from weariness and the sweat dripping from their sides scored by the spurs and the quirt, showed how fierce had been the struggle. Further riding would have been brutality; for many of those splendid animals who had carried their riders through treacherous ground without mishap or stumble and with no other guidance than a touch of the reins on the neck in a killing race could scarcely sustain their saddles. Their legs were cut, bruised and strained, but the cow pony dies game, and it is hard race that makes him lie down." Was the buffalo becoming smarter or was the cowboy becoming older?

Pablo and his cowboys gave a sigh of relief when the last buffalo were safely in the corrals beside the railway at Ravalli. Their work, however, was not completed until the proper number of animals — between 12 and 20 depending on size — was driven or dragged up the loading chutes and into each car. As for the humans responsible for the operation, there were risks and hazards every step of the way. Serious delays and accidents occurred at the loading chutes where belligerent old bulls constituted a large proportion of the herd.

A very serious accident was narrowly averted on the Ravalli loading platform when the buffalo were being loaded for shipment to Edmonton. One of the biggest bulls broke the heavy rope by which he was being dragged by block and tackle to his stall in the car. When he discovered his freedom, he dashed down the chute, catching a heavy stockyard gate with one horn and tearing it off its hinges. With the plank gate still hooked to his horn, the bull headed toward the open range. The fact that Alexander Ayotte and Howard Douglas, the two Canadians who represented Canada in the buffalo negotiations were standing precisely in the bull's path, didn't worry the animal in the least.

But it did worry the Canadians who could see that the bull was charging straight for them. The Canadians had neither time for a caucus nor farewell. Their fate was altered, though, when the bull slipped and fell on the wet plank floor of the loading deck, giving Messrs. Ayotte and Douglas enough time to fall backwards over the deck fence and to the ground. Both men were stunned and a third man who had been standing with them, broke his arm in the fall.

Like a California earthquake, the Montana buffalo loading had its "aftershocks" too. When Ayotte recovered from his fall, he took a stroll along the train of cars loaded with buffalo. While walking close to one car, his attention was arrested by two bulls engaged in a fight . Ayotte paused to peek between the slats to see who was winning. At that instant, the fighting bulls so rocked the car that a man walking on its roof lost his balance and fell off, landing right on Mr. Ayotte's head, who then mumbled, "A man isn't safe anywhere in buffalo country."

75   Benham, D.J., Thrilling Buffalo Hunt of 1907, *Manitoba Free Press*, Winnipeg, Oct. 19, 1907.
76   Indenture, Feb. 25, 1907, Between Michel Pablo, Ravalli, Montana, and His Majesty, King Edward the Seventh, (Re purchase of buffalo) Copy of Indenture seen at Glenbow Archives, Calgary.
77   Benham, D.J., The Thrilling Buffalo Hunt in 1907, *Manitoba Free Press*, Winnipeg, Oct. 19, 1907.

"The buffalo, in spite of his great size and somewhat ungainly appearance, is as agile as a cat and the remarkable speed at which he travels is as surprising as his power of endurance which permits him to maintain a killing pace for hours in flight. Starting with an easy lope, he soon develops a swinging gallop, and it requires a good horse indeed to outstrip him in a dash at a break away. The race soon degenerates into a runway with the buffalo in the lead when exhaustion causes the horse to lag. The buffalo has an advantage in the fact that he can travel seemingly as easily up and down precipitous mountain sides or along the open prairie with equal facility. Even the little calves seem capable of developing unlimited speed and can keep pace with the herd on the wildest route or in swimming the strongest current."[78]

D.J. Benham

Chapter 15

A Haven For The Herd Of 1907

The geographic centre of the buffalo world shifted, in a few historic days at the end of May and beginning of June, 1907, from Montana to Alberta and the political focal-point moved from Washington, D.C. to Ottawa, Canada. The new focus was Elk Island National Park.

The Elk Island National Park story began in 1903 when W.H. Cooper, Game Warden for the North West Territories, watched a herd of elk struggling to survive against hunters in the Buffalo Hills. The herd's numbers were dropping and Cooper took his concern to Frank Oliver, a Member of Alberta's Legislature at the time. Oliver suggested the circulation of a petition requesting federal government assistance. More than 60 residents signed a request for a protected area of 16 square miles to be fenced and withdrawn from homesteading.

After another year or two, the local residents volunteered to capture at least 20 elk for release in the reserve in return for the federal government's agreement to provide fencing. The fence was completed in 1907 and one of the signers, Ellsworth Simmons, became the caretaker. By 1908, the reserve was the home for 24 elk, 35 mule deer and the unexpected first big importation of Michel Pablo's buffalo.

In 1907 a new urgency for the large animals' park became clearly apparent. The Government of Canada, which had bought the big Montana herd expected to number between 300 and 400 head, had scheduled the bisons' accommodation on 200 square miles of well-fenced range at Wainwright. But the fence work at Wainwright wasn't ready and, Michel Pablo, in spite of the problems, was on schedule for delivery. The daily press kept the public well informed with respect to the travelling herd. The journey from the point of shipment in Montana to Calgary took 48 hours and was made without loss of animals. Two buffalo cows, though, met death in the freight cars between Calgary and Edmonton and one old bull "in a state of wildness nearly demolished his portion of the freight car."

Eight of Pablo's cowboys, including himself, made the trip to Edmonton where the official transfer was made. The train then moved on to Lamont,

60 miles northeast of Edmonton. There, with only two-and-one-half miles to the northeast corner of the pasture, the buffalo plunged wildly through a strongly reinforced chute to their haven of peace and grass.[79] On October 22, 1907, the second shipment of Pablo buffalo consisting of 211 head was delivered. Thus, with over 400 buffalo at Elk Island National Park, the need to complete the 70-mile perimeter fence at the Wainwright range increased.

Minister of the Interior, The Honourable Frank Oliver was obliged to deal with many requests for small or large herds for local parks across the west. Among the most ardent applicants was the Calgary Board of Trade which publicly regretted the Government's error in sending the first shipment to the Edmonton area which will "prove unsuitable." The remedy, the writer noted, was to "bring the second shipment to this part of Alberta and locate it near Calgary. Southern Alberta is the natural home of the buffalo and the herd would thrive here. . . The government might locate it on one-half of the Sarcee Reserve, renting the land from the Indians. . ."[80] The Calgary Board of Trade couldn't be blamed for wanting a major tourist attraction — but Frank Oliver didn't see the situation quite the way Calgary saw it.

A proposal to place the principal part of the herd, or even all of it, in a national park in the Moose Mountains in southeastern Saskatchewan was accompanied by considerable political pressure. The Saskatchewan Game Protective Association was the main instigator. Richard S. Stuart, Member of Parliament for Qu'Appelle Constituency, wanted to know, on June 8, 1908, if the Minister (Oliver) could offer any encouragement with respect to the establishment of a National Park and Game Preserve in the Moose Mountains and "the placing therein of a herd of buffalo and other wild game."

The Hon. Frank Oliver's reply held special interest. "When the project of purchasing a herd of buffalo in Montana was first brought up, the Moose Mountain timber reserve was the place I had in mind for the location of the herd. But afterwards, when I heard of the resentment that was felt locally against the removal of the herd from Montana, I thought it would be rather doubtful policy to place such a large herd of buffalo within what you might term easy reach of the boundary line."[81]

Another Member asked: "What would the distance be?" The Minister answered: "About forty miles which is not a very long run for a band of buffalo. I thought it would be better to place them temporarily and afterwards make arrangements for an area of grazing land where they would be practically out of reach of anything of that kind."

The debate in the House of Commons turned out to be a full scale review of the Government's involvement in buffalo matters. The eastern members appeared eager to learn as much as possible about the mysteries of the bison and the western members seemed to be just as anxious to pose as authorities. Another Member, John Herron, a former North West Mounted Policeman and rancher, could speak from experience. He had some sound advice for the Minister and a few words of warning concerning the Elk Island National Park range.

"As I had some experience with buffalo in the early days," Herron declared, "I have great sympathy for the government in procuring this herd. I think they did well to secure the buffalo which are natives of our land but I rather think it was unfortunate that they were placed in the northern country where they are at present, (meaning Elk Island). Does the government not anticipate a great deal of trouble in securing and removing them from the present place to the new park laid out for them?. . . I understand that they are in a wooded or partially wooded country. I doubt very much if the government will ever be able to secure the buffalo from that timbered country, get them loaded on the cars and moved to another part of the country. You cannot do that with ordinary domestic cattle in a timbered country. It is impossible to get them out of the timber until they are ready to come. I feel certain that there will be a great disappointment in getting them out. Has the government taken that into consideration?"

The eight-foot fence enclosing the buffalo range at Wainwright was ready in June, 1909. Once again the buffalo, this time at Elk Island, were the objects of a roundup. All those gathered would be loaded in the railroad company's reinforced cars for the trip to Wainwright. The idea, of course, was to transfer all of the Elk Island buffalo but, after corralling and loading 325 head, there remained at least 48 animals that became known as the "mavericks." These buffalo never did leave Elk Island Park. They became the impetus of a new herd which, by 1927, grew to 729. The same park census showed 227 moose, 454 elk and 288 deer, the reason why the Elk Island range became overgrazed and the wildlife required supplementary feed.[82]

The House of Commons continued to hear much about the new herds. Most men in public life shared pangs of guilt after the big herds were allowed to become practically extinct, and the display of new interest in Canada's park herds was like salvation for a bad conscience. Frank Oliver, as Minister of the Interior and the one upon whom the main responsibility for parks and buffalo fell, did everything in his power to encourage interest on the part of fellow Members. When asked in the House: "How many buffalo do we have all told?" he probably beamed and then delivered an excellent review. The following is an abridged reply:

"We have about 950. . . We received our first shipment in June, 1907, 199 head. . . We received our next shipment in October, 1907, 211 head. . . We received our next shipment in July, 1909, 109 head. . . We received our next shipment in October, 1909, 28 head. . . We received our next shipment in June, 1910, 46 head. . . We received our next shipment in October, 1910, 28 head. . . There are still about 70 head to be delivered from the Pablo herd. We have already received 15 head from Mrs. Conrad and expect 15 more in the spring. Then we shall have the only buffalo herd of any account on this continent."[83]

The Minister might as well have said, "The only buffalo herd of any account in the world," because it was too boastful to be well received by the Americans. President Theodore Roosevelt — who wanted his own Congress to buy the Pablo herd for its American heritage value and was refused — was genuinely embarrassed. Ernest Thompson Seton, an internationally noted authority on wildlife, passed through Edmonton just a few days before the arrival of the first Pablo shipment. He not only congratulated the Government of Canada for having succeeded in the purchase but added confidently that the American President regretted very earnestly his failure to win the great buffalo prize for his country.[84]

A New York editor offered, at the same time, consolation to the President who was popular on both sides of the international boundary. "President Roosevelt has been making every effort to 'roundup' the famous herd on the Flathead Reservation. . . But despite his watchfulness and earnest efforts to keep the herd in the United States, the buffalo have been driven off before his eyes, so to speak, and into Canada."[85]

Unloading Michel Pablo's buffalo at the National Buffalo Park at Wainwright, Alberta, 1909
(Provincial Archives of Alberta)

78   Benham, D.J., The Thrilling Buffalo Hunt In 1907, Manitoba Daily Free Press, Winnipeg., Oct. 19, 1907. (Benham attended the Roundup, rode with Pablo's cowboys and wrote as a Free Press correspondent.)
79   Edmonton Journal, June 1, 1907.
80   Calgary Herald, June 11, 1907.
81   Handsard, House of Commons, Ottawa, Session of 1907-'08, p. 10102, June 8, 1908.
82   Lothian, W.F., A History of Canada's National Parks, Vol. I, 1976, Parks Canada.
83   Hansard, House of Commons, Ottawa, Session of 1910-11.
84   Edmonton Bulletin, May 8, 1907.
85   Edmonton Bulletin, May 17, 1907.

N.K. Luxton,
Banff, Alberta
October 2, 1961

Dear Mr. McCoy:

I am sending you two copies of the Buffalo photos that I took on the roundup in Montana in 1908. Had another issue printed in U.S. as you say in your letter. The whole booklet is my own, including the story and a short history of the herds.

Having grown up in Winnipeg along side of them, you might say, I knew their history fairly well. Then I came to Banff shortly after Sir Donald A. Smith presented his bunch to the Dominion Parks Branch. This herd was replaced after the Pablo herd came to Canada. I have been informed the Smith herd was exterminated on account of inbreeding. Or perhaps they were sent to Wainwright and joined the Pablo bunch. It is no trouble to comply with your request. Sorry, I am a flu patient just at present, so don't feel so good.

The Buffalo story in Banff is a sad one. We can boast of (only) three cows and a bull in the herd just at present. At one time I can remember almost a hundred. These four are difficult to see, though they are the greatest attraction for the tourist. One morning, up to 2 p.m., fifteen hundred cars passed through the gate to see the buffalo. Five carloads only saw them. Some day we will meet and have a chat about them.

Yours sincerely,
N.K. Luxton[86]

Chapter 16

A National Park Home For The National Herd

Why did the members of Frank Oliver's committee fix upon Wainwright for the buffalo park asked many Westerners? It was a highly favored feeding range, especially for winter grazing in the years of the big herds. The area was home to the relatively short prairie grass which possessed high protein and better-than-average curing qualities, all in all, superior nutritional qualities for winter grazing and decidedly better that the inter-mountain ranges or foothills. These were facts of which Frank Oliver's friend and handyman, Howard Douglas, officially the superintendent of the Banff National Park, had knowledge.

Oliver faced a mounting dilemma with the first of "not less than 300 or more that 400" of Michel Pablo's critters soon to arrive on Canadian soil. He needed a big spread of good grazing, well-fenced in short order. The only facility offering even temporary accommodation was Elk Island National Park, 30 miles northeast of Edmonton. There, the government was in the position to withdraw needed parkland from areas being offered to homesteaders if more grassland was required.

Frank Oliver instructed Howard Douglas to find a proper location, get something ready to accommodate at least 400 head of bison but preferably twice to four times that many. Douglas, with a double portion of pioneer resourcefulness, plunged into action and quickly produced a plan for the temporary use of Elk Island National Park in addition to the preparation of a permanent block of the favored grasses found close to the new railway point about to be named "Wainwright."

The park's name itself brought confusion. Often it was called "Wainwright Buffalo Park," sometimes "Prairie Buffalo Park," and correctly "National Buffalo Park." But whatever it was called, Canadians took satisfaction in the thought that by gaining the custodianship of the biggest remaining herd of prairie buffalo in the world, they had "stolen a march on Uncle Sam." Wainwright, about 125 miles southeast of Edmonton, enjoyed success and it became known as, "the town that was born lucky." Its popularity with homesteaders, especially those from Ontario and United States, was proved when the village, incorporated in 1908, graduated to a town in just two years. Certainly much of its progress was due to the buffalo experience.

Douglas knew that Calgary, Moose Mountain in southeastern Saskatchewan, Edmonton and Winnipeg wanted the park. But he believed the 234 square miles of grassland, aspen groves and surface water at Wainwright was an ideal range. Time confirmed his judgement but other forces were less helpful in securing longevity for the park and its herd. Bovine diseases and wartime contingencies saw military officers replace cowboys and the buffalo liquidated.

Fencing took time and there were delays in making the great transfer from Elk Island. But by late May, 1909, about 400 head of the Elk Island buffalo were being trapped in new corrals as close as possible to the loading tracks at Lamont. They were fed well with good hay for some days before being herded up the chutes and into the reinforced freight cars, some of which were borrowed from the Northern Pacific Railway and had been girded with steel for the Pablo buffalo shipments from Ravalli, Montana. Simultaneously, the most recent Pablo buffalo to be shipped to Canada on the government account, were being entrained at Ravalli and forwarded directly to the new range at Wainwright. The two shipments were expected to arrive at Wainwright at approximately the same time.

The first buffalo to enter the new, well-fenced kingdom of grass were 232 head that arrived on a train of 23 freight cars at 6 a.m., June 13, 1909.[87] Spectators, notwithstanding the early morning hour, were already numerous on the outside of the fence in the unloading area. By 8 o'clock, when unloading was expected to begin, every nearby point offering a direct view, was occupied. For all except the very young animals, this was not their first time in a freight car. Spectators who anticipated another furious refusal to leave the cars must have been disappointed because the cars were vacated with a mad rush. The stubborn critters were not without memories or learning ability.

A plank and wire chute about 100 feet wide and almost a mile in length had been constructed from the small corral at the base of the unloading chutes to the huge corral covering a thousand acres just inside the park fence. The idea was that the incoming buffalo would be held for a day or two where they would be fed well and given a chance to settle down, thereby escaping the urge to stampede when they saw opportunity. The arrangement appeared to have the desired effect.

"Not a sound was heard from the buffalo as they were driven from the cars," an Edmonton reporter wrote. "But when in the corrals an old bull's eye would occasionally flash, his head go down and with tail up he would dash around the corral till he found the entrance to the chute down which he would go at breakneck speed. The buffalo made no attempt to break through the fence, having discovered the futility of this while in confinement in Elk Island Park."[88] He may have been the only reporter who took serious note of the condition of the buffalo at the end of their most recent train journey. He assured readers that the buffalo had survived the transfer as well the recent hard winter in Alberta.

But press reporters can make errors too and either this reporter or another was guilty of playing with the figures. While one reporter impressed most readers by his assertion that the holding corral was one thousand acres, the next reporter announced the big enclosure was two thousand acres. Perhaps it didn't matter greatly because, as corrals are known, either figure made Wainwright the biggest on record.

In the four years, 1907 to '10 inclusive, Michel Pablo shipped a total of 620 head, many more than the Canadians expected to receive and far more than he expected to find and capture on his rugged range. Pablo proved himself to be a man of honesty and honor. He reported that he believed he still had 28 buffalo on his range and would ship them later if he could capture them. But with every successive roundup, the wildest and fastest escaped and the remaining 28 were like the "survival of the fittest" — sure to be the most difficult to land in freight cars. Nobody expected to see many of them. If they or any of them were captured and delivered they would cost the Canadians no more or no less than those in earlier deliveries, namely $245 per head delivered at Edmonton, even though it might cost Pablo a thousand dollars per head to capture the remaining "outlaws."

When Edward Ellis, superintendent of the national park at Wainwright, wrote his first annual report at the end of 1910, he mentioned several small shipments of buffalo stragglers from Pablo's range. He was particularly encouraged by the steady growth in buffalo numbers by natural breeding. The park herd in the year 1910-11, benefited by 100 head from natural increase, while suffering death losses of only seven, leaving a total herd population of 809.[89] After another five years, the corresponding report claimed a total population of 1710 buffalo and conveyed the superintendent's conviction that the park buffalo were becoming tamer and easier to handle.

As the Wainwright herd grew, so did the park staff and organization, and so did the need for policies that would hold the herd to manageable numbers. By 1921 it was clear that slaughtering and meat sales would have to be increased or breeding curtailed. Coming so soon after the herd was acquired at a fairly high price, nobody wanted to waste the herd's potential. Given that there would have to be more slaughtering, a small but serviceable abattoir was constructed in 1921 among the park buildings. The new facility was initiated with a contract awarded to a group of professional butchers to slaughter and dress one thousand buffalo culled by park staff.

Slaughtering became a wintertime occupation, not because the weather would help to prevent the meat from spoiling, but buffalo hides were prime in November, December, January and February and they represented a big part of the return from the animal. The premium paid for top quality hides by the buffalo robe and fur coat trade made it amply worthwhile to kill during the best months. And for many years, according to E.J. "Bud" Cotton, the Easterner who had tried the life of a western cowboy in 1912 and was a park warden on the Buffalo Park from 1914 to the concluding roundup in 1940 — and that presided with a high powered rifle in dropping every buffalo when its turn came to be dragged onto the abattoir floor — was "Sureshot" Sam Purchell. Although recognized as a Buffalo Park specialist, Sam was not a bookkeeper and left no records. Bud Cotton said of his colleague's accuracy: "Sam fired 39,001 rifle shots to kill 39,000 buffalo."

The slaughter and sell policy adopted in 1921 was to hold the buffalo population to reasonable numbers while converting a modest cash surplus to revenue. It was worked moderately well but the planners were challenged to find a use for surplus animals to avoid the waste represented by the killing of animals still capable of breeding. Why not transplant part or all of the prairie bison surplus to the Canadian north where the wood buffalo subspecies was already established and surviving? The merit of such an option loomed larger than the risks that lurked. The Ottawa politicians were already hearing criticisms of annual slaughter that ended the lives of animals which had cost the Canadian taxpayers $245 per head or more to recover.

Some observers pointed to probable intermixing of the two strains in the north and the subsequent loss of identity and genetic control in both. Quiet whispering was heard about the reckless disregard for disease dangers in regions where disease would be difficult to combat. But public opinion strongly supported the idea of establishing meat herds in the far north and pleas for caution were shouted down by calls for approval. Proposals were advanced to ship between 1500 and 2000 head of the prairie buffalo from the National Buffalo Park to the north. Most people said it was economical and sensible. Politicians, who would rather follow than lead, nodded their heads.

In 1925, the first year of the transfer, 1625 yearlings and two-year-old buffalo were taken from the big Buffalo Park herd and made ready for the journey in June when the north has almost constant daylight. While current plans were being explained, it was announced that further shipments of approximately 2,000 buffalo from the same herd would be made over the next three years. Disaster might be lurking but the engineers were showing exactly how these shipments could be made without excessive cost, and Canadians would witness one of the best land-use programs ever tried in their rugged north. The transfer of the unwilling buffalo would entail a 800-mile journey by rail and water to the area of Great Slave Lake and the problems, some of the planners were promising, would be no greater than capturing Pablo's buffalo on the Flathead Reserve in Montana and entraining them to a Canadian buffalo park.

First, there would be a general buffalo roundup for the purpose of segregating the poorer individuals for slaughter. Park cowboys would then cut out the 1625 good young animals for the north. Orders were issued to brand the latter group with a "W" brand, described as "the gamb joint W." The gamb joint is the hock joint of the hind leg, a very sensitive joint and not a very sensible place for hot iron applications. Nobody seemed sure of why the animals going into the northern remoteness would need branding unless there was fear of confusion with the wood buffalo strain already there.

The first 200 buffalo for the north were branded on June 12, 1925 and were started on their way, followed by shipments of similar size at weekly intervals. The branding, however, became a complication. The Edmonton Humane Society sent its representatives to protest what was called needless cruelty and according to Bud Cotton, the Society's representative came equipped with a court injunction. There was a confrontation and although the details are lacking, it appears consignments after the first 200 went forward without brands, indicating an early victory for the humane guardians of the animals.

Most Canadians saw the 1925 project as a worthy experiment, capable of making the north more productive. But government leaders are not compelled to tell everything and they were extremely slow in revealing all of the reasons for moving thousands of Wainwright buffalo to the north.

But with public interest high, the editor of the Edmonton Journal assigned one of his best writers, H.F. Mullett, to accompany the herd of '25, starting at the branding squeeze on the Wainwright range and furnishing day-to-day reports until delivery was made by the sternwheeler, Northland Echo, and barges at Labutte Landing in Wood Buffalo Park. Mullett probably tried to be impartial but readers believed his sympathies were strongly on the side of the buffalo.

"It all sounds easy, this branding of two hundred 'baby buffalo'," he wrote, "but the babies are husky lads and lassies of anywhere from four-hundred to eight-hundred pounds with no sense of obstruction — fleet as all wildlings are — bulletheaded beyond any other wildlings and imbued with but one determination, to avoid at all hazards the white bars of the corrals and get back through the line of cow ponies to the safe shade of the green poplar bush.

"Round and round circle the cowboys heading the buffalo toward the corrals. Round and round mill the buffalo, intent on getting through the line of horses. There is a gap of a foot between two ponies, the gap widens to two feet — shizz, and fifty buffalo in a cloud of dust skim lightly back to the brush and the work is all to do over again; in the squeeze, the little herd of wild-eyed and uneasy buffalo, their movements sideways stopped by the unyielding bars of two-by-eight lumber, press forward. The gates swing open ahead to what looks like an outlet. The first buffalo springs forward like a bullet from a gun. Then, as if by magic, a gate ahead of him slides across, barring the road to freedom. At his tail another gate swings silently into place, four solid walls against which he cannot move. The brand, a wavy 'W' signifying Wainwright, is done but lightly on the right thigh. It will not be seen when the winter coat grows, but it forms at least some mark of identification for the future."[90]

The remaining chore was to chase, pull or push the 200 buffalo into the loading chute and on into the freight cars, some of the same steel-ribbed cars made unbreakable for Michel Pablo's bovine outlaws. As the journalist noted, buffalo character was as variable as that of humans. A few of the animals loaded without a fight but most were ready for a "life or death" battle rather than walk peacefully up the chute and into the freight cars. One bull — described as "The Fighting Fool" — seemed to want nothing more than to annihilate the human race. "He is," in Mullett's words, "a great full-chested, bewhiskered two-year-old, a chunk of eight hundred pounds of devil, fight and dash, and he won't go up that chute, no siree, not if it is the last thing he does on earth. Aided and abetted by a slightly smaller but equally obdurate lady buffalo who ought to be above such things, the two give the grinning heathen in the dust storm a real thrill.

"The big fellow tries to climb the fence but falls. A cowboy, eluding death by a hairsbreadth, swarms cheerfully up the sides of the corral. 'Rope him, Slim,' he calls. The obliging Slim drops a lariat neatly over the horns of 'The Fighting Fool.' Half a dozen cowboys grab the line and run up the chute with it, and then the tug-of-war commences in earnest. It is pull cowboys and pull buffalo, with only a few inches between the contestants."

It was a long tug but the six cowboys with their thousand pounds of combined weight, won the pull. A couple of hours later, the seven carloads of buffalo emigrants were on their way, 500 miles by rail and 300 on river barges pushed by the sternwheeler, Northland Echo. The first 1634 buffalo from the Wainwright Park were unloaded at Labutte Landing in 1925 and a total of 6673 were delivered over the next four years.[91]

86 N.K. Luxton, Letter to his friend, Mr. McCoy, on file in Glenbow-Alberta Archives, Calgary.
87 Edmonton Journal, June 14, 1909.
88 Edmonton Journal, June 14, 1909.
89 Ellis, Edward, Superintendent, Annual Report for the National Buffalo Park, Wainwright, Alta., April 1, 1911.
90 Edmonton Journal, June 15, 1925.
91 Ibid.

"A buffalo is now so great a prize, and by the ignorant it is considered so great an honor to kill one, that extraordinary exertions will be made to find and shoot down without mercy 'the last buffalo.' There is no possible chance for the race to be perpetuated in a wild state, and in a few years more hardly a bone will remain above ground to mark the existence of the most prolific mammalian species that ever existed, so far as we know."[92]

William T. Hornaday

Chapter 17

Gift-Wrapped Trouble For The North

Natives and early fur traders viewed a buffalo as a buffalo and a bison as a bison, regardless of the differences found between the wood buffalo strain and its better known prairie cousin. Similarities are always more obvious than differences. The typical representative of the wooded north was slightly bigger and more pugnacious than its prairie counterpart. It was also partial to what the north offered for habitat, poplar and aspen groves, sheltering white spruce forests with intermittent stretches of open grazing and wetlands to furnish still more variety. A herd could find about everything it needed for good nutrition on a short tour and adopted much shorter migration routes than those followed by the southern herds and which took up to a year.

Although most people living in central regions a century ago had no knowledge of the wood buffalo and its distinguishing characteristics, William Hornaday, Director of the New York Zoological Park, who travelled extensively in frontier Canada, certainly wasn't one of them. In his book, *The Extermination of the American Bison*, published in 1889, he wrote: "The wood buffalo when I was on the Peace River in 1875, were confined to the country lying between the Athabasca and Peace Rivers, north of latitude 57°30', or chiefly in the Birch Hills. They were also said to be in some abundance on the Salt and Hay Rivers, running into the Slave River, north of Peace River."[93]

Scientists admitted bewilderment in attempting to estimate wood buffalo populations in the 19th century. It is quite certain that numbers never reached the staggering figures advanced for North American or "plains" or "prairie" buffalo. One of the most cautious guesses about wood buffalo numbers in their better years came from a man who insisted on anonymity when he said: "While the North American prairie buffalo in the early '70s of last century numbered as high as 50 million, I'm saying the wood buffalo at the same time probably totalled a small fraction of one million."[94]

Hal W. Reynolds of the Canadian Wildlife Services supported the belief that wood buffalo numbers where they would be expected to show the greatest concentration "south of Great Slave Lake and west of the Slave River" dropped to a perilous 250 head in 1891.[95] The slow recovery in the following years was accompanied with pessimism: "Saving the wood buffalo looks like a lost cause."

One major problem was that the wood buffalo had no real friends except the alleged ones who, more than anything else, wanted the animal's skin and edible flesh. There wasn't much sentiment at Fort Chipewyan for the "wood buffalo" designation. Most people referred to them simply as "the buffalo." The same practical people offered the best of reasons for the failure of the subspecies to increase their numbers more quickly — the Indians, hunters, poachers and north country wolves, were greedy and over-killing.

The Canadian government did pass some rules for buffalo protection. There was the 1877 Buffalo Protection Act, in 1893 the Dominion Government passed a law to protect the surviving wood bison, and the 1897 enforcement mandate was assigned to the North West Mounted Police. But enforcement was hopelessly inadequate. The country that appealed to buffalo also attracted wolves, hunters and poachers, the latter two blaming the former for their own misdeeds.

In 1907 a police outpost was established at Ft. Fitzgerald and the first formal patrol of the region occurred. Two well-known personalities, Ernest Thompson Seton, biologist and writer of note, and Inspector A.M. Jarvis of the North West Mounted Police, took it upon themselves to penetrate to Fort Smith and Fort Chipewyan. It was a mission with a double purpose: to observe the local buffalo and to check if more than one kind of "wolf" was contributing to the starvation of the Chipewyan Indians by irresponsible slaughter of the buffalo.

Everywhere these two men went in the north, they heard about the recent epidemic of buffalo killing by "wolves" that were never seen and rarely left bones and other refuse from slaughtering. When the evil-doer needed a ruse to help divert suspicion from himself, the "two legged" wolf turned into a traditional four-legged one.[96] The "wolf" cry ended with a quick departure from the country of certain suspects.

With the captive prairie strain rehabilitated in park herds and biologists finding new interest in the northern subspecies, the Government of Canada with a spurt of unsuspected enthusiasm passed an Order in Council in 1922 that created Wood Buffalo National Park. The park was at once Canada's biggest, spreading itself across the boundary between Alberta and the Northwest Territories, the larger part of its 17,300 square miles or 44,800 square kilometres in Alberta. The parkland offered an inviting mix of forests, lakes, streams and swamps, traditionally favored hunting and fishing country for Chipewyan, Cree and other tribesmen. It also had a ready-made animal population, all healthy and, as far as anybody could judge, genetically pure wood bison. It was expected that with reasonable protection the park could accommodate at least twice as many buffalo as the 1,500 to 2,000 believed to be there in 1922. There was no reason to think that the northern herds would not always be healthy.

There was some satisfaction in the thought that the combined capacity of the Buffalo Park at Wainwright and Wood Buffalo National Park gave western Canada convincing claim to world leadership in buffalo conservation and breeding. There was also the easily overlooked breeding value of the two breeds or strains that might have gained much in genetic purity by their separation for a thousand to 10,000 years. It was a quality that should have been safeguarded meticulously until more was known. For a short time, Canadians had a golden opportunity to boast about their buffalo showpieces.

But genetics was a new science and apart from a few biology scholars, Canadians didn't give it much thought and people in government weren't concerned with buffalo genes. Politicians and civil servants had another problem. Foot-and-mouth disease had an ugly connotation and public workers were not allowed to forget it even though Canada, up to that time, had never experienced it. Outbreaks of anthrax had occurred a few times, chiefly among sheep, but concerted efforts had stamped it out. Contagious abortion or brucellosis, more widespread and insidious than realized, could attack as undulant fever in humans. But the most costly of these and other hated diseases was tuberculosis, widespread and versatile in its attacks. Humans, and farm and wild animals including the buffalo, were vulnerable.

It may be that buffalo susceptibility to tuberculosis was minimal until the animals felt the harassment of capture and exposure to attempted domestication. The Canadian experience certainly encouraged the thought that the pursuits and distress caused by corrals and freight cars, and the close confinement that followed had something to do with the susceptibility that appeared to follow.

The source of the infection in the Canadian herds, if there was a single source, remained in doubt. Even the nurse cow brought from Prince Albert by James McKay and Charles Alloway, when they were in search of orphan calves near Battleford in 1873, did not escape suspicion. Did the homesteader's milk cow — never tested for TB — transmit the infection to the buffalo orphans, and through them to buffalo that were sold from the McKay and Alloway herd to Col. Samuel Bedson, to "Buffalo" Jones of Kansas, to Charles Allard of Montana, to Michel Pablo and finally to the Government of Canada in 1907? It is doubtful but the theory may be worth noting.

There were other additions of buffalo to the Wainwright herd that might have brought tuberculosis infection with them. There were two shipments from the Conrad herd in Montana and a sizable herd of mixed origins from the Banff National Park. Fortunately for the politicians, the existence of the disease in the herd was a well-kept secret and the policy makers resolved to reduce the herd. But how?

The idea of an annual slaughter program was initiated in 1922 but the public objected and the plan was suspended in 1923. All the while, the Wainwright herd was growing. In 1913 it numbered 1,188 head; by 1923 it had grown to more than 6,780 and was creating new problems. The growing numbers not only defeated the idea of herd reduction as an aid in disease control, but the animals which had increased by 500 per cent in ten years were overgrazing the big range. The situation demanded positive and immediate action. Either increase the rate of slaughter, an action not acceptable to the public, or find new pasture for a big cut of surplus. It was then that the decision was made to send one thousand or more of the surplus to Wood Buffalo Park, annually, for at least four years, beginning in 1925. In all, total of 6,673 animals were transferred between 1925 and 1928.

If anybody had strong objections to throwing a big herd of the pure plains buffalo onto the same range as that occupied by the only known herd of wood buffalo in the world, there is no record of it in the Debates of The House of Commons or press. And if anybody had knowledge of the widespread presence of tuberculosis in the Wainwright herd, he did little or nothing to share it with the public for some years later. The transfer, however, was objected to and challenged by the American Society of Mammalogists and by individual biologists. Both believed that interbreeding would result in loss of both subspecies of bison and that the wood bison population would become infected with disease.

Exactly how many of the Wainwright buffalo met death in the park and were subjected to post-mortem examinations was not known or revealed. But W.F. Lothian, author of the *History of Canada's National Parks*, Vol. IV,[97] noted that, in 1923, 264 park buffalo were killed and dressed under the supervision of Dr. I. Christian, veterinarian in the federal service, Dr. A.E. Cameron, who became Inspector General in the Veterinary Service of the Department of Agriculture, and Dr. Seymour Hadwen, at that time employed by the Ontario Research Foundation. Although their report indicated "that 75 per cent of the animals slaughtered had some form of tuberculosis lesions" — the shipments to the north began in 1925.

Further along in author W.F. Lothian's summary, it is stated that: "Dr. Hadwen recommended the elimination of the herd to avoid the spread of infection but the proposal was not acceptable to park authorities. Dr. Hadwen then offered suggestions to the Department of the Interior for reducing the percentage of disease in the herd. The proposals included improved methods of feeding the buffalo in winter and the slaughter of the older animals whenever possible."[98]

But instead of acting promptly "to avoid the spread of infection," a decision was made to forward sizable droves of untested young buffalo to Slave River country. The consequences should have been clear enough to remove all doubt about the wisdom of Hadwen's advice. Nevertheless, four annual shipments went forward to the north as planned. Thus, the two strains interbred and lost the identity and purity of both. No longer was there a pure or healthy herd of Canadian buffalo.

From time to time, there was criticism about the extent of slaughtering in the parks such as Buffalo Park at Wainwright, also about the making of movie films of rodeo tactics in the park or the idea of shipping buffalo surplus as far away as Slave River. Park administrators must have been discouraged at times but they could take satisfaction from the knowledge that some of their policies were winning public approval. Nobody could criticize the prolificacy of the herds; their reproductive rates had exceeded all expectations. And as tourist attractions, the same could be said. Relatively few tourists saw Wood Buffalo Park but pleasing to the authorities was the report that visitors to the National Buffalo Park at Wainwright had grown to almost 20,000 in 1929, the last year before the Great Depression.

Most people in public life insisted that the transfer of prairie buffalo to Wood Buffalo park was a success, even though early reports indicated a disorder that few humans would have suspected, namely, homesickness. The big creatures wanted to return to their Wainwright pasture and many of them started. Traders coming to Edmonton told of seeing a herd of 50 swimming the turbulent Slave River and turning south and making their way through the northern jungles to arrive at Fort Chipewyan on the western end of Lake Athabasca. There they were blocked by lake water and swamps west of the fort.[99] A bigger herd was reported swimming the broad Peace near its mouth and heading south toward Wainwright, some 700 miles farther on. There is no proof that any of the prairie buffalo went all the way but it wasn't the first time that buffalo demonstrated a highly developed homing instinct. Somebody in a jocular mood commented that the buffalo frenzy to return to the familiar prairie haunt was not the direct result of being brain-washed by the Wainwright Board of Trade.

Nor was there any inherent animosity between the two bison strains when, by 1928, the prairie immigrants would outnumber the thoroughly climatized northern representative. It may have been expected that calf crops following the delivery of shipments of prairie buffalo would be predominantly hybrids, the prairie buffalo ratio being almost four to one. As a possible equalizing factor where the biggest, strongest and most wicked fighters became the most influential breeders, it's to be noted that the wood buffalo males held the advantage in both size and aggressiveness. In any case, the two original strains were rapidly losing their distinguishing characteristics. With every successive generation, the entire wood buffalo herd was looking more like hybrids. There were pure members of the plains buffalo race elsewhere if they should be needed, but no other wood buffalo of pure parentage, or as far as anyone knew.

It didn't take much to understand that the surest way of ending disease in the buffalo herd was by destroying all animals known to be carrying the infection, and to start over again with a relatively small but healthy herd. Members of a new herd could be selected for purity of breeding. Other options were sure to be suggested but Canadians who had paid dearly for their experience with animals infected with tuberculosis or contagious abortion, or both, should be wiser. They should not forget that such diseases do not go away and unless they are prepared to live with the hateful disorders, the cattle or buffalo owners must act decisively. Where a public herd is involved, large scale slaughter will be unpopular but procrastination, a common forerunner of blunder compounded, should be avoided.

It was never intended that the two big parks, Wood Buffalo and Wainwright, would be bridged by the buffalo themselves; distance would be too great for that. But for better or for worse, 6,000 of the prairie buffalo — between one-quarter and one-half of which were probably infected with tuberculosis or the brucellosis disease, or both — were moved by rail and water and released on the 44,000 square kilometre Wood Buffalo Park where they fraternized with about 1,500 wood buffalo, thought to be the only surviving herd in existence. Fraternize they did and before long the two subspecies were being fused into a hybrid strain, neither wood buffalo nor prairie buffalo, but sharing the exact same diseases.

From 1940 onward, the wood buffalo was believed to be extinct. But in 1957, Dr. Nick Novakowski of the Canadian Wildlife Service was making an aerial survey in the northwest corner of Wood Buffalo National Park when he spotted a small herd in a remote area near the Nyarling River. Ten years had passed, then 17 without a sighting and extinction seemed increasingly certain although the biggest conservation park in the world did offer countless hiding places. With nigh hysterical hope an investigation was conducted. Skins and skulls and other parts were studied and specimens were forwarded to the National Museum in Ottawa for further study. Finally, it was confirmed that these Nyarling River buffalo were, indeed, the closest remaining representatives to the original pre-1925 wood bison left on earth.

The immediate challenge was to make these buffalo secure against crossbreeding with hybrid stock. Eighteen head were captured and transplanted to a still more remote and isolated refuge which became, in 1963, the Mackenzie Bison Sanctuary, an area outside the park. A second transplant consisting of 23 of the same Nyarling River herd was taken to an equally well-sheltered home at Elk Island National Park, far from the danger of interbreeding with the hybrid buffalo and safely distanced from any current threat of anthrax. In 1975, Elk Island became the source herd for a recovery program. It looked like good and practical conservation.[100]

For the small herds of modern-day wood buffalo, the return to four-figure populations was inevitably slow. But the assurance of genetic purity, relatively speaking, and freedom from tuberculosis and brucellosis brought satisfaction. However, Wood Buffalo Park and Wainwright Buffalo Park continued to be plagued by misfortune. The former's animal population growth was impressive but its hereditary make-up was mixed and its health record was seriously tarnished by tuberculosis and brucellosis, and in later years by anthrax. The northern parks' buffalo population reached 12,000 in the 1960s, 9,000 in the 70s, dropped to 4,000 in the 80s and to just under 2,000 in 1994.

It was Elk Island's herd of plains buffalo, the offspring from the small group of "outlaws" which proved too fast and smart to be caught in the roundup when the animals were moved to the new Buffalo Park at Wainwright in 1909, that had the best record of all. With population limits imposed by the small size of the grazing range, Elk Island held generally to 400 or 500 for many years, always at the north end of the park, thoroughly separated and maintained from the 23 head of rediscovered Nyarling River wood buffalo. The members of Elk Island's bigger herd distinguished themselves by evading the epidemics of tuberculosis and brucellosis that struck widely in the next few years.

But while Elk Island was winning praise for its excellent park record, the bigger Buffalo Park at Wainwright with a bison population of 8,000 in 1924 was experiencing the misfortune of all time, pathological, nutritional and political, leading to its complete liquidation as a reserve for buffalo and other wild animals. The story of disease in the buffalo at Wainwright was skilfully suppressed but slaughtering in the park abattoir continued as a herd-reduction measure and the healthy meat was sold. The presence of tuberculosis in the herd was not necessarily an added danger to human health because all carcasses and meats were required to pass the same strict inspection by government inspectors as meat products for the most discriminating trade elsewhere.

The government, by its park trade, was clearly in the meat business, not a very profitable business as some sale prices for buffalo meat during the Depression years would show. A Member of the House of Commons, on March 21, 1938, presented the government with a list of questions to find out how many buffalo were slaughtered in 1936 and '37, if tenders were called for the sales, who were the successful tenderers and at what prices.

The Hon. T.A. Crerar, Minister of Mines and Resources, answered on behalf of the government, showing that P. Burns and Company of Calgary, was the purchaser in 1936 and Canada Packers Company of Toronto in 1937. The prices were as follows:

P. Bums, 1936: Buffalo

For choice quality/carcasses - three cents per pound
For all other saleable, good and top medium - two cents per pound
For aged and boner carcasses - one-half cent per pound

Canada Packers, 1937: Buffalo

For choice quality buffalo carcasses - three cents per pound
For all other saleable, good and top medium - one and three-quarter
  cents per pound
For aged and boner carcasses - three-fifths of a cent per pound.[101]

A short time later, veterinarian Seymour Hadwen of the Ontario Research Foundation was back at Wainwright. He had been present for a buffalo slaughter test in 1923 which revealed the distressing information that 75 per cent of the animals slaughtered had tuberculosis lesions. His advice was to eradicate the herd, thereby avoiding more serious problems later. But park officials could or would not bring themselves to take the extreme measure.

Naturally, the disease worries became worse rather than better and in September 1939, Hadwen was back, invited to make another visit and another report. The disease picture was no brighter and he repeated his earlier advice. The veterinarian recommended the destruction of the entire herd including the elk, moose and deer found in the park. He paid tribute to the park staff whose members performed their duties with good conscience and loyalty. Again he raised the question why the Elk Island herd remained clean while the Wainwright herd suffered so severely. He offered no explanation but criticized policies that ignored the dilemma.

By this time, Canada was at war and the demands of World War II were making instant revisions in national goals and priorities. Wainwright Buffalo Park

Plains bison in National Buffalo Park at Wainwright, Alberta, 1930 *(Glenbow Archives)*

was one of the first victims, one that gave an indecisive government an immediate "way of escape" from its diseased buffalo dilemma. The country's revitalized Department of National Defence needed or presumed a need for a big block of land for purposes of military training. The big park — almost 200 square miles — was proposed. The tuberculosis-riddled buffalo would have to be destroyed and would take their disease infections with them. Public criticism of herd destruction would be minimized. Even at that, the government people were in no hurry about telling everything.

Still sensitive about the widespread state of tuberculosis in the park herd, the Hon. T.A. Crerar, Minister of Mines and Resources, was on June 24, 1940, making some disclosures about the buffalo which had already been destroyed. The questioner was George Black, Member for the Yukon and he was visibly irked that he should be obliged to get the first information about the peoples' business from the press instead of the government. Glaring at Crerar, the Member declared: "A report appears in the Ottawa Journal of this morning to the effect that the government has had destroyed 3,000 buffalo, more than 1,000 elk, 500 moose and 500 deer which had been in Wainwright National Park. Is that report correct? If so, why were the elk, moose and deer not released to form an addition to the wildlife of Canada?"

The Honourable Mr. Crerar replied: "The report is correct. The buffalo, elk, moose and deer which were in Buffalo Park were destroyed some months ago. . . An opportunity was given to various public bodies possessing parks or other facilities to secure any of these animals they might wish before the destruction took place. The destruction of the animals in Buffalo Park at Wainwright was made necessary by the fact that they were badly infected with tuberculosis. There are several other parks in which we have buffalo, elk and other animals. For instance, in Riding Mountain Park there is probably the largest herd of elk on the North American continent. It was not thought desirable or necessary to turn these animals loose. . . at any rate this action was not taken."[102]

After the Minister broke the long and unholy silence, raising more questions than he answered, reporters and politicians in opposition began searching for other items of government news they might have missed in the previous weeks. They discovered that November, 1939, was slaughter month at the Wainwright Park and about 5,000 of the big and beautiful wild animals, most of them buffalo, met their death. Sam Purchell, whose inglorious distinction was in having killed more blameless buffalo than any other person in history, was again the park's sharpshooter making his total kill ever greater. Two killing gangs with two park wardens in each were at work in the fields, followed by pickup trucks which transported the animals to the abattoir.

Elk to the number of 750 were the first to be shot and removed. They presented bigger field problems because, as the wardens believed, they could not be rounded up like buffalo and had to be hunted and shot in the traditional manner. On November 30, 1939, ten carloads of elk meat were shipped from Wainwright to Indian reserves in Saskatchewan and Alberta. Buffalo meat had been gaining popularity with both Indian and non-Indian consumers until Hon. T.A. Crerar told the Canadian people officially, that "the destruction of the animals in Wainwright Buffalo Park was made necessary by the fact that they were badly infected with tuberculosis." Many people reacted in anger at the thought of what they had been buying and eating. The government was indeed open to criticism in its handling of disease in the park herds but the prescribed handling of the carcasses and meat was exactly as that practiced with beef, pork and mutton in all abattoirs having government meat inspection.

This was explained to the Canadian people, perhaps at the Government's request, by Grant Dexter, one of Canada's leading journalists. He was well aware that rumors were flying and hoped to set them at ease. "Reports, particularly from the west, indicate a fairly widespread belief that all this meat is of doubtful quality, that all the animals are badly infected with tuberculosis. It is also being said that the government is allowing diseased meat to be given to the Indians and that this is one of the contributing causes to the prevalence of TB among the Indians. It is not denied at Ottawa that the Wainwright herd is infected with TB and this is one of the reasons why the slaughter policy was adopted. But it is stated officially that the strictest precautions are being taken to prevent any infected meat reaching the market or being given to the Indians.

"There seems to be a general impression that the normal custom is to destroy all carcasses that show TB infection. This is not so. The infected parts of a carcass are condemned and destroyed and the good meat is permitted to be sold. This is true of every (inspected) slaughter house in Canada."[103]

After 32 years, the Wainwright Buffalo Park was "retiring" from one job and taking another. On the authority of the War Measures Act it was made available to the Department of National Defence for training purposes. All the big game animals, except the herd of crossbred stock known as cattalo, were gone. The Department of National Defence accepted the property with its 170-mile long fence that was constructed at a cost reported to be a thousand dollars a mile in March, 1940. There was no reason to believe the Buffalo Park at Wainwright would ever see another buffalo. Attention shifted to Wood Buffalo Park in the north and, as time was to show, a park that was capable of completely overshadowing Wainwright in generating disease troubles for its buffalo herds. That is now another story.

The Wainwright Park served the purpose for which it was chosen and those who selected its location had no reason to apologize. It was served by four superintendents. Ed Ellis moved from Banff National Park to become the first in 1908, and A.G. Smith was the last and occupied the position for 24 years. The park's statistics included hundreds of loyal workers including cowboys, tens of thousands of buffalo, elk, moose, deer and cattalo, and hundreds of thousands of visitors and tourists who were impressed by what they saw.

92   Hornaday, William T., The Extermination Of The American Bison, p. 525, published by the Government Printing Office, Washington, 1889.
93   Ibid.
94   Soper (1941) reported that the population reached an estimated low of 250 during 1896-1900.
95   Reynolds, Hal W., Wood Bison, Past, Present and Future, Canadian Wildlife Service Paper, C.W.S. Regional Library, Edmonton, 1980
96   Jarvis, Inspector A.M., whose story was related by "The Old Timer" in the Third Column, Edmonton Journal, Jan. 15, 1965.
97   Lothian, W.F., The History of Canada's National Parks, Vol. IV, Parks Canada Library Published in 1981.
98   Dr. Seymour Hadwen was a cultured Britisher, born Leeds, England, 1877. He obtained his post secondary education at McGill University and held the post of research professor of animal diseases at University of Saskatchewan between 1923 and 1927. It may be noted that the author of this work was on the staff of the University of Saskatchewan from 1928 to 1946 and got to know Dr. Hadwen moderately well when he returned from time to time to visit friends and pursue certain studies. This author recalls occasions when he repeated his convictions about the TB-infected buffalo.
99   Manitoba Free Press, Aug. 3, 1925.
100   Reynolds, Hal W., The Canadian Wildlife Service Program, To Restore Wood Bison, Canadian Wildlife Service, Edmonton office,1980.
101   House of Commons Debates, March 21, 1938, Vol. II, page 1529
102   Crerar, Hon. T.A. Debates, House of Commons, Session of 1940, Vol 2, Jan. 24, 1940.
103   Dexter, Grant, Winnipeg Free Press, Jan. 6, 1940.

"We hope that before long the annual prize list of the Manitoba Agricultural Society may contain premiums offered for the best specimens of crosses between bison and domestic cattle and who knows but at some future day, this province may possess a breed famous the world over, the bulls of which will be exported at fabulous prices."[104]

The Winnipeg Daily Free Press

Chapter 18

The Lure Of The Hybrid

By the end of 1939, the big Wainwright herds were gone, all except the breeding animals in the cattalo research project that began, in 1916, on six sections of prairie land on the east side of the main buffalo range. For many of Canada's progressive cattlemen who sensed a possibility of gaining greater efficiency in beef production by crossing buffalo and domestic cattle, or using sires carrying some degree of buffalo breeding, the cattalo project was the most important part of the National Park program. A hybridizing venture of such proportions was new in Canada but rested clearly upon ancient convictions that crossbreeding offered the surest "short cut" in achieving new strains and better production. The favorite examples were the mule and the husky dog. The latter, originating in a cross between the wolf and domestic dog, was conceded to be superior to either parent strain in meeting the needs in northern dog team transportation.

Similarly, the mule, a moderately well-known draft animal on western farms, came by crossing the horse female or mare with the donkey male or jack and was — in the opinion of farm users — unsurpassed by either parent species in stamina, hardiness, versatility and longevity. It was recited many times that the mule had "no pride of ancestry and no hope of posterity." But it held its friends and it didn't surprise anybody on the western frontier when it was reported in 1893 that: "A carload of mules arrived on Monday last from Minneapolis, destined to the Mormon settlers at Lee's Creek."[105]

The interbreeding of domestic cattle and the prairie buffalo was discussed by Selkirk settlers beside the Red River on the site of today's Winnipeg, as early as 1813. Lord Selkirk — with the mind of a scientist and the spirit of a generous uncle — advanced proposals that he considered practical and useful. Among them was the idea of drawing upon the limitless resources of buffalo in building farm herds and supplying dairy foods and farm power as well as meat. "If cattle and buffalo are related, why not interbreed them on Red River farms?" he reasoned, thereby reducing the costly necessity of importing livestock from overseas. He bemoaned the absence of cows and cows' milk in the settlement and believed the settlers and their children would accept the milk from buffalo ahead of that from "mares."

After three or four years, the Red River bovine herd was still discouragingly small, showing only five or six domestic cattle and one buffalo heifer that was proving to be particularly useful. She was seen pulling a Red River cart at times and occasionally hitched with one or two horses or milk cows, pulling a plow. The popularity of the buffalo heifer must have made a very favorable impression upon the settlers because by 1820, according to John Pritchard of the settlement, there were 18 buffalo in varying stages of domestication in the community.

William Laidlaw, who was Lord Selkirk's appointee to the position of manager of the experimental farm, lost none of his hope of capturing more buffalo calves for raising in captivity but progress was slow and the attempts to make inter-species crosses were totally unsuccessful. Laidlaw complained that his failure to raise a hybrid was due to the snobbish pasture manner of "the English bull on the farm."

If personal enthusiasm could be taken as a guarantee of success, "Buffalo" Jones would have become the great name in developing a North American Cattalo breed, ranking with Amos Cruickshank of Shorthorn fame in Scotland, Warren Cammon in connection with the Polled Hereford in the United States and Richard C. Harvey of Alberta who achieved a high goal with his "Romnellet" sheep.

Nobody in the business had more fertile imagination than Jones and in 1888 he had a private herd of 127 buffalo of pure breeding, most of which were animals he captured ingeniously as calves and raised by hand. Like Walking Coyote, James McKay, Charles Alloway, Col. Sam Bedson, Charles Allard and Michel Pablo, he was an obvious factor in saving a remnant of the North American herd in the '80s. Even his exaggerated evaluations were well received and generated both entertainment and public interest. But one question remained. Did Jones really believe all that he claimed in support of buffalo and cattalo? Was buffalo flesh really "far superior to that of any other domestic animal and was its tallow as rich and palatable as butter?" Was its fur softer "than lamb's wool" and was it when woven into cloth, "the lightest and warmest fabric ever manufactured?" Was buffalo underfur equal to swan's down for making "perfectly waterproof hats?" Was the Cattalo "without a superior as a beast of burden" and was the milk of the buffalo "infinitely richer than that of the Jersey cow?"[106]

Jones made his mistakes, two in particular. The first was in overestimating the value of the buffalo or the hybrid as a domestic animal and, second, his failure to recognize the magnitude and seriousness of the sterility problem in first cross hybrid males. Perhaps he did gain an understanding of the incidence of infertility in the hybrid males in his later years or maybe the breeding impediment to progress was a disappointment about which he did not care to write or talk.

When Jones sold the last of his herd to Allard and Pablo of western Montana in 1893, the North American centre of interest in hybridization moved back to Canada and appeared to remain there. The new leader was the Ontario-born Irish Canadian, Mossom M. Boyd, with lumbering interests inherited from his father and farming enterprises at Bobcaygeon, Ontario, and Prince Albert, Saskatchewan. Fine livestock, including Clydesdale and Percheron horses, Aberdeen-Angus and Hereford cattle, and Oxford and Persian sheep, were his specialties. He was one of the first North American breeders to have success in producing Polled Herefords. A bull calf, registered as Bullion 4th and born at the Prince Albert farm in 1912, was sold to an American breeder for whom he became one of the greatest show and breeding bulls of the Polled Hereford strain.

It may be that Mr. Boyd's interest in crossing his Hereford and Aberdeen-Angus cattle with prairie buffalo was a product of the influence of "Buffalo" Jones. About 1893 he was trying to buy one or two buffalo bulls but was having trouble in locating them. One of his first bulls was bought in Mexico and delivered by rail. Another was obtained as a loan from the Dominion Department of the Interior and still another was acquired by trade in which Boyd paid with some Persian sheep and several young buffalo hybrids. But Mr. Boyd died in 1914 and interest in the experimental breeding flagged.

Conservation of a great national heritage was the incentive that brought the buffalo back to Canada in 1907 and, having acquired the big herd, it became imperative that it be placed in proper habitat where it could be seen and enjoyed by all citizens. The choice of site proved generally acceptable although its use for experimental studies had not been seriously considered. But servants of the Dominion Department of Agriculture were suddenly being swamped with questions about the possible use of buffalo in farm practice. They

Buffalo bull "Napoleon Bonaparte" imported by Mossom Boyd, Bobcaygen, Ontario (Boyd Family/MacEwan Collection)

were asked: "Is there any hope of incorporating the best buffalo characteristics into our farm herds, characteristics like cold weather hardiness, the ability to winter graze when the pastures are heavily blanketed with snow and carcasses with high proportions of lean meat?"

The Department of Agriculture wanted to become involved and when the animals owned by the late Mossom Boyd were offered, the government department bought four bulls and 16 cows of the "ready made" test herd and shipped them to temporary quarters at Scott Experimental Station in Saskatchewan. Two years later, the herd was moved to Wainwright where they remained until 1950 when the cattalo project was centralized at Manyberries, Alberta. The new Wainwright home for the test animals was a six-section block contiguous to the Buffalo Park on the east side, with double fencing between the two ranges. The buffer strip between the fences was six rods wide, enough to cool the ire of the most belligerent. The double fence worked well; a single fence of wire between two angry buffalo bulls would mean, at the very least, a ruined fence.

According to E.J. "Bud" Cotton, who began working at the Buffalo Park in 1913 and rode as a cowboy and park warden for most of the next 30 years, the buffalo X cattle hybrids were the least lovable of all the animals with which he worked. "The buffalo," he said, "would wave his short tail in the air and warn you when he was going to charge but not the hybrid; he'd just charge, without warning and without reason. "You'd think," Cotton added, "that the animal with one domestic parent and 50 per cent domestic blood would be more docile than the totally wild bison. But it didn't work that way. The meanest hybrid in my memory was one whose mother was a Jersey cow."[107]

A specimen named King was, for many years, the Park's showpiece. Guessing his weight was an unending pastime for both local people and travellers. There were no scales capable of weighing him except at one of the grain elevators in Wainwright and nobody wanted the job of escorting this ever-angry leviathan to the elevator and guaranteeing to return him to the pasture. His domestic parent was believed to have been a Shorthorn and his colors, like a rainbow, were bright and numerous.

Cattle dealers and drovers who depended upon their skill in guessing weights for their living, admitted that they had no experience with animals of such colossal weight as King's and then made guesses ranging from 2,400 to 3,500 pounds. Even the dealers were heard to say, "He's the biggest critter I've ever seen." When he was proclaimed, "The biggest bull in the world," nobody uttered a word of agreement or disagreement. But when somebody described him as, "Big and mean and sterile" — every Wainwright head nodded understandingly. King, however, was growing old and when a cut of expendable animals was shipped to market, King, at close to 20 years of age, went too.

If King had an apprentice to confirm Bud Cotton's unflattering opinion of the hybrid's evil disposition, the white-face bull known as Quinto Porto might have been it. He wasn't as big as King but no less notorious as a fence breaker and he made a reputation for himself. He treated all fences as if they were not there. Bud Cotton is quoted as saying, he would never forget the bull's performance when, "with a lariat loop around his neck, he plunged through the buffalo-proof fence, taking three cowboys and one saddle horse on the restraining end of the lariat and a portion of the fence itself . . . with him."

The last of the Park herd was destroyed in 1939, leaving only the test animals in the cattalo breeding program to be moved later. As the Department of National Defence moved to occupy the Wainwright property, the Department of Agriculture made plans to receive all the working parts for a better bovine breed at the Manyberries Experimental Station. Hopefully, the search would continue without more than the slightest interruption. The studies were bound to become more complex, more entrenched in genetics and more scientific.

In Dr. Hobart Peters, who directed the Manyberries studies throughout the cattalo years, the researchers had a scientist as a great teacher and a practical agriculturist as a critic. He understood the problems, chief of which was sterility: "While the cattalo had no difficulty in becoming good beef producers," he said, "the bulls had a fertility problem from the very beginning."

"The female hybrids appeared to have a normal conception rate but all male hybrids were sterile. As the domestic beef carcass was considered superior to those of the bison, backcrosses to the domestic were made. The first backcross males were sterile but eventually some fertile bulls of the second, third and fourth backcrosses were obtained and mated with hybrid and backcross cows."[108] It wasn't a victory but it was an advance and the realization that the herd could produce its own males for breeding gave hope for the time when the herd could be "closed" to outside or "foreign" strains, an acknowledged "long step" forward in breed building. That time for the closure of the herd came in 1956. The herd that at one stage could not produce any except sterile males was, by then, in a position to supply its own sires and go on to conduct line breeding, also thought necessary in breed building.

The studies ended formally when the cattalo test herd was shipped from the Manyberries Experimental Station to market in 1964. It was the conclusion of another chapter in the history of the race, ending very much like other buffalo chapters, in extermination, one way or another. If the only purpose was the

Cattalo bull "King" at National Buffalo Park, Wainwright, Alberta 1919, weight estimated at between 2,500 and 3,500 pounds. *(Glenbow Archives)*

creation of a breed incorporating the best of the two bovine species, then the years of effort and millions of dollars of expenditure were a loss. A few hundred animals of mixed breeding were produced and might have been declared a breed and called Cattalo. But they, too, are gone. There is no new breed but the breeding project was not a total failure or loss.

At best, Canadians have been extremely slow in gaining a proper understanding of their most colorful big native animal and should welcome the new light cast upon the buffalo and its halfbreed offspring. Should the time come when the buffalo and his mixed-blood progeny will be wanted and needed as the only eligible candidates to utilize the mediocre grazing of the vast and frosty north — the preliminary study will not need to be repeated.

An Agriculture Canada worker in Lethbridge, Dr. D.G. Keller, admitted: "There is probably little advantage in bison crosses in Canada where we already have a variety of high-performing straight-breeds and crossbreeds and where extreme hardiness is not as critical as it used to be because management and winter feeding patterns have changed."[109]

Dr. Peters said in connection with the decision to end the hybridization project: "Being an honest scientist is more important than being popular." The director of the project was as popular as he was honest. Rancher and neighbour George Ross described Peters as: "A foremost expert in crossbreeding. When he came to Manyberries, all the cattle had white faces but by the time he left, there were cattle of every color in the rainbow and they weighed more and ate less."[110]

138

104 The Daily Free Press, Winnipeg, Jan. 5. 1877.
105 The Lethbridge Herald, Aug. 24, 1893.
106 Jones, C.J. "Buffalo", Forty Years of Adventure, (Compiled by Henry Inman), p. 49 Published by Crane and Co, Iopeka, Kansas, 1899.
107 Cotton, B.J. "Bud", Private conversation, Calgary, July, 1983.
108 Peters, Hobart F., Experimental Hybridization of Domestic Cattle and American Bison. Paper presented at the International Congress of Animal Breeding, September, 1964.
109 Keller, D.G., Research reveals Drawbacks with Cattalo, Western Producer, Dec. 14, 1978.
110 Canadian Cattlemen, 1964.

"The plains burned in every direction and blind buffalo were seen wandering about. The poor beasts have all their hair singed off; even the skin in many places is shrivelled up and terribly burned, and their eyes are swollen and closed fast. It was really pitiful to see them staggering about, sometimes running afoul of a large stone, at other times stumbling down hill and falling into creeks not yet frozen over. In one spot we found a whole herd lying dead. The fire having passed only yesterday, (the carcasses of) these animals were still good and fresh, and many of them exceedingly fat. ,. At sunset we arrived at the Indian camp, having made an extraordinary day's ride and seen an incredible number of dead and dying, blind, lame, singed and roasted buffalo. The fire raged all night toward the S.W."[111]

Alexander Henry

Chapter 19

They, Too, Had Their Enemies

Although built "like battleships" and buttressed with courage to match their strength and size, the buffalo had their enemies too. There were extremes of weather, prairie fires that trapped whole herds, glare ice on which the versatile buffalo became almost helpless, diseases and 10,000 years of predators. The near-total destroyer was not the sabre-toothed tiger, grizzly bear or grey wolf but the human with a bow-and-arrow, gun or some ingenious idea for wholesale slaughter. Humans talk about conservation but if they like the experience of killing or are making money at it, they don't seem to know when to stop. Pot hunting from which the hunters saved the tongues, tenderloins and humps, and let 90 per cent of the carcass rot in the field or killing day after day for no other purpose than selling hides for $2.00 each were evil practices which almost cost the environment a noble race.

The human may have been the worst offender but certainly not the only predator in the life of the buffalo. Man's closest rival in the slaughter may have been the grey wolf, sometimes called the timber wolf, the biggest member of today's dog family and weighing between 55 and 100 pounds. The best known member of that family is, of course, the widely distributed coyote, weighing about half as much and smart enough to keep safely beyond striking distance of the buffalo. Their pack attack was cruel but skilful, making them appear as specialists that had perfected their strategy from generations of study. Were it not for their savage cruelty, their methods would win praise; they are creatures of singular interest inviting more study than they have received. Their modern habitat corresponds with that of the wood buffalo in the Canadian north. Some research studies have been carried out, the earliest being the relationship between the wood buffalo and wolves was conducted by Ernest Thompson Seton.

Seeing a herd of wood buffalo, with or without calves, resting or grazing in a northern meadow, with four or five members of a grey wolf pack loitering nearby, might convey the impression of a peaceful natural community. But things are not always what they seem. The "peaceful community" may be, in reality, a battleground one moment and the place where a strategy is being planned the next. The true state of the ongoing contest comes alive when the canine aggressors sense a chance of making a kill in the face of a coordinated defence. In the absence of calves, the predator's attack will be aimed at a mature animal handicapped by age, illness or injury. Likely, the animal chosen would be one that was no longer an asset to the herd and in a practical sense, the herd would be stronger without it. But if there are no easy adult victims in the herd and young calves are present, the challenge to the hungry wolves is much different. As the patient research workers in the Canadian Wildlife Service know, "Wolves are natural predators of wood buffalo."[112] It is a conflict millions of years old.

The attackers discovered long ago that when there were buffalo calves present, hunting in packs was still the surest way to a good meal. A pack of four or five made hunting more effective but the manner of choosing the animal for the kill remains a puzzle, like the force which guides the whooping crane from its winter home in the Arkansas National Wildlife Refuge on the Texas Gulf Coast to the nesting grounds in Wood Buffalo National Park, about 3,900 kilometres each way. At the instant of an attack, the target calf knows instinctively to dash to the ever-willing protection of the mother or one of the nearby bulls. Even young bulls of a year or two are ever ready to fight for the protection of the infant. The enraged bull, fighting like a demon, may still be unable to deliver a direct blow to the more nimble wolf but it would be an unworthy wolf that would not accept a warning.

Carbyn and Trottier, in the course of a three-year study, made numerous pertinent observations of buffalo-wolf interactions, some of them with the help of 43 wolves to which radio-collars were attached. On May 28, 1980, they observed eleven wolf attacks. They found reason to marvel at wolf strategy, buffalo calf speed and agility and particularly, the loyal protectiveness of the young buffalo bulls that "bunched up" around a threatened cow and calf and defied the wolves.

Again and again, the wolves appeared to give up the pursuit until the buffalo relaxed their defences and the target calf and its mother wandered from the main herd. Then the wolves bounded back for attack. Often a calf was knocked down and sometimes it was injured and bleeding but observers were impressed by both the speed and resurgence of a buffalo calf. After the eleventh attack with repeated injury to one calf, the wolves really appeared to abandon the chase and if that calf did survive, the bulls deserved much of the credit. Musk-oxen had the reputation of producing a solid fence of bulls' heads facing an enemy, behind which the calves and females found the comfort of security. It could be suggested that the buffalo and musk-ox learned something of value from each other.

According to Carbyn and Trottier, as written in the abstract of their report: "Five apparent defense strategies to protect buffalo calves from wolves were noted:

1) To run to the (mother) cow. 2) To run to the herd. 3) To run to the nearest bull. 4) To get out in front and centre of a stampeding herd and 5) To run through a body of water."[113]

Another piece of nefarious work by wolves against the buffalo was long overlooked. It was the phenomenon of the buffalo ox, sometimes seen as a monstrosity. The ox was easy to recognize in a herd, being bigger than other males, somewhat flat-sided and at least one hand taller at the hump than most mature bulls. He lacked the fine balance, however, and particularly the attractive degree of masculinity that characterized the buffalo bull. Little is written about the buffalo ox but two visitors, at least, Henry Y. Hind who was in the west for the purpose of a survey in 1857 and '58, and the Earl of Southesk who was here as a holidayer and hunter in 1859 and '60, displayed interest in the native ox. The Earl learned that the meat of the buffalo ox possessed superior quality and he was interested in shooting one. He was successful in locating one in a prairie herd but not in bagging it.[114]

But how was the presence of the buffalo ox in a wild herd to be explained? The conspicuous giant was quite correctly called a buffalo ox. According to the Earl, the tall ox, in all probability, had been one of the buffalo calves singled out by

Buffalo calf *(L.W. Carbyn/MacEwan Collection)*

A fox feasts on remains of a buffalo carcass after the kill by wolves (L.W. Carbyn/MacEwan Collection)

a wolf pack for a kill and in the course of the attacks, the little fellow was mutilated and emasculated but not killed and he recovered to become a buffalo ox. Farmers would have called him a "buffalo steer." It's also possible that Indians, for reasons that are not certain, were responsible for some calf emasculations.

Buffalo deaths by drowning — often involving huge numbers — were not uncommon in the wild herds. A Canadian Wildlife Service brochure, entitled *North American Bison* and published in 1974, revived the account of the 1795 drowning tragedy in which a fur-trader counted 7,360 dead bodies lining the shores of Qu'Appelle River and Lakes.[115] An average herd of that size would likely have a total weight of almost 3,000 tons, a severe test of ice at any season.

That may seem as an item from ancient history but another buffalo drowning as recently as 1974 came close enough to matching the sad and disastrous result. It was another springtime catastrophe, another case of buffalo bunching and multiplying the pressure on a small area of ice weakened by spring thaws. It was water from the Peace and Athabasca Rivers flooding the big delta region. When flood water subsided, Wood Buffalo Park workers counted 495 dead bodies but when the many carcasses swept away or buried in mud and debris were considered, it was estimated that the total number of buffalo deaths from drowning would be about 2,000.

Fire was a common enemy. Prairie settlers with but feeble protection from the fires carried in by wind, found some assurance behind fireguards. Wild animals, on the other hand, fled, believing instinctively that their best hope was in keeping ahead of the fire demon. Prairie fires could hurt the plains buffalo in two distinct ways, one by loss of grazing and the other by direct injury from the cruel flames, resulting in wounding or death. The bison's natural speed and stamina aided greatly in escape but there were occasions when, running in panic, a herd allowed itself to become trapped by the shifting flames, with serious consequences.

Even the custodians of buffalo parks learned something of the dangers arising from prairie fires. Workers at the National Buffalo Park at Wainwright had their opportunity for a first-hand demonstration of fire dangers in the autumn of 1909. The report that reached the press suggested total loss of the park herd following the burning of the grass, the destruction of the fence and the dispersal of the animals. The story was greatly exaggerated, however, and park workers were successful in recovering the animals that escaped and making repairs to the fence.[116]

Alexander Henry, the highly voluble wintering partner of the North West Company, was in the best possible position to know and understand the buffalo that completely dominated the prairie ranges at the beginning of the nineteenth century. It was with distress and sympathy that he wrote about the poor brutes he saw in 1804, "the dead and dying, the blind, lame, singed and roasted buffalo."

Henry Y. Hind, making a survey of western potential on behalf of Canada west — meaning Ontario — where the idea of annexation of the west was growing, was in Manitoba and the Territories about half a century after Alexander Henry and held many of the same sympathetic feelings. It is easy to sense something mystical about the role Hind assigned to the blind ones. "Blind buffalo," he wrote, "are frequently found accompanying herds and sometimes alone. Their eyes have been destroyed by prairie fires; but their quickened sense of hearing and smell, and their increased alertness enable them to guard against danger and make it more difficult to approach them in quiet weather than those possessing sight. Hunters think that blind buffalo frequently give the alarm when they are stealthily approaching a herd in an undulating country. When galloping over stony ground blind buffalo frequently fall, but when quietly feeding they avoid the stones and boulders with wonderful skill."[117] Hind was quite critical of both Indians and non-Indians for their failure to exercise humane methods.[118]

If a writer of that time wanted a balanced judgement about the future of the race, he could do nothing better than consult Ernest Thompson Seton. This man was becoming recognized as the leading naturalist in Canada. Born in Durham, England, in 1860, he came as a child with his parents to Lindsay, Upper

Canada. His earliest interests were in the same areas that gripped him lifelong, namely, natural history and art. But these attractions did not preclude his adventure as a Manitoba homesteader that led to his appointment as Provincial Naturalist in the same province.

Quickly, Seton became an international figure, travelling extensively. He travelled the Arctic in 1907; he became Boy Scout Chief for America and worked at it; he founded a prestigious school featuring wildlife and wood craft; he wrote more than 40 books, the best-known of which were *The Life Histories of Northern Animals* and *Wild Animals I have Known*. With a view to his own experience, how would he have summarized a chapter dealing with the enemies of the buffalo? His list of enemies in order of importance would look something like this:

1   Ice-covered rivers on which the ice still looks strong but is becoming ever weaker.

2   Indians and non-Indians with guns.

3   Prairie fires.

4   Predators like grey wolves.

5   Epidemic diseases (would be nearer the top in recent years, lower in early years).

6   Bogs.

7   Blizzards.

Seton knew all about the buffalo's front-end blizzard protection and the instinct that turns its head to the wind and furnishes a measure of wind break for the lightly-clothed rear quarters. He also knew from experience that there were winter spells when the best of clothing wasn't enough. He had all the information about the American winter of 1871-'72 and the Canadian winter of 1886-'87, destroyers of cattle and bison. He had the full story about the herds, hundreds of thousands of buffalo, that crossed the Missouri River and never returned. The buffalo was still the most winter-hardy animal on the continent but what Seton was saying was: "Don't ignore that killer winter that returns unexpectedly." It was a message for cattlemen as well as others.

Seton stood by his belief that river ice in Spring season was the most treacherous of all killers: "All winter the buffalo herds of the colder range were accustomed fearlessly to cross and recross the ice-bound rivers. Springtime comes with the impulse to wander farther north. The herds travel slowly on their route; river after river is crossed but a change sets in; the ice grows rotten; to all appearance it is the same but it will no longer bear the widely extended herd; the van (vanguard) goes crashing through to death and thousands more are pushed in by the oncoming herd behind."[119]

111   Henry, Alexander, the Younger, New Light On The Early History Of The Greater Northwest. The Manuscript Journals of Alexander Henry and David Thompson, Edited by Elliott Cous. Vol. I, Francis P. Harper, New York, 1897.

112   Carbyn, L.N. and Trottier, T., Descriptions of Wolf Attacks On Bison Calves in Wood Buffalo National Park, Canadian Wildlife Service, Edmonton, Journal of the Arctic Institute of North America, Dec. 1988.

113   Ibid.

114   Southesk, The Earl of, Saskatchewan and the Rocky Mountains, p. 111, James Campbell and Son, Toronto, 1875.

115   North American Bison, Brochure, Canadian Wildlife Service, Ottawa, 1974.

116   Man. Free Press, Oct. 6, 1909.

117   Hind, Henry Youle, Report of Progress, Assiniboine and Saskatchewan Exploring Expedition, Printed By John Lovell, Toronto, 1959.

118   Hind, Henry Youle, Report of Progress, Assiniboine and Saskatchewan Exploring Expedition, Printed By John Lovell, Toronto, 1959.

119   Seton, Ernest Thompson, Life Histories of Northern Animals, Vol. I, p. 267, published by Charles Scribner's Sons, New York, 1909.

"For centuries aborigines of the plains utilized the meat and hides of the buffalo without making the slightest impression on their fabulous numbers. This was left for the white man to accomplish. Peak of the slaughter was reached sometime after the middle of the past century — a crescendo of such sadistic butchery of a big game animal as the world has ever known. Millions were wiped out in a few decades."[120]

J. Dewey Soper

Chapter 20

Anthrax — A Word With A Deathly Ring About It

Anthrax is a word with an ugly connotation, identifying an ancient bacterial disease that brought death to millions of humans and animals around the world. Canadians were lucky in escaping it for a long time. That the buffalo were, in the words of Ernest Thompson Seton, "a race in which epidemic disease seems to have been unknown," was further indication of good fortune and cause for thanksgiving. But good luck offers no guarantees and buffalo fortunes suffered reverses in form. After becoming the helpless victims of tuberculosis and brucellosis, they were suddenly confronted by another destroyer. Wildlife specialists asked: "Now it's anthrax. For Heaven's sake, what's next?"

The bad news for the buffalo was contained in a report from the Parks Administration to the Council of the Northwest Territories, dated September, 1962. The narrative began with the introduction of a Canadian Wildlife Service biologist making a routine field survey on August 26, 1962. That the biologist would and did find several dead buffalo on the range in the Hook Lake area, about 80 miles north of Fort Smith, should not, in itself, produce much surprise, considering there was a population of 10,000 or more of the bison on the range.

It had always been park policy, as far as it was practical, to check on buffalo deaths and try to identify the cause of such losses of life and record the information. If and when the cause of death was uncertain, it might take some days to get the information. In the case of one of the animals found dead on August 26, the laboratory evidence at the end of a week raised suspicions of anthrax and after another week that included additional tests at the Health of Animals Laboratory in Lethbridge, anthrax was confirmed as the cause of the animal's death.

Immediately, the north saw bulldozers and heavy digging equipment moved in, with workmen coming and going. The bacterium responsible might seem strange and insignificant but everyone was eager to learn the mysteries of the organism. The most practical lesson to be learned was that the organism was a tough foe, determined to survive. Its special safeguard against extermination was its ability to produce spores with the ability to survive under the most unfavorable conditions. The anthrax spores could live for long periods in the residue from buffalo carcasses, on vegetation and in the soil — perhaps for 20 years in the soil. The men of the north had to accept that this enemy would be difficult to destroy or outlive. It would take energy and patience and imagination to defeat it.

While the buffalo might be the biggest sufferer, it was not alone in susceptibility to the disease. All herbivorous animals, domestic and wild, were susceptible, also the omnivorous ones like humans and pigs and some of the carnivores. A preventive vaccine was used with success and, of special interest, its history traced back to the laboratories of the famous Louis Pasteur, where the discovery of the vaccine was one of his first successes. Modern antibiotics were also found to have proven value in treating the disease in humans. But treatment of anthrax infected buffalo somewhere in and beyond the 45,000 square kilometre boundaries of Wood Buffalo National Park was difficult to comprehend.

The impression was widespread that this outbreak of 1962 was western Canada's first experience with anthrax in animals, but that was not so. There had been the outbreak in the sheep flocks of the big English company, the Canadian Agricultural, Coal and Colonization Co., with its ten big farm and ranch units of 10,000 acres, each situated along the main line of the CPR in Saskatchewan and Alberta. It was known more commonly as the "76", the cattle brand that came with the herd of 7,000 head bought for the ranching enterprise. The "little big man" behind the huge operation was the short but highly voluble Englishman, Sir John Lister Kaye, who spent lavishly to furnish buildings and breeding herds. He appeared to deal exclusively in round numbers: his ten land units along the railroad consisted of 10,000 acres each; to stock his ranches, he bought the 7,000-head herd from the Powder River Ranching Co. of Wyoming; next, he bought 500 work horses, most of them pure bred Clydesdale mares, for farm use. Finally, there was the big flock of sheep trailed in from the States of Oregon and Washington.

After travelling for months, eight or ten miles per day, the big flock arrived at Maple Creek in September, 1889, a total of either 10,000 or 20,000 head; both figures have been used and it would be folly to attempt to adjudicate the dispute at this time. All that will be said is that a surviving picture of the big flock penned at Maple Creek seems to sweep away all doubt about Sir John's flock being the biggest ever trailed into western Canada. But Sir John stepped aside in 1895 and wasn't present when anthrax hit the flocks six years later, very much the way the disease struck the Wood Buffalo Park herd in 1962, except that early observers believed they knew the sources of infection.

It had become common practice for the big sheep ranchers to hire itinerant shearing gangs to move in and remove the fleeces in the spring. Shearing at that time was performed by hand and it wasn't a job that inexperienced men wanted anything to do with. Sir John's old company with a new name, Canada Land and Ranch Co., contracted with a shearing gang from Australia. But members of the gang had been shearing in Australia, in a part known to have had anthrax. In coming to shear in Canada, they brought their greasy working clothes with them. Such garments looked like the ideal carriers of disease organisms. If an anthrax spore could live for 20 years in the soil, it should be able to live for 30 years in the accumulations of wool grease on the bib of a shearer's overalls, heavy with animal fat.[121]

There was no positive proof but soon after the shearing was completed and the shearing gang had moved on, many of the Canada Land and Ranch Co. sheep were sick and Dr. J.C. Hargrave, government veterinarian at Medicine Hat was consulted. He visited the flock and pronounced the disorder as anthrax, then ordered a quarantine on 17 townships of surrounding country.

A good summary of events appeared in the Northwest Farmer, herewith quoted: "The report comes from Swift Current that an epidemic of anthrax has broken out among the sheep of the district and several hundred have died. Dr. J.C. Hargrave was promptly on hand and identified the trouble and is now taking prompt measures to stamp out the plague. He has ordered a quarantine on 17 townships and it is proposed, once the trouble has been stamped out, to burn over the affected district so as to kill the germs of the disease that may be on the ground. It is estimated that over 600 head have succumbed to the disease. It was in the flock of the Canada Land and Ranch Co. at Crane Lake that the disease first broke out. This company has probably the largest sheep flock in the west and is doing all it can to stamp out the dreaded disease of both cattle and sheep."[122]

The principal methods employed consisted of quarantining, vaccinating and burying all dead sheep and the methods appeared to work. Before the end of the year, the area was declared free from anthrax and there were no further outbreaks.

It was a good and successful western effort but it had to be recognized that the problems in eradicating a virulent disease from completely domesticated sheep are but shadows of the difficulties arising where the subjects are undisciplined critters ranging over wild and mountainous wastes with three-quarters the size of Nova Scotia.

At the scene of trouble in 1962, workmen counted 23 dead buffalo on July 28. On August 14, the disease was confirmed as anthrax and after four more days that part of the north sprang to life with a tempo never seen before. A new crew began constructing a camp and headquarters beside the turbulent Slave River to receive men and equipment for a massive attack against the unseen enemy.

Sanitation and rules resembled those to be seen at a modern quarantine hospital and everyone was required to comply. Everything was predicated on the prevention of anthrax infection from contaminating clean areas. Workmen and all others coming and going, regardless of who they were or what their rank, were required to pass through the decontamination facility and have their working clothes sterilized by boiling. Whether they realized it or not, they were receiving an introductory course in bacteriology at no cost.

By the 20th of August, 40 men, five caterpillar tractors, two bombardier type vehicles, one muskeg tractor and one helicopter for use in locating dead buffalo bodies were ready for operations. Obviously, the locating, liming and burying would be a crucial part of the work.

By the 5th of September, 276 carcasses were treated and interred at a depth to discourage the most durable bacterium, and herders were engaged in keeping resident buffalo on the move outward and preventing new animals from entering. An added reason for preventing animals of all species from entering the area was the planned intention of running a fire over as much of the ground believed to be contaminated as possible, thereby destroying disease organisms on or near the surface. The extremely varied character of the ground cover — everything from muskeg vegetation to forests — made it impossible to obtain a uniform fire treatment but the burning was still considered a useful aid.

Further confusion arose after the Hook Lake trouble was confirmed as anthrax and the governments involved acted very properly to cancel public hunting in the general area. There had been public hunting in the Hook Lake region in two previous years and it was expected to be the same in 1962. What was especially annoying to the professional hunting guides and hunters was that the cancellation of hunting privileges came late, after many would be hunters, including some from the United States and Europe, made preparations for their safaris and hero returns with buffalo bull trophies.

Disease control never comes at bargain prices and the campaign of 1962 was not an exception. Nor should the estimated expenditure of $100,000 for the first three and one-half months of the war against anthrax at the remote point midway between Edmonton and the Arctic Circle be seen as excessive. One westerner said: "If we were sure the cures will work, they'd be worth five times that much." The thought that the infection could remain viable even longer than the men directing the control campaign were likely to live, was inescapable.

And among the risks was the awful possibility of the disease getting into the big northern herds and flocks of other species, especially the northern caribou that cover thousands of migratory miles annually and upon which uncounted Eskimos and other northern groups depend for food and survival. There are many wild agents like scavenger birds and predator wolves that could carry the anthrax infection. Indeed, when such birds and animals are feeding upon the dead meat from anthrax victims, it is difficult to see how they could escape being carriers and spreaders.

The progress report presented to the Council of the Northwest Territories soon after the anthrax outbreak was detected admitted the disease could be carried to the migrating caribou herds. "Presumably, wolves that feed on diseased carcasses could transport the infection into areas inhabited by caribou in most winters. Only time will tell how successful such measures may be," said the Parks Canada author of the 1962 report. "It is frightening to think what could happen if anthrax did get into the migrating caribou herds."[123] The relatively new anthrax danger increased the need for a predator control program as one means of reducing the spread of the disease.

Most Canadians will confess a passing interest in the two buffalo strains but will not become excited about the differences which may or may not justify a subspecies distinction. They will still approve of giving the two strains or families or subspecies some individuality by allocating the big Wood Buffalo National Park for the exclusive occupation of the Wood Buffalo strain which has a preference for the north but no wish to see the relatives every day. The same citizens will be moderately interested in the size and location of an expanded prairie range for the Plains Buffalo but most of all, they will have some strong and stubborn views about good health in the new herds. They will recall the government mistakes in former years and will demand tuberculosis-free and brucellosis-free herds — an entirely reasonable demand. And finally, the same observers probably know enough to be hopeful rather than demanding in their remarks about anthrax, that wicked enemy of both man and animals and about which there is not much that can be said with positive confidence.

Perhaps the herd of plains buffalo that reappeared after being lost for about 20 years in the Pink Mountain country of northeastern British Columbia has an important message for biologists and others. This herd, which escaped or became lost, totalled some 200 head at the time of its disappearance. Two decades later, and after feeding an ever present population of predators and probably some hunters, the herd — free from tuberculosis, brucellosis, anthrax, malnutrition or loneliness, reappeared with some 600 healthy and vigorous animals.

120   Soper, J. Dewey, The Mammals Of Alberta, p. 373, Published by the Dept. of Industry and Development, Government of Alberta, 1964.
121   MacEwan, Grant, Highlights of Sheep History In Western Canada, p. 51, Published by Alberta Sheep and Wool Commission, Alberta, 1991.
122   MacEwan, Grant, Highlights Of Sheep History In The Canadian west, Published by the Alberta Sheep and Wool Commission, 1991.
123   Parks Canada report on the anthrax outbreak in 1962, presented to the Council Of The northwest Territories and carried by the Lethbridge Herald, Jan. 26, 1963.

On a recent trip we took a supply of this famed food and one night decided that buffalo pemmican instead of bacon would be just right for supper. The driver, Joe, was asked to help himself.

"My gran'father made fifty trips to York Factory, an' all he lived on was pemmican," said Joe. 'He was a strong man, my gran'father, you bet, an' nearly eighty when he died. He allwus tol' me jam an' butter an' molasses was no good, an' you can't carry nuthin' on that stuff. I'm glad to get buffalo pemmican; I'll run all night now, an' all day tomorrow an' all the next night. My gran'father said you can't stop working when you eat buffalo pemmican! By Jove! I'm glad to taste that stuff."

Joe seized the axe and hewed off a chunk of pemmican commensurate with his voracious appetite. The piece he cut off fell to the brush by the camp fire; he picked it up and went at it. Pictures of his forefathers running across hot portages with 500 pounds, ceaselessly chasing after dogs and other Herculean feats of strength lit up his imagination. He had been eating and chattering for fully twenty minutes, the pemmican following the natural channels. Joe, always talkative, was gradually growing quiet, till at last dead silence reigned.

"Hello, Joe; what is the trouble?" was asked. "Don't you want any more pemmican?"

"No thank you," he replied. "I've had 'bout enough."

"Don't you like it?"

"'Well, no, not very much; I don't think them people at Wainwright made it right. My gran'father said there was lots of grease in it, an' Saskatoon berries but I finds this dry. I don't think I can run tonight."

"Let me have a look at it," said I. "Perhaps you have a bad piece."

Joe handed over the small portion left, and to my astonishment, I saw that it was not pemmican, but a piece of black poplar bark three quarters of an inch thick which in the uncertain light, Joe had picked up and eaten instead of the pemmican.[124]

H.M.S. Cotter

Chapter 21

Winnipeg Herds Had A Special Role

Winnipeg's pronounced sentiment for prairie buffalo came slowly and naturally, like French Canadian pea soup came to Quebec, like fiddlehead stew came to New Brunswick and the love for horse racing to Edmonton. For thousands of years the prairie buffalo were as "bread-and-butter" to the native people in that part and when the Selkirk settlers came to become the first real farmers, the thoughtful Earl of Selkirk, himself, was the first to conclude that the most practical way of meeting the settlement's needs for milk, butter, cheese, leather and farm power would be by domesticating buffalo.

Then came the years of heavy slaughter. Most people had no compunctions about overkilling. "How can you be overkilling when millions of buffalo remain?" was being asked. But suddenly, unbelievably and shockingly, the big herds vanished and the small herds were going the same way. Most people rationalized: "If the settlement can't live with the buffalo and the Indians can't live without them, let them go."

By the end of the '70s, only a remnant of the majestic herds remained and it would have been difficult to find even half a dozen humans with serious thoughts about rescuing the species from the thin edge of oblivion. Of the few who were known, one was the Montana Indian who had been hunting on the Canadian side of the boundary, presumed to be a safe distance from a hostile mother-in-law, Walking Coyote, described elsewhere on these pages, and two were conservation-minded citizens of Fort Garry, soon to become the city of Winnipeg. Scottish halfbreed, James McKay, and his Irish friend, Charles Alloway who became a private banker in Winnipeg, travelled west to the area of Battleford in 1873, expressly to capture some orphan buffalo calves whose mothers had been killed by hunters. To improve their chance of keeping the motherless calves alive, they took with them a domestic cow in milk. The two pioneer conservationists arrived back at Fort Garry with three calves and in the next year, they added two more and thereby laid the foundation for the first captive herd in Manitoba in that decade.

After Mr. McKay's death on December 2, 1879, the buffalo and other McKay livestock were sold by auction on January 20, 1880; thirteen head from the orphan calves were sold to Col. Samuel Bedson, warden of Stony Mountain Penitentiary, for a total of $1,000. To pay for his new herd, Bedson borrowed that amount from Donald Smith, later to be known as Lord Strathcona.

The little herd was taken to Mr. Bedson's farm at Stony Mountain where it grew rapidly, reaching a total of about 100 head in 1888 when Col. Bedson felt obliged to sell. Enough pure buffalo and hybrids were cut out and returned to Donald Smith to discharge the loan and the balance of the Bedson herd was sold to "Buffalo" Jones of Garden City, Kansas; the 83 head shipped to Kansas were sold at a price reported variously above $15,000.

More important to buffalo history than the sale price was the fact that the Bedson herd was becoming the best guarantee of the survival of two genetic links between the dwindling wild herd from which James McKay's orphan calves came and two rejuvenated herds with a good potential for useful influence in useful rebuilding programs.

One of those rejuvenated herds was to pass from the James McKay Estate to Col. Bedson, then to "Buffalo" Jones. From Jones, herd ownership would pass to Charles Allard and Michel Pablo of Montana. After Allard's death, a share of the buffalo was distributed according to the terms of his will but Pablo continued to graze his herd on the Flathead. There it grew to be the biggest herd of prairie buffalo on the continent until it was purchased by the Government of Canada in 1907, then delivered to Elk Island National Park, near Edmonton, and the National Buffalo Park at Wainwright. It will never be possible to determine the exact percentage of McKay and Bedson buffalo blood carried by the Pablo stock in 1907 when the biggest privately owned herd in the world began its return to the land where forebears grazed. It did, however, give practical assurance that some of the Pablo herd delivered at Elk Island Park and Wainwright traced directly to the orphans that reproduced for James McKay and Charles Alloway. It seemed to confirm the importance of the small Winnipeg herds of the '70s and '80s.

The other branch of the same strain of McKay and Alloway animals, turned back as payment of a loan debt to the distinguished Donald Smith became foundation stock for Winnipeg's Assiniboine Park and Banff National Park herds. It should be enough to show the important role of Winnipeg stock in the buffalo rehabilitation of a century age.

Donald Smith, by the strange circumstances of the loan made to Col. Bedson, became an active owner and breeder of buffalo. His adventure resembled somewhat that of the man who had never attempted to understand the terminology of the race track but made an unpremeditated bet in a claiming race and came away as a greatly surprised but enthusiastic owner of a thoroughbred.

In Donald Smith's case, the experience served to reveal what most people would not have suspected in him, a well-camouflaged but genuine fondness for the wild creatures. If friendly interest by a man of influence and means was what the ill-treated buffalo needed, Smith was their ray of hope. As his interest in park herds grew, so did his generosity in making gifts of breeding stock from his Silver Heights herd, thereby helping various community or park herds get started, notably in Winnipeg and Banff.

When a display of buffalo was wanted for a World's Fair, Donald Smith supplied it. And when in early 1898, the three buffalo at Banff National Park were looking lonely and lost amid the mountains and Winnipeg was having similar difficulties in obtaining a proper foundation for a park herd, Donald Smith donated most of his private herd at Silver Heights to the Dominion Government to be allocated where the animals could do the most good. Fifteen Silver Heights buffalo were shipped to Banff and four were placed with Winnipeg for its new River Park. That left Smith with only seven head.

For Winnipeg, the allotment of four buffalo for a new city herd was a triumph and wasn't won without a struggle. Winnipeggers heard the street rumour that the Donald Smith herd to which they chose to believe they held a moral claim, would be given to Banff. Anger mixed with fear and a petition to the Dominion Government was started, praying that the Silver Heights herd or a portion of it be left permanently at Winnipeg. In a few days, the petition had over 600 signatures.

At the same time, Winnipeg's Mayor Andrews wired The Hon. Clifford Sifton, Winnipeg's Member of Parliament and Minister of the Interior in the Laurier government, making the same request for buffalo. The "game of politics" was being played with familiar skill and four or five days later, June 4, 1898, the Minister replied, advising that Winnipeg could keep four of the Donald Smith animals on permanent loan. The number may have seemed disappointingly small but it should have appeared as quite enough for a community that did not have accommodation for any buffalo. Moreover, the Ottawa ruling was that representatives of the city would be permitted to choose the animals to be retained. H.A. Chadwick — who was the lessee of Deer Lodge at the time and had considerable experience with buffalo — was asked to make the official choices and was willing to do it but the Mayor and certain of the aldermen wanted the job or the prestige that would accompany. In the end, the Mayor, Commissioner McCreary and two or three aldermen constituted the selection committee, with H.A. Chadwick acting in an advisory capacity.[125]

The group of four to qualify for permanent Winnipeg residence consisted of three young cows and a three-year-old bull that became known as Shaggy or Old

Shag. He proved to be an excellent choice, a popular Winnipeg favourite and the one that headed the River Park herd for the next 16 years, although sometimes "in absentia." He was big and powerful and had no difficulty in demolishing corrals and walking through wire fences and like, just to wander.

Early in Shaggy's career, while still living at Silver Heights, he established his claim to the role of leader of the herd and, one way or another, turned back all threats to his supremacy — at least until a younger bull "called his bluff" and settled the long-standing arguments as to who was the better bull. The confrontation came in November, 1902 and was expected to be a bloody battle to the death. Shaggy, at the time, was being confined to a log corral at Silver Heights.

Shaggy and the younger bull, it was said, had been bellowing angry boasts and insults at each other for months and observers believed the feud would never be settled except in a battle, bison style. For human spectators, there would be nothing very ennobling about such a battle but it had its entertainment-seeking promoters. The gates were thrown open and the two bulls dashed at each other but to the disappointment of the spectators, the older bull paused as if to consider his age and then with a few snorts of disdain, he "coolly turned his back on his erstwhile tormentor, slowly moving off in unconcerned dignity, indifferent to the possibilities and showing his preference for the green grass growing all around. He then and there abdicated the monarchy which he had held undisputed for years."[126]

Author Tyrrell noted that "Old Shaggy was said to have been the largest and finest buffalo ever bred in captivity." The aging bull died in October, 1914, and the *Manitoba Free Press* paid him a deserving tribute: "After sixteen years of captivity within the city limits of Winnipeg a monarch has died. There was little or no notice taken of his demise. And yet he was a friend of many. For years he has been a source of interest and education to young and old alike. Many men now prominent in Winnipeg knew and loved the old fellow when they were boys in short breeches. He is the shaggy-maned old bison who has headed the herd at Assiniboine Park for the past sixteen years. . . Shag, however, will not be forgotten. The remains of the old-timer will be turned over to a taxidermist and after he has been stuffed and mounted he will be placed in some public building."[127]

Members of the Winnipeg Parks Board discovered the obvious, that they had much to learn about the mysteries of the buffalo race. If the wild creatures had their own rules of conduct, they were loath to disclose them and their first years at Winnipeg's River Park were marked by problems and reverses that might have been avoided. Old bulls suffering from boredom wrecked fences and corrals and then went astray, sometimes taking the whole herd with them. Deaths from no very obvious reasons were occurring and the Winnipeg herd was in a period of declining numbers. According to a press reporter writing in 1909, the city herd had been reduced to two lonely individuals and was likely to be "extinct in a year."[128]

The Parks Board, about this time, decided to establish a modern zoo at the new park, of which the buffalo herd would be a part, and appointed J.P. Turner to the position of superintendent. He may have noticed it at once that the bison were showing signs of nutritional deficiency, probably due to being corral-fed for much of the year and not getting enough good grazing when green grass was at its best. When brought to the attention of city officials, feeding changes were made and buffalo vigour returned. The reverses of that year left some important messages for buffalo park managers everywhere and park populations began to rise again, especially at Assiniboine Park.

One week after the public was informed about Donald Smith's gift to the city of Winnipeg, it was announced that the new "livestock" would be on public display at the Winnipeg Industrial Exhibition. Critics thought the decision was risky: "these wild animals in totally strange surroundings could wreck the fair and inflict loss of life. And how would they be transferred to and from the Exhibition?"

They were reasonable questions but those who knew T.A. Preston, the man who had been Donald Smith's buffalo herdsman, had complete confidence about his skill and he said he would make the deliveries. He understood the buffalo and they appeared to understand him. Perhaps he did not disclose everything he knew about handling the fearsome critters but he was particular about starting them in the exact direction of the Exhibition and then keeping at a steady gallop until inside the grounds. In any case, he delivered the little herd at the special log corral constructed for it without mishap.

At the show, the four city buffalo were judged to rate with the foremost attractions. Most viewers were seeing the species at close range for the first time and instinctively paused to study the strange shape and proportion. Adult visitors pulled green grass and threw it over the corral fence and children offered peanuts and candies at arm's length between the corral logs and were disappointed when their offerings were not appreciated.

The four buffalo were believed to be the first of their species to be presented at a Canadian exhibition and probably found no pleasure in the crowds who came to gawk and make meaningless remarks. The best part of the fair for the big brutes was when Preston opened the gate and cleared the way for the mad rush. Trying to guide the herd from Silver Heights to the exhibition grounds was not without risk but Preston's experience told him that the return to home pastures would require no special effort on his part. The instant the heavy gate was opened, the four animals set out in the precise direction of Silver Heights, the first and only home they knew. They were glad to be home and able to chew their cud in peace on their own bedground.

Two facts appeared to have been confirmed: one was Winnipeg's instant pride in its buffalo and the second was the buffalo's pronounced homing instinct which most people didn't realize existed. On two occasions in the next few years, the same small herd demonstrated its bird-like sense of direction, leaving behind the stories to which Mr. Preston could attest.

It was on a pleasant summer evening, July 17, 1907, that the Assiniboine Park herd, by this time numbering 10 head, broke from its fenced paddock, swam across the river as if the leaders knew where they were going, then promptly disappeared. It wasn't uncommon for aging bulls to break out and wander away on a private tour of exploration, from which some returned and some never did. But it wasn't common for entire herds to go "absent without leave."

Somebody recalled the buffalo bull, Horace Wilson, that walked through a heavy River Park fence and was absent for some days before he was seen at Carman, Manitoba, 50 miles from Winnipeg. While preparations were being made to send a crew of park employees to recover Horace Wilson, the old bull grew tired of waiting to be "recovered" and about the time the workmen arrived at Carman, he was back at the Park, presumably looking for the hole in the fence through which he escaped and now needed in order to rejoin his stay-at-home friends.

But in the more recent buffalo escape from River Park, the park authorities proceeded at once to search for the "10 lost buffalo." It was the human's privilege to call them "lost buffalo" if he chose but the fact was, the buffalo were not lost. They were found grazing on Silver Heights grass — merely a long and hard gallop and a test of stamina in swimming the Assiniboine.

Sooner or later, the run-away bison would have to be brought back to the park, even though it necessitated forcing them into the water to recross the river against their stubborn wills. However, nobody wanted to provoke them needlessly so it was decided to leave them at Silver Heights until the winter season when they could be driven back to the park on six or seven inches of ice, thereby escaping the necessity of a plunge. That seemed sensible enough to people in the park office but the buffalo had other ideas.

The whole story was told in two short items of news appearing in the *Manitoba Free Press* of the time. The first item reported on the escape, in two short sentences: "The buffalo escaped from the city park Tuesday, swam the Assiniboine River and made for their old quarters near Silver Heights, where they are now enjoying life. There are 10 in number and all in good condition."[129]

The next report explained the return — but not the way the members of the park staff planned it or expected it: "BUFFALO BACK IN PARK. Two of the buffalo which escaped from the city park some time ago and made their way to Silver Heights, their old pasture ground, have returned to the park after swimming the river again. They were being left at Silver Heights to be brought across the river on the ice next winter but broke out Friday and saved the city the trouble of taking them back to the park."[130] Winnipeg citizens were being well entertained and some were saying, as they chuckled, that their buffalo must really have a pretty good sense of humour.

It is good that most stories — including those about buffalo — have cheerful conclusions. But reality demands that while one member of a race or herd is praised for an apparent superiority in ideals and memory, there is generally another like the buffalo given country-wide publicity in February, 1958, that had to be shot to restrain him. He too was a Winnipeg resident when he was making fame for himself but his stay was short. He was the one-ton bull brought from Elk Island Park after being selected especially to restore vigour to the Winnipeg herd where the breeding problems were believed to be due in some measure to inbreeding.

The robust fellow arrived at his future home in a well-spiked hardwood crate and was not in a friendly mood. He didn't like humans at the best of times, it seemed, blamed them for every wrong and his grudge was growing. His remedy for all buffalo ailments, it appeared, demanded destruction of the entire Family of Man and in his first hours of freedom in Manitoba, he did his best to do something about it. He allowed the zoo keepers to draw the first spikes in his crate and then completed the demolition in his own way. He then wrecked two fences, plunged across the Assiniboine River and continued to drive frightened residents to cover until he was dropped by gunfire from a Mounted Police weapon.

Banff National Park which at one time had over a hundred head of the diminishing plains buffalo strain or subspecies, brought strength to the efforts of the pioneer Winnipeg trio, James McKay, Samuel Bedson and Donald Smith, who had attempted, with some success, to forge "a chain of genetic links," that would help to ensure the survival of the bedeviled race. It was meaningful, therefore, that most members of the founding herd at Banff came from the same stock that gave rise to the Winnipeg Park herd. It was another case of the Donald Smith buffalo that came from Bedson and before that from James McKay who with Charles Alloway captured a few orphan calves at the rear of a Métis buffalo hunt near Battleford in 1873 and with them started a new line of captive breeding stock.

There were other similarities between the Winnipeg and Banff herds. Both started in small ways and with gift animals from Donald Smith. In the case of Banff, there were actually two donors who made their contributions about the same time, one of them being Toronto lawyer, T.C. Blackstock, by whose generosity two buffalo females and a bull were shipped from Texas. But regardless of which gift was made first, the bigger and more influential one was the herd of 13 head from Donald Smith who was about to become Lord Strathcona. With the two gifts — Banff in 1898 had a total of 16 head — all thriving and proving instant successes as tourist attractions.

About this time, both Banff and the state of the buffalo benefited by the coming of two citizens with generous interests and loyalties, Norman Luxton and Howard Douglas. The former was born at Fort Garry where his father was one of the founders and editors of the *Manitoba Free Press*. Norman, became one of the leading instigators of the plan that saw the big Pablo buffalo herd in Montana being purchased by the Government of the Dominion of Canada and moved to reservations in the Canadian midwest.

Howard Douglas was appointed superintendent of the Banff National Park in 1896 and during the period of negotiations for the purchase of the Pablo herd, he watched and directed very much like "a general manager." In 1910, when the biggest buffalo transfer in world history was completed and nearly all the Pablo buffalo were settled in the new National Buffalo Park at Wainwright, Douglas was appointed to the position of Commissioner of National Parks for Canada and moved to Edmonton.

The "Paddock" as the Banff buffalo range became known, was enclosed on three sides with a high wire fence and the sheer rock walls of Cascade Mountain on the fourth side. It was constructed and named in time to receive and accommodate the gift herd from Lord Strathcona in '98. And to keep company with the Banff buffalo was a small population of moose, elk, deer and mountain sheep, all under the supervision of Edward Ellis.[131]

The buffalo were, indeed, the main attraction said Norman Luxton. He rejoiced when the park herd increased and sorrowed when it dropped. The herd that numbered less than 20 in 1898, rose to 40 in 1903 and one writer mentioned 107 in 1909. But there came problems, mainly in finding sufficient grazing space. The general rigidity of the Banff terrain made an expansion of pasture almost impossible and then the construction of the Trans Canada Highway in the '50s and '60s substantially reduced the existing grazing area and herd reduction became necessary.

Norman Luxton mourned. In a letter to an acquaintance whom he addressed simply as "Mr. McCoy," in 1961 when the herd was at an extremely low point in numbers, he said: "The buffalo story at Banff is a sad one. We can boast of three cows and a bull in the herd at present. I remember when there were almost a hundred. These four are difficult to see, though they are the greatest attractions for the tourists. . ."[132]

When Mr. Luxton made the remark that "the buffalo story at Banff is a sad one," he was thinking only of herd numbers. He would have been the first to agree that one of the best park herd stories of them all was the lifetime account, as far as it was known, of the "Patriarch of his race," the bull, Sir Donald. His death in the Banff Paddock on April 6, 1909, left historians believing that at 36 years of age, he was the oldest on record and, almost certainly, the only one in his age category that was born in the wild herd and still living in the early part of 1909.

He looked and acted like the Monarch, and for 30 years he never failed to respond to a challenge from a rival bull and never experienced a defeat from a challenging male. After being captured as a motherless calf, he spent his first seven years at James McKay's Deer Lodge farm, six or seven miles west of Winnipeg and there came to fighting maturity. After McKay's death in December, 1879, the herd was bought by Samuel Bedson and the bull in question lived at Stony Mountain for eight years and then back to the district west of Winnipeg where he remained as a member of Donald Smith's Silver Heights herd for 10 years or so until being shipped to Banff.

Over those years there were probably scores of herd leadership arguments that had to be settled by the time-honoured duels. In going to Banff, Sir Donald's first battle for leadership was no doubt with the prairie buffalo bull imported from Texas — the other gift bull in the Banff herd at that time. Nobody knows how many times the native Manitoban and native Texan fought for the herd leadership but Sir Donald was the perennial victor for the first five or six years when, with Sir Donald showing his advanced age and the Texas bull displaying more of the stamina of youth — there came the day when the younger bull triumphed and made his victory convincing.

It had to happen and the old fellow deserved a medal for having subdued "junior" for so long. Now the oldster was not only beaten but badly damaged. Early in the battle, he lost one horn which left him bleeding profusely and then he received the jab of a horn in an eye. Sir Donald was beaten and knew he was beaten. He still looked like a monarch, a one-horned and half blind monarch, but the old spirit was wounded and he chose to wander and graze alone. The other members of the herd ignored him as if he wasn't present and he accepted the indignity that wasn't restricted to the bison race.

Howard Douglas, speaking at Montreal on February 18, 1909, announced that the bull that had become for tourists and others the hero of his race was failing and park authorities had decided that the time had come for Sir Donald to be dispatched and allowed to join his forefathers in the mythical "sand hills." In a few weeks, Douglas explained, he will be put to death and his body stuffed and mounted for museum display.[133]

Park rangers were not looking forward to putting their old friend to death and as it happened, they didn't have to do it. Sir Donald "beat the park officials to it" and the attendant coming on duty on the morning of April 6, 1909, found the old monarch dead in the paddock. It appeared that his partial blindness caused him to fall over a log, leaving him unable to get up. Then, as the buffalo specialists explained it, the other members of the herd, for reasons of vengeance or to put an old friend out of his misery, undertook to mutilate the dying bull. Young bulls gored his prostate body and buffalo of all ages used their feet to trample, bruise and crush the helpless body.

The only part of the carcass that seemed to offer anything for the taxidermist was the big handsome head lacking a horn. The hide was punctured and made useless but the head was recovered and mounted for hanging in some public building.

The concluding scene at the paddock, left the park employees puzzled. They had tried to drive the herd away from the dead body but found the buffalo objecting to their presence and threatening to charge the visitors and pin them against the fence. The point of it all was strange but it did appear that the members of the herd that had trampled their old leader to death when he was dying, were now determined that no others would be allowed to take their dead leader away from them.[134] Why shouldn't the buffalo that lived close to Nature on North American soil for about as long as humans not have some mystical ideas and ideals too?

"Sir Donald" at Banff National Park *(Canadian Parks Service)*

124 Cotter, H.M.S., Buffalo Pemmican a la Mode, The Beaver, May, 1924, The Hudson's Bay Company, Winnipeg, Man.
125 *Manitoba Free Press*, June 10, 1898.
126 Tyrrell, C.S., The Strathcona Herd, The Beaver, March, 1933, The Hudson's Bay Company.
127 *Manitoba Free Press*, Oct. 14, 1914.
128 *Manitoba Free Press*, City's Buffalo Almost Extinct, Feb. 22, 1909.
129 *Manitoba Free Press*, July 18, 1907.
130 *Manitoba Free Press*, Sept. 9, 1907.
131 Crag and Canyon, Banff, June 13, 1903.
132 Luxton, Norman, Letter to "Mr. McCoy," Oct. 2, 1961, Original in Glenbow Archives, Calgary.
133 *Manitoba Free Press*, Feb. 18, 1909.
134 *Manitoba Free Press*, April 21, 1909.

"Because the trade in bison remains was a rather ephemeral practice and its participants for the most part nameless people, the demise of the industry went largely unnoticed. This is unfortunate since the commerce provided a rather substantial income for many penniless settlers and Métis. ..... Many a homesteader bought his first seed, supplies and equipment with money he earned by hauling bones to town. An even large number of Indians and Métis survived by chasing over the plains in search of remains from the creatures they previously hunted in the flesh. Thus, with classic irony, the once great Canadian herds became, in death, the salvation of some of their own executioners. This contribution of the bison to the prairie provinces has generally been overlooked, so it is fitting that now, nearly one century later, the last chapter in the buffalo story be written."[135]

Leroy Barnett

Chapter 22

No Peace For The Buffalo — Not Even For Their Bones

An aging Cree, the wise man of his tribe and acknowledged seer, warned his people of the greedy and grasping ways of the members of the paleface race. "They took our land," he said, with anger in his voice." They plundered our soil; they would have killed the last beaver if they could have found it; they destroyed the buffalo that was our food and took everything they could sell. They left only the bones but, wait and see what comes next; as soon as they find out how to sell them, they'll be back to get the bones too."[136]

Sure enough, they found a market for the bones — in the manufacturing of phosphate fertilizers and in making charcoal filters needed in refining sugar. As an item of industry, the buffalo bones did not survive for long but while the supply lasted, they were important.

Wild furs were the first of the "easy money" resource in the west and the traders flourished until beavers and other popular fur-bearers became scarce. The collection and sale of the buffalo bones — aftermath of the most savage mass killing in North American history — was next to appear. Its life was short for the very simple reason that there were no buffalo to replenish the raw materials. Its survival was for a decade or a little more, beginning in 1883 when the CPR was able to offer freight service from numerous collection points. Dealers and brokers who acted as middlemen consigned the bones in carloads to their favoured factories or firms in the United States.

Gathering bones in ox-drawn Red River carts or horse-drawn farm wagons became the prevailing livelihood with the Métis and homesteaders who, it seemed, were perpetually short of cash. They needed the returns from the sale of bones to pay for their groceries, tobacco, Epsom salts, overalls and Dr. Bell's Medical Wonder.

Picking and shipping of buffalo bones began in Kansas where the opportunity to ship by rail was earlier than on the Canadian side. Moreover, Kansas was the scene of some of the most intense hide-hunting. The first carloads of bones to be sent to the American markets from Canadian points were shipped from

Buffalo bones, Saskatoon, 1893 *(MacEwan Collection)*

Regina and Moose Jaw respectively in 1883 and were followed soon thereafter by rail shipments from Swift Current, Medicine Hat and Calgary, all main line points and, hence, among the first to have shipping opportunity.

It may seem appropriate that Regina, with Pile Of Bones as its original name, should have been a leader in the bone trade. But the Pile Of Bones from which the name came, had no connection with the bone trade. Presumably, the landmark pile was made by the Indians, the purpose of which remains in doubt. In any case, it's a good name, distinctive and easy to remember and understand, and there will be some observers who will wonder why it was ever changed.

Hon. James R. Wilson, the son of a homestead farm at Hanley, Saskatchewan, went looking for a job with wages in 1885 and took work with Baker and Lee, the leading dealers in bones at Moose Jaw. In that summer season of '85 his principal duty consisted of weighing buffalo bones. Most shipments outward were being sent to fertilizer and sugar companies at Minneapolis, St. Paul, Chicago and Detroit. The Moose Jaw price for the bones received was $7 per ton and the sellers were pleased.

Most parties delivering bones in that spring were homesteaders rather than Métis; it was the year of the North West Rebellion and most of the latter people were with Louis Riel at Fish Creek and Batoche. The struggle ended, however, and late in the summer Riel's friends began returning with their carts and oxen and about one thousand pounds of bones, the customary cart load. Almost as cheerful as ever, the men from the northern districts were glad to be back at their "profession," back to the bones that allowed an all summer occupation and all-winter holiday.[137]

Regina and Moose Jaw were enjoying their mainline railway locations slightly earlier than Swift Current, Medicine Hat and Calgary and were thus one season ahead of their westerly neighbours in being ready to ship bones. But there was no monopoly in the trade. Once the railway was in operation — every district with extensive resources of buffalo bones on top of the ground, good camping facilities with lots of water and grazing for the oxen and horses hauling the carts or wagons and somebody to fill the role of dealer to keep the accumulated bones moving to market — had an equal chance of being a leader in the bone business. Little known places like Pense, Maple Creek and Belle Plaine had the necessary resources and matched the bigger places in performance.

At distant Battleford, the pioneer editor, Patrick Gammie Laurie, saluted Pense and "the Creek," two of the smallest points on the western map and suddenly, two of the biggest in output. "There is a great rustling among the dry buffalo bones. Mr. A. Blair handled over a hundred tons at Pense this season already, besides large quantities at Belle Plaine and other points west. Six dollars a ton is being paid... It may be of interest to the public to know that one hundred carloads of bones were shipped over the CPR to various points last year and this year the amount will be more than doubled. This fact conveys some idea of the enormous herds of bison that roamed this vast breadth of rolling prairie."[138]

As new railroads were built, new supplies of bones became available for industrial-use. The grade for the Long Lake Railway which was to run north via Lumsden and Saskatoon to Prince Albert, was built in 1889-90. Saskatoon, at once, became the centre of a fruitful area for bone gatherers and witnessed the departure of many trainloads of the "crop" from the first harvests. The "Bone Trail" that entered the city from the southwest became and was for many years an important channel of transportation. The bone shipments from Saskatoon began in 1890 and because nearby districts were the first to be picked, 1891 and '92 were peak years.

Owing to railway expansion at that time, there was an almost constant shortage of freight cars and the bones were being delivered at loading points faster than they could be shipped out. Consequently, bones awaiting freight cars were being placed in piles beside the rail track. Some of the piles grew big and disorderly; just as many, however, were symmetrical and tidy with each pile conforming to the exact size and shape of a box car. The orderly arrangement removed much of the guess-work about quantities when negotiating sales and ordering cars. The big bony heads that easily resisted fracture were set in place

Buffalo bones stacked for loading at rail siding, Saskatoon, 1891 *(Canadian Pacific Railway/J.R. Metcalf)*

carefully to form the outside wall or framework of the car-shaped pile and the smaller bones were then thrown into the central space.

A Saskatoon settler of '85 recalled that the piles of bones awaiting the availability of box cars often extended from 23rd Street to a point on the river close to where the railroad bridge of later years was built. A newspaper item of 1891 reported another Saskatoon pile of bones waiting for freight cars as containing the bones of an estimated 168,000 buffalo.[139]

Mrs. Grace Fletcher, James Leslie and R.W. Dulmage, all of whom operated stores in the pioneer town, handled most of the bones shipped from there. But even some late comers were kept busy. W.H. Duncan opened a store late in 1890 and, like the others, accepted bones in lieu of cash. Reporting from his trade records, he told of billing out four carloads of bones on September 6, 1890, seven carloads on the 9th, four on the 10th and six on the 17th of the same month, making a total of 21 carloads in 11 days which seems most significant for a newcomer in the business.

Mrs. Fletcher who came to Saskatoon in 1885 and opened the first general store on her side of the river, had a large share of the bone trade. James Leslie, prominent throughout the formative years of the town, gave up teaching school to open a store in 1890. In the same year, Andrew Blair of Regina who had been dealing extensively in bones along the main line of the CPR, agreed to buy all the bones Mr. Leslie could collect. Then, in 1892, Leslie sold his store and went ranching at Brighwater Marsh near Dundurn but continued to act as a broker in the bone business. He had an arrangement with the Northwestern Fertilizer Company of Chicago to take all his deliveries at slightly higher than the prevailing prices. In consequences, Leslie in the early part of 1893 was handling all the bones being delivered at Saskatoon, including the stocks accumulated by Mrs. Fletcher and Mr. Dulmage.

But the bone business was on the verge of trouble. Chicago was in the grip of financial panic and because there was no telegraph operator at Dundurn, telegrams being sent to Leslie to halt all bone deliveries were not reaching him. What he did not know was that the consignees were refusing to accept delivery and with 35 carloads of bones being held in Chicago by the transportation company, Leslie was facing bankruptcy. Fortunately, the financial situation eased and the Chicago company was able to settle for the freight and bones but was obliged to tell Leslie to ship no more bones that season. Leslie escaped bankruptcy but his losses were heavy.[140]

The bone trade was never the same again. The fact was that after 10 boom years, bone resources were largely depleted and manufacturing techniques in sugar and fertilizers were changing. Andrew Blair who had been a leader in the western trade gave the hint and the Calgary Herald reported it. "Mr. A. Blair of Regina who has bought bleached buffalo bones for the American Sugar refineries for some years past, is in the city. Depression of trade and new methods of refining have reduced the demand for charcoal made from buffalo bones and price consequently rules lower than usual."[141]

The homesteaders who needed the few extra dollars from the sale of bones and the Métis who not only needed the money but loved the job missed the pursuit. Most of the bones from the Saskatoon area were gathered by the latter who lived at Fish Creek and Batoche. It suited most of them to trade their bones for groceries and tobacco and very little cash changed hands. Nevertheless, these men from the north generally ended the bone season with a debt to the trading merchant.

One of the "Captains of Industry" among the Batoche people was Edouard Dumont, a burly brother of the celebrated Gabriel Dumont. W.K. Fletcher who could speak from memory about the bone trade, recalled Edouard coming to his mother's store in Saskatoon at the end of the hauling season and addressing her in a dignified way, saying: "Madam, I owe you $45. I don't have any money but I will send you a cow and a calf." Mrs. Fletcher replied: "That's fine Edouard; send them in the spring." And in the spring, several cows and calves would arrive to balance the accounts of Edouard and certain of his friends.[142]

It was the custom of the bone gatherers to set fire to the prairie grass in early spring or late summer, leaving the white bones clearly visible on the blackened prairie and making discovery a simple matter. "In the spring of 1888," James Leslie wrote, "I went by trail (from Saskatoon) to Moose Jaw. The country south of Beaver Creek had been burned and the buffalo bones showed white, making the whole country look like a very stony Ontario summerfallow."[143]

To indicate further something of the abundance of the bones, Mrs. W.P. Bate wrote to tell of a homesteader of her acquaintance, working alone with a team and wagon, gathering three carloads of bones in three weeks. It was his "first harvest" and, indeed, a very good one.[144]

The first bone picking in a new area was generally confined to districts close to the railroad but as the nearby parts became depleted, the gangs went farther afield until, ultimately, the carts and wagons were going from 50 to 100 miles for their loads and Saskatoon was the shipping point for a district extending from Young on the east to Rosetown on the west, and from Osler on the north to Bladworth on the south. The Goose Lake district that included Zealandia and Rosetown were especially rich, as were the Blackstrap coulee running east and west at Dundurn and the Hanley district that was already popular with homesteaders.

James Leslie, by his own figures, shipped 750 carloads of the buffalo bones out of Saskatoon and estimated that the total shipments from that point between 3,000 and 3,500 carloads. Loaded cars carried about 20 tons on the average and contained about 250 heads, implying that the massive skull bones and all other bones from 250 skeletons were thrown together in each car. Thus, it becomes easy to speculate that the bones from more than 750,000 buffalo were loaded for export from Saskatoon alone and the revenue returned ultimately to pay for or helped to pay for oxen and horses, harnesses, wagons, buggie axels, manure forks, plows, seed drills, wood-working tools, the first lumber for buildings, barbed wire and staples for fencing, outfits of winter clothing for all members of the family and dozens of other gadgets previously overlooked. Almost everybody had a good word for the buffalo bone trade and the revenue it generated but at least one editor recognized its shortcoming and should be commended for his imagination.

He was the editor of the Nor'-West Farmer and wrote in 1884: "We notice that an enterprising merchant in Regina is collecting and shipping bones by the carload to Minneapolis. If Regina boasts of a live Agricultural Society, they will do well to step in and stop this export. The bones will ere long be required at home. Even the reputed fertility of the western prairie cannot afford to let the best of all fertilizers be shipped to other fields. Keep the bones and use them."[145]

135 Barnett, LeRoy, Buffalo Bone Industry in Canada, Part II Alberta History, Historical Society of Alberta, Spring, 1979.
136 Attributed to an elderly Indian on the Fort LaCorne Reserve in Saskatchewan, approximately 1944.
137 Wilson, James R. was well known to the author where, in the city of Saskatoon, they shared the troubles of the drought-stricken '30s and attended the same church.
138 Saskatchewan Herald, Battleford, July 26, 1866.
139 Saskatchewan Herald, Battleford, August,1891.
140 From information in correspondence with James Leslie in his late years and from conversations with his son, Dr. Russell Leslie, Superintendent of the Experimental Farm at Morden, Man.
141 Calgary Herald, March 15, 1894.
142 Fletcher, W.K., Letter from Melfort to author, Nov. 25, 1936.
143 Leslie, James, Personal letter to author, Nov. 1936.
144 Bate, Mrs. W.P., Saskatoon, Letter to author, Nov. 20, 1936.
145 Nor'-West Farmer, Winnipeg, October, 1884.

"Bison are vastly superior to cows in making humans feel guilty. The human race looks back at the wanton slaughter of millions of buffalo in the last century and shudders. It feels pangs of remorse about how 'sportsmen' shot bison from the train windows just to see them fall, and how hunters were encouraged to wipe out vast herds of bison as one means of bringing plains Indians under control. The feeling of guilt prompted the Canadian government at the turn of the century to purchase three small herds of bison, one from near Prince Albert and two from the United States, and place them in a park near Wainwright, Alberta."[146]

Keith Dryden

Chapter 23

A Beautiful Buffalo! Where's My Gun?

A Saskatoon acquaintance, who was correctly described as a rail train "buff," admitted that every time he saw a train on rails, he felt an urge to climb aboard. So it was with many hunters. Long after the almost complete extermination of the prairie buffalo, even the view of a museum specimen was enough to arouse the urge to reach for a gun. Buffalo were for killing and the long "dry spell" between the last of the wild herds and the introduction of limited hunting in the Northwest Territories, didn't end the interest and desire.

Most people believed they would never again see real buffalo hunting but 1910 brought the first of several surprises. The able and reliable Michel Pablo of Western Montana, from whom the Canadian Government bought more than 400 head of buffalo, the biggest herd in the world at the time, devoted almost three years to delivering the animals to Elk Island National Park and the Buffalo Park at Wainwright.

By the summer of 1910, not more than 55 head of tough, old, outlaw bulls remained on the big Pablo range. These rebels had eluded capture and it seemed a waste of effort to spend more time in their pursuit. As a gesture of good will and gratitude to the Canadians involved in the sale and transfer, Pablo proposed to stage the world's last wild buffalo hunt. The 25 or more invitations were sent out via Howard Douglas, Dominion Commissioner of Parks. The proposal was that Pablo would collect a fee for living accommodation but the hunters would become the owners of hides, trophy heads and meat if the latter was wanted. Pablo would furnish everything needed for the hunt, experienced hunting horses with saddles, guns and ammunition. It was presumed that every hunter would be successful in taking at least one bull with a good trophy head worth at least $500 and a hide worth $100.

The guest list included: Commissioner Howard Douglas, Norman Luxton of Banff, Sheriff W.S. Robertson and James Ross of Edmonton, and Col. James Walker and S.A. Ramsey of Calgary.[147] Nobody was gored and if anybody fell off his horse, it wasn't recorded. Hunters shot at least one old bull and returned home with a trophy head, proof that "Grandfather really did participate in the world's last wild buffalo hunt."

But it wasn't the last buffalo hunt at all. There were still some wild buffalo of the wood buffalo strain in the Canadian north and it was legal for the native people to hunt them for meat, as long as they did not hunt within the park. With the rehabilitation of the northern herds of wood buffalo and the transfer of more than 6,000 prairie buffalo from the National Park at Wainwright, there were more and more members of both strains living outside the boundaries of the northern park. The Northwest Territories Council met in Ottawa in January, 1959, and gave approval to a limited hunting season between September 15 and November 30 of that year. The Council had taken stock of a big increase in buffalo numbers since hunting had been banned in 1893. At that early date, it was believed the total buffalo population was under 3,000 and falling. Sixty-six years later, the population had risen to 17,000, with about 3,000 animals roaming outside the park, mainly on both sides of the Slave River, north and east of the National Park.

Thirty licenses were issued, each conveying the right to kill one buffalo. The animals available were predominantly wood buffalo and crossbreeds from the plains buffalo interbreeding with the wood strain. And as pointed out by Dr. Nick Novakowski of the Canadian Wildlife Service, most hunters would be looking for the somewhat bigger, darker and shaggier ones with the better claims to the north. The adventure did not come at bargain prices. The license was $25 for residents of the Northwest Territories and $200 for non-residents. It was expected that the hunt would be particularly popular with sportsmen from the United States and the cash outlay wasn't likely to be much of an obstacle. Outfitters provided horses and saddles, guns, food supplies and native guides but not at a figure under $500. There was also the airfare from Edmonton to Smith that was inescapable and outward shipping charges on heads, hides and meat.

But cost didn't seem to deter the visitors who were mainly from the United States. By the middle of July, 40 applications were received. It was feared that the 700 treaty Indians and Métis living in the area might be disgruntled by the prospect of foreign hunters taking the big game and trophies to which they had first claim but the cash returns derived from guiding services put an end to any resentment felt. By the end of the first official year of hunting, 29 licenses were issued, each one conveying the right of ownership to one buffalo carcass shot beyond the limits of the Wood Buffalo National Park.

Views about the ethics of the hunt and the rightness of the thrills hunters were getting from their kills varied. A journalist who interviewed the first hunters to return to Fort Smith after shooting the legal limit of one buffalo each, reported that the reactions measured in thrills or "kicks" were extremely diverse. If it took a vicious charge by an old bull to produce the maximum thrill. Two hunters working together told about it in almost gleeful terms. The bull was believed to weigh 2500 pounds and was tough and mean and fast. Although the first bullet stopped him, it took 14 more to effect a kill. It was in subduing this old fighter that the two hunters from Burns Lake, British Columbia, found what they described as the greatest hunting thrill of their lives.[148]

The next two to be interviewed, both Edmonton businessmen, were less ecstatic about the adventure but praised the buffalo as "the greatest of game animals." The men, both of whom had hunted big game animals of other kinds in Saskatchewan and Alberta in earlier years, were satisfied with their first northern adventure but insisted that the big animals made easy targets, too easy for sporting purposes. One of the men was quoted as saying that shooting their two bulls was not a severe test but added: "They are easy to shoot but hard to kill."[149]

Another hunter said that shooting his buffalo was like "shooting cows in a farm pasture. They couldn't see too well and their hearing was worse. The only thrilling part was in killing them. They're tougher than boiled shoe leather; I'll give 'em credit for that."[150] Banff's well-known Claude Brewster reported: "Hunting buffalo is similar to hunting moose but a lot more dangerous. Buffalo won't hesitate to charge the hunter and they are hard to knock down."

The 1960 season was extended by two weeks and 100 licenses were offered. Hunters assumed that their buffalo safari would become an annual outing. But 1962 brought an outbreak of anthrax, a potential killer of humans, buffalo, cattle and other animals, both domestic and wild. The control program ended public hunting in the north for more years than anybody would have guessed.

The urge to kill a noble and guiltless animal like a buffalo was not to disappear, nor was the desire to cater to the needs and whims of the hunters for monetary gain. Inevitably, the character of the hunt was changing, almost beyond recognition. The leading actor in the new drama was, for better or worse, to be the "game farmer" who by raising animals of the conventional game varieties in well-fenced farm fields was in a position to sell the privileges of entering the said farm fields and blasting away at the peace-loving animals that couldn't escape. To some observers it looked like a game of slaughter more than of hunting. There was little more to be said for it except that the people who paid for the right to make quick and easy kills appeared to like it and so did those who collected the target fees.

Canadian farmers have always been encouraged to diversify their agricultural activities. Mixed farming was extolled as a form that minimized risks and soil depletion. The good farmer, it was said many times, wouldn't be caught "carrying all his eggs in one basket." Hence, farmers looking for new avenues of production, didn't overlook the possibility of adding game farming in some form to their operations. Interest widened in the early 1980s and provincial governments offered encouragement and made game farm licenses available. Alberta, in 1985, had not more than a dozen licensed game farms but at the time of writing in 1992, had close to 100.

The scheme for handy slaughter in farm fields was, of course, promoted for profit but had a fairly substantial body of support, much of it from provincial government departments. Conservationists and animal rights supporters disapproved and the resulting controversy became widespread and bitter. Nevertheless, buffalo, elk, deer and some other kinds were renamed "livestock" and a trade in breeding stock animals for private hunting grew.

An Alberta case winning the widest attention was a herd that belonged to an Indian reserve northwest of Edmonton. The Alexander Band obtained 50 buffalo from Elk Island Park herd in 1979 and did well with them in both herd growth and financial returns. It didn't go unnoticed that some of the oldest bulls in the herd had the meanest expressions and the best heads for trophies for wall displays. With many of the American hunters who had visited western Canada over the years, the heads were always the most important of valuable parts obtained from a buffalo hunt. Good heads suitable for mounting were valued at $1,000 each while the remaining parts of the carcass, including the edible portions, would not command more than $100.

The Band got the idea of capitalizing on the aging bulls that would normally be culled. These old and cranky fellows were segregated and offered to American trophy hunters as something very special. The visitors were impressed and didn't object to paying extra for the opportunity of making their own selections and shooting the best at close range. Satisfied customers told their friends and the Indians realized that they had developed a profitable trade.

Some Alberta hunters disapproved, saying it was "too much like shooting fish in a bowl."[151] An observer from the reserve was especially eager to make the point, however, that what they were doing was legal. Another observer who was visibly amused by the arguments, said: "I don't like the idea of using wild animals for private commercial slaughter but if the California big game and big money men would rather have our best old head than 5,000 American dollars, I'd say, 'Let's be neighbourly and take their money before they change their minds.'" Nevertheless, the old bulls didn't surrender quickly and according to a story from the reserve, it took from ten to a dozen California hunters "a week to kill eleven bulls."[152]

146   Dryden, Keith, A Treatise On Bison, Western Producer, Saskatoon, Dec. 11, 1969.
147   Strathmore Standard, Nov. 10, 1910.
148   Edmonton Journal, Oct 3, 1959.
149   Ibid.
150   The Albertan, Calgary, Oct. 10, 1959.
151   Damgaard, Niels, Calgary Herald, Feb. 9, 1987.
152   Masterman, Bruce, Calgary Herald, Feb. 12, 1989.

"I was more than ever struck with the likeness of the old (buffalo) bulls to lions. As we saw them standing apart on the low ridges and sandy knolls, eyeing us from afar with an air of savage watchfulness, — each neck with a luxuriant mane, swelled into greater largeness by the hump beneath it, each short tufted tail held straight out from the body in bold lion-like defiance."[153]

The Earl of Southesk

Chapter 24

Good For A Long Run

The most impressive feature about this mishappened animal's running is its stamina. If there is an explanation for its marathon performances – a thousand-mile tour of migration, or a wild stampede, or a 25- to 50-mile run to escape a prairie fire — it would probably be found in its "mishappened form." Two-thirds of the animal's weight is in the thorax where the vital organs, heart and lungs are encased, safeguarded and aided. The buffalo's running speed is not as fast as that of a pronghorn antelope or an English thoroughbred horse but fast enough to leave a farm horse far behind.

In the first years of buffalo captivity, there was little trafficking because of the difficulties and dangers in moving the animals from place to place. Purchasers and sellers were afraid of a herd on an open trail and skeptics prophesied that the proposed shipment of Pablo buffalo from Western Montana to Alberta would be a failure. But the art of handling and moving buffalo changed. James McKay, "Buffalo Jones," Pablo and Bedson discovered that bison could be driven more or less like cattle. It wasn't as easy but it could be done, and practical owners decided that the additional economy by moving buffalo on their own feet and legs justified the added risks.

The first buffalo herd to be moved overland by driving appears to have been the little band of 13 head that Col. Samuel Bedson bought at James McKay's sale at Deer Lodge in January, 1880 and then had to deliver to his home at Stony Mountain, some 21 or 22 miles away. It wasn't a big herd or a great distance but under the circumstances, it was a daring undertaking, complicated by the birth of a buffalo calf at the most inconvenient moment. And if the distinction of driving the first herd of buffalo overland belongs to Bedson and the honour of moving the largest total number of buffalo by any means to Michel Pablo, who holds the record for the longest buffalo drive? Probably that honour belongs to the Government of Canada, for its performance in transferring more than 6000 head from the National Buffalo Park at Wainwright to Wood Buffalo Park in the north. Whether the transfer was a colossal biological error is debatable but, the fact remains, it was a 700-mile journey, a little more than half of which was made by railroad and the balance made by barge on the Athabasca River.

But if it is an object to identify the longest overland buffalo drive on this continent, the story must return to that fabulous buffalo trafficker, C.J. "Buffalo" Jones who became a familiar figure in the Canadian west when he bought the Bedson herd in 1888 and planned the delivery that included an open trail drive from Stony Mountain to the Winnipeg Stock Yards and then railroad freight from there to Garden City, Kansas. And for anybody seeking excitement, there were buffalo plunging through stone walls, buffalo scaling stockyard fences, and buffalo breaking away from the stockyard enclosures and running non-stop all the way back to Stony Mountain.

The last known adventure in Jones' career it took place after his life-story was written and about the time he disappeared rather mysteriously. The story of the long drive began on the William Goodnight cattle ranch in Texas about the beginning of the present century. The owner kept cattle and some buffalo in which he had an indifferent interest. His wife, however, had a merciful feeling for animals and was sympathetic to the buffalo. All things considered, Goodnight concluded that he would be better off without the buffalo. Then, by coincidence, Jones who was always ready to buy or sell buffalo, came that way and asked the owner, "How much for the bunch?" Goodnight, in a moment of impatience, replied, "Give me $10 and take as many as you can round up away."

It took considerable time to collect the 200 or 300 head and get them started on the trail toward Flagstaff, Arizona. Jones and his two or three cowboys plodded on, across much of Texas, all of New Mexico and deep into Arizona, about a thousand miles. It took them almost 12 months. But Jones, it appears, finally, had enough. Suddenly, it seems, he left one of his cowboys in charge, took a train to the east and according to story, wasn't seen again. The cowboy, Owens by name, remained faithful to his former boss and the herd of buffalo until the courts declared him to be the owner of the herd. He did very convincingly, however, prove his claim to the distinction of being the man behind the longest buffalo drive on the continent.

Specimens and founding herds became wanted for parks and zoos all over the world. Canada, United States and Mexico were the only countries where the strain was indigenous and most solicitors looked hopefully to Canada. Crated representatives of the race were seen fairly often travelling by express, to roam where they had never roamed before. Germany, for example, was anxious to save its European bison from extermination and was ready to try some mild outcrosses with Canada's prairie strain. Twenty head were loaded out from Wainwright in 1935 and escorted to Berlin Zoological Gardens.[154] The more common requests were from British and European parks, seeking young buffalo for display and with the requests came some strange questions about their feeding, care and management. An English correspondent wanted to know if the Canadian buffalo they hoped to obtain were "house broken."

Numerous requests for buffalo came from Canadian communities, some of them very remote. New herds were wanted in Indian and Métis settlements in northern parts of the western provinces. Where feed and climate were considered reliable, the authorities made special efforts to furnish the buffalo to eager native people. The Waterhen area of northern Manitoba, 250 kilometres northwest of Winnipeg, seemed to meet the requirements. In 1984 a captive herd of 34 wood bison was established and in 1991, another 13 animals were released, four with radio collars. One bull remained within a 50 kilometre radius of the release site.[155]

The bison that became part of these experiments were bred and raised at Elk Island Park and, needless to say, they never saw their beautiful parkland again. In 1964, a herd of 24 head was shipped to spend the rest of their lives on the tiny Island of Brunette, seven square miles of loneliness in Fortune Bay on Newfoundland's south coast. Visitors to the island say its topography, climate and vegetation make it difficult to describe and impossible to match, leaving the biologists with two questions: first, could the island support the buffalo and, second, could the buffalo accept the island?

Seven years later, in 1971, only four of the founding animals were known to be alive with accidents accounting for some of the casualties. One of the buffalo drowned when being unloaded for release and two fell from a cliff and drowned in the sea. What happened to the other animals was never confirmed. However, six young buffalo were born on the island. The provincial wildlife biologist saw hope in the results of the first years, proving that the Brunette-born buffalo calves can survive. Journalists conjectured that the reason for the deaths on that Atlantic island about the size of a wheat farm on the Regina Plains, was probably suicide or a broken heart.

Buffalo travel both before and after accepting a degree of human control, invites contemplation. In their wild days, they travelled far and grazed in distant and beautiful places. In later years they travelled ugly city streets, suppressed their instinct to stampede or run away with the carts and harnesses to which they were tied, walked in Calgary's Annual Exhibition and Stampede Parade, travelled under protest to Montreal to be a part of the street parade at the World's Fair, Expo '67 and then travelled back to the more mundane business of farming — buffalo farming and ranching if you please!

153   The Earl of Southesk, in his book, Saskatchewan and the Rocky Mountains, p. 118, Edmonston and Douglas, Edinburgh, 1895.
154   Western Producer, Saskatoon, June 1, 1936.
155   Hal Reynolds, 1995.

"There is no animal in the world more clannish than the buffalo. The male calf follows the mother until two years old when he is driven out of the herd and the parental tie is then entirely broken. The female calf fares better, as she is permitted to stay with the mother's family for life, unless by some accident she becomes separated from the group . . . When separated by a stampede of other cause, they never rest until they are all together again. . . [161]

Ernest Thompson Seton

Chapter 25

A New Role for the Buffalo — Farming and Ranching

Indian elders prophesied that the buffalo would return, and return they did. But not the way the native people expected. There was no glorious descent on celestial wings from the abode of the Great Spirit. Rather, they returned to the Blackfoot Indians at Gleichen with the help of three big cattle-liners furnished by the Government of Canada.

It was early November 1967 and Canadians were celebrating the centennial anniversary of Confederation and doing it proudly. Anniversary projects were being pursued with imagination and financial assistance from the public treasuries. Canadians from coast to coast were studying their country's history, many of them for the first time. With varied emotions they were revisiting the fur-trade years, the acquisition of Rupert's Land, the land survey, the coming of the North West Mounted Police, the Land Act, immigration, homesteading and the destruction of the great herds of buffalo. History warned of extermination with a clear call for measures of restoration.

One of the acts to mark the centenary was a National Parks' proposal to place one or more small herds of their buffalo in a test of suitability for farming and ranching purposes. The Ottawa news release announced the intention to call for bids for a test herd of 25 healthy buffalo from Elk Island Park, east of Edmonton. "The idea of buffalo ranching had been around for years," the release noted, "but has met stiff provincial resistance until now."[162] Alberta was an example of that "stiff resistance" to use buffalo or other wild races in captivity. The arguments between government departments and farming and ranching interests had persisted through the years until seen as a wasted action.

Buffalo, according the Alberta Game Act, were big game animals that could not be kept legally in captivity except in locations constituted by license as game farms. To obtain such a license, the proposed farm was required to contain at least 160 acres of suitable land, adequately fenced and geographically furnished to ensure feed, good water, shelter and solitude. The game farm license fee was $100 and the Act warned that contravention of its provisions were punishable by fines of up to $100 or three months in jail.

Most citizens showed only slight interest in the "buffalo laws" at first but it seems the species touched the population in more ways than government workers had suspected. Even the Provincial Liquor Control Board found reason for concern. It took the position that the long familiar horseshoe-and-buffalo trademark of the Calgary Brewery for its beer would have to be removed from the company's bottles lest the handsome bison image be accused of promoting the product!

The next restriction appeared to be intended to force the famous pair of buffalo owned and used by the Calgary Exhibition and Stampede for parade and advertising purposes, to retire from the Calgary street parade where it was driven like a team of oxen. The two distinguished bison had been purchased as calves in Colorado by the veteran Stampede director, Dick Cosgrave, six years earlier and were very popular with Calgarians and visitors. Their orderly conduct in the excitement of the parade had impressed millions of viewers and many observers had difficulty in understanding the bureaucratic view that they should be removed from the parade.

But the interest in buffalo was finding a greater importance on farms and ranches where it had been slow in expressing itself. Imaginative herd owners like Col. Bedson, "Buffalo" Jones and Michel Pablo tested the potential in the '80s and '90s of the previous century but the results were not overwhelming and the agricultural industry was not ready for buffalo. But change was coming. A new chapter was about to be written in the deep and lonely valleys of the Alberta foothills where cattle ranching had its beginning three-quarters of a century earlier. The new hero was Fred C. Burton who bought his picturesque setting near "the end of the trail" toward Tornado Mountain in 1931 and lived there until his death in 1977. Burton had no proof that the breeding and raising of buffalo would be profitable but he admired the big and majestic animals and had a stubborn conviction that he should be free to breed and raise their kind on his ranch if he so wanted.

Although there was no privately-owned herd of buffalo in Alberta prior to 1951, there was the big federal government herd at the Range Experiment Station at Manyberries where it was being used in connection with the hybridization studies started a Wainwright and then transferred to Manyberries. Fred Burton visited Manyberries and enquired if he could buy some of the surplus young animals. "No," he was told because private ownership of such wild animals would be contrary to provincial policy and federal workers had no wish to become involved in provincial jurisdiction. "Then, how will you dispose of surplus young stock?" Burton asked. He was told that it was the practice to truck the saleable stock to the Calgary Stock Yards as if they were cattle intended for the meat trade.

"If I were present at the sale pens on the proper day, could I not make a bid to buy the critters?" Burton questioned again. The specialist at Manyberries wasn't very sure but said that as far as he knew, there was nothing to prevent Burton or anybody from making bids to purchase animals brought to the yards for sale. "The way to find out is to try it."

Burton learned that a truckload of yearling bulls and heifers would be forwarded to Calgary on a certain day. After driving much of the night, he was at the sale pens at an early morning hour and made the first bid on the eight buffalo from Manyberries, two bulls and six heifers, and was declared the buyer. Burton should have been worried about loading them on his old truck and starting out over the hundred-mile trip to the ranch. But Fred C. wasn't one to worry and he delivered what his son, Tim, called "Dad's Pets" to the ranch without mishap.[163] When nearing home, a neighbour waved and shouted: "What are you going to do with those monstrosities?" Said Burton: "Going to milk'em and start a dairy. Whiskey milkshakes will be our specialty."

The herd grew rapidly. Most cows calved with ease every second year and the calves weaned themselves at seven or eight months. And the Burton buffalo did not give much trouble by breaking pasture fences and wandering away. A fence with three or four strands of barbed wire was generally adequate but animals which appeared too circumspect to break through a barbed wire fence, could and would leap over fences of standard height with ease. Only one bull in the history of the Burton herds became a chronic fence jumper. But nobody worried because he always returned to jump back into his own pasture and join his friends.

The Burtons bought six hybrids of cattalo from the Manyberries Station but were not greatly impressed by them and did not keep them very long. No hybrids were ever produced by the intermingling of cattle and bison on the Burton place and that was quite satisfactory because the owners concluded that they did not need them or want them.

The buffalo herd grew to 65 head and was kept at about that size but its importance in history is due to two other factors. First, its existence ahead of other private herds and second, its place in the legal dispute about buffalo being owned and raised like farm cattle. The day on which Fred C. Burton was summoned to appear in court to face a charge of keeping wild animals contrary to the Game Laws of Alberta, and the subsequent outcome, shaped the provincial outlook of buffalo as farm and ranch livestock.

Fred C. was no stranger to the provincial statutes and probably welcomed the opportunity for a showdown. He engaged Charles Bennett of Claresholm to represent him and quipped good-naturedly that he hoped his neighbours would visit him if he took up residence in jail. The case took a day. The Provincial representative appeared confident and expected a judgment that would furnish fresh "muscle" for the enforcement of the Act. But the decision favoured Burton.

Mr. Burton died in 1977 and the ranch and buffalo were taken over by his son, Fred G. or "Tim." The herd received the same good attention that became a Burton tradition until 1991 when, in the face of increasing difficulty in keeping the buffalo in their own pasture, the herd was liquidated. Many of the animals were bought by new breeders, mainly in the Peace River region where interest was running high. It marked the end of 40 years of buffalo on the Burton ranch but buffalo have a habit of returning. Quipped Tim Burton, "Don't be surprised if you see another herd in these valleys."

In the same romantic foothills there were several younger herds that owed their existence to Fred C. Burton. There were herds on the historic A7 Ranch started by A.E. Cross, one of Albert's "Big Four Cattlemen," and on the celebrated Rocking P, where Roderich Macleay began to build a "cattle empire" in 1900 and left it, in 1953, to his daughters, Mrs. Maxine Chattaway and Mrs. Dorothy Blades.

Ernie and Dorothy Blades and family made their home on that portion of the original ranch that retained the Rocking P brand and name. Their initial purchase, in 1972, consisted of eleven head of young animals at a price of $800 each. They were brought to their new home in two truckloads and in recalling the delivery, Mr. Blades said there was fear at one point that the truck would be demolished. One young buffalo was killed by the others during transit but they settled down fairly quickly after being placed in their corral. Apparently the new owners weren't aware of a certain buffalo idiosyncrasy. The animals travel better if a canvas or tarpaulin covers the truck rack, thereby forcing the critters to travel in the dark.

Marketing surplus stock was never a problem. Blades owned his own slaughter house and refrigeration facilities which made it relatively easy to sell carcasses at about $1.50 per pound in recent years. Europe is a promising potential market for frozen carcasses delivered by air. More speculative will be the demand for buffalo hides and trophy heads from bulls of at least three or four years of age. Canadian producers have seen hide-and-head sets selling for up to $800. And understandably, returns from the sale of breeding stock will fluctuate widely. Mr. Blades, on one occasion, consigned five surplus young animals to an auction sales at Fort Macleod and received $1650 for one bull and an average of $1350 for the five. In 1992, Blades could count 1300 cattle and 76 buffalo on his rolling range east of beautiful Chain Lakes and the visitor wasn't likely to hear an unkind word about either cattle or buffalo running peacefully together.

The federal government's gesture of an anniversary gift of 25 breeding buffalo of the purest prairie strain — 22 females and three bulls — for the tribesmen living in Gleichen, seemed perfect. The twilight procession that formed behind the three cattle-liner trucks carrying the buffalo was no less appropriate, except it looked more like a reptilian monster slithering over the Blackfoot grass than an expression of joy and gratitude for the gift arriving with the compliments of Prime Minister Lester Pearson and his Cabinet. Following behind the big trucks were scores of Indian farm cars and trucks in various states of repair and still bearing traces of baked mud from the pot-hole season on the reservation trails, two or three school vans recruited to accommodate a hundred eager youngsters who had heard countless stories about buffalo but had never seen one, and a dozen or more saddle horses, with or without saddles.

The 25 buffalo were unloaded without mishap into a new corral and fed and watered. There then followed a great outpouring of oratory and the darkness did nothing to shorten the speeches. A government spokesperson said that if this experiment on the Blackfoot property was a success, it would be repeated on other reserves and in farming districts. It was up to the Blackfoot people to demonstrate their skill and dedication; it would be entirely up to the native residents to ensure that fences were high enough and in the best of repair, and that feed and water were always available and adequate.

Rev. Maurice Goutier, well-known in Blackfoot circles, was the next speaker. He expressed confidence that his Indian friends would accept the buffalo as one of the major challenges in their lives. [164] But the oratory was just beginning. Elders, inspired by the buffalo, insisted upon sharing their wisdom. The happy night wore on and a golden glow was showing clearly in the eastern sky before the last of the self-appointed buffalo caretakers threw additional hay to the buffalo, checked the corral fence and the lock on the gate and went home.

The arrival of the buffalo and the remarks from the government representative were taken as the clearest expressions to that time of the Feds endorsement of buffalo as worthy candidates for acceptance in farm and ranch production wherever a serious interest exists.

The critics were entitled to their opinion but more farmers were saying with reason: "If the government at Ottawa thinks the buffalo deserves consideration for a place in livestock farming in the years ahead, I'd be a fool to refuse them a trial."

Many of those who invested in test herds lost interest and dropped the project. Others like William Nilsson, who was already a big cattle operator at Clyde, Alberta, about 40 miles north of Edmonton, reported satisfaction. In the early

1970s when beef cattle producers were feeling hard times, Nilsson set out aggressively to find a way to bring diversity to his operations. He entered the building business in his area and yielded at the same time to the challenge of buffalo production. He wanted to buy a small starting herd but that wasn't easy to do because he knew of only two small herds in Alberta at the time. Nor had the government announced a sale by tender. Alternatively, he went to South Dakota and returned with 28 head, including some bought for his Alberta clients. In any case, the Nilsson herd grew to a total of 90 head in 1978 and Mr. Nilsson wanted more. When he heard that the Canadian government anticipated offering five lots of 25 head from Elk Island Park, he notified Ottawa that he would submit a tender for all of the five small herds. Ottawa, however, preferred to sell the animals to more than one buyer.

It was the very first sale involving more than one small herd. The accounting showed six purchasers for the 125 animals and a total return of $91,886, or an average for $739 per head. Of the six purchasers, two were located in the Province of Quebec and Mr. Nilsson was one of four from Alberta. The other three Albertans were Ray Croteau of Bonnyville, Mike Kapala of Gurneyville and Ken Miller of Milk River. The Nilsson purchase consisted of 13 animals acquired for an average price $692, bringing his total buffalo count to over 100 head, the biggest privately-owned herd in the province at that time.

By 1980, the Peace River area might have claimed the distinction of having the highest concentration of privately-owned captive buffalo in the west. Weather was forceful factor. Wet harvest seasons and the difficulty of selling tough grain drove grain growers to search for alternative avenues of income. Farming people like Matt Boake, with an abundance of grazing land beside the Pouce Coupe River where it discharges into the Peace River, elected to produce the low-risk forage crops and employ the buffalo to convert them to saleable form. The turning point for him came in 1980 when he made his initial bison purchase of four heifers. The Peace River program became popular with more buffalo per unit of land area than any other farm or ranch in present-day Alberta. It is easy to understand why Peace River has such a strong and active association of buffalo producers.

Saskatchewan, like Alberta, was traditionally buffalo country and there was never any doubt about buffalo in farm herds doing well in that part. William Bintner, farming at Barrier River, south of Melfort, has had his own herd since 1980 when he started with some animals brought from Wyoming. In 1992, the Bintner herd numbered about 50 head and was distinguished by the much-travelled herd bull. Bintner trucked "Sasquatch" to the National Stock Show at Lenve with a showring rating like a "supreme court" in its own right, and returned with the show's Grand Championship for buffalo bulls.[166]

For a while, Mr. Bintner was specializing in buffalo meat for discriminating markets. One of his elite outlets was a Saskatoon hotel which he served for 10 years and another was a food store with a national name. With the new prestige and the influence of an internationally recognized herd sire, the fame of Saskatchewan bison was sure to travel far.

Alberta public servants with an interest in the buffalo, made an effort in February 1992 to obtain "round figure" statistics and satisfied themselves that they had a hundred farms and ranches in the province on which buffalo were being kept and bred. The total population indicated 7,537 animals of all ages, of which 2,647 were mature breeding females. It was then presumed that the 1992 calf crop was sufficient to bring the total population to 9,913, close enough to 10,000 to suit most needs.

Obtaining reliable counts of buffalo owned on Canadian farms and ranches has not been easy, due in part to the strange and lazy habit of counting buffalo as cattle instead of giving them the identity they deserve. The Canada Year Book, at the time of writing, was not even indexing the buffalo or bison. The old and admirable race was both dishonoured and ignored.

161   Seton, Ernest Thompson, Life Histories of Northern Animals, vol. II, Published by Charles Scribners' Sons, New York, 1909.
162   Edmonton Journal, April 13, 1967.
163   Burton, Fred G. (Tim), Interview at the Burton ranch, Oct.21, 1992.
164   Canadian Cattlemen, Article by I.H. Williams, August issue, p.10, August, 1968.
165   Canadian Cattlemen, I.H. Williams article, Aug. 1968 issue, p.10.
166   Western Producer, Saskatoon, Feb.20, 1992.

"Apparently, during the days of the great free-roaming herds, the buffalo were free of any of the serious animal diseases. However, they have been found to be highly susceptible to tuberculosis when brought in contact with that infection. . . There are now about 18,000 buffalo in the Wood Buffalo Park area. Unfortunately, the Wainwright animals appear to have carried tuberculosis infection thereto. Slaughtering under federal government veterinary inspection during the period 1946-1955 disclosed a 40 per cent incidence of tuberculosis among the slaughtered animals. . . It should be noted that tuberculosis is transmissible — under favourable conditions — from animal to animal of almost any species, from infected animals to mankind, and vice versa. All species of the bovine family, the deer family, swine and all birds are susceptible.[156]

T. Childs

Chapter 26

Dilemma — Horns And All

Any nation processing a big herd of unhealthy buffalo, diseased to the point of being a possible source of further infection, yet popular with wildlife lovers, has the makings of a national dilemma. Canada "rode on the horns" of such a dilemma for 70 years, waiting for politicians to declare decisions that should have been ratified at least a generation earlier. The biggest visible change in buffalo administration was in redistribution of the national herd but nothing was done to ease the crisis of tuberculosis among the buffalo. The Wainwright park was stripped of its animal population while the still bigger Wood Buffalo Park — 44,000 square kilometres or 17,300 square miles and, thus, bigger than Switzerland or Denmark — became the new geographical centre of buffalo population and disease in Canada.

Nobody knew the exact source of the tuberculosis infection that presumably entered Alberta soon after the beginning of the present century and completely changed buffalo history in the Canadian west. There was speculation that the diseases were introduced by the Michel Pablo animals or other importations after 1907 but there was no supporting evidence. Nevertheless, tuberculosis and brucellosis were first discovered in Wainwright buffalo in 1919.

When Dr. Seymour Hadwen, pathologist at the Ontario Research Foundation, was invited in 1923 to consider the health of the Wainwright herd and issue a report, he seized the opportunity to attend the slaughter and post-mortem examinations of 264 park buffalo. Shocked by what he observed, he gave as his opinion that between one-quarter and one-half of the Wainwright buffalo were infected with tuberculosis or brucellosis or both. He advised substantial herd reduction be achieved by progressive slaughter of old animals and any that gave the slightest sign of suffering from tuberculosis. There is no reason to believe that Hadwen was consulted about the plan to reduce the prairie herd by sending 6,000 or more buffalo from the Wainwright park to share the environment with disease-free wood bison in Wood Buffalo National Park. He would have recognized the hazards, spreading the disease and destroying the genetic purity of both strains.

Canada's Department of Agriculture regarded it as a great double triumph when, in 1985, it announced that the nation's cattle herds were, at last, brucellosis-free and a short time later, tuberculosis-free. The same, however, cannot be said of Canada's buffalo herds and as long they are infected, the possibility of reinfecting of cattle herds exists. Therein is the reason for the repeated demands from cattlemen and cattlemen's organizations for the complete destruction of northern herds known to be infected with tuberculosis and brucellosis. Anthrax, while an environmental contaminant, is not actively carried by the animals except during an outbreak when dying animals further contaminate more area.

The surprise attack of anthrax in the wood buffalo country, east of the Slave River and north of Fort Smith in 1962, was its first appearance known to man, thereabouts. It is almost a sure killer and doesn't waste much time in completing its work, polluting the soil and surroundings with spores capable of perpetuating the organism for many years to come. Tuberculosis had become so widespread and commonplace that the mention of the name was said to produce little more than a yawn in the area of Wood Buffalo Park, but not so with anthrax. The word shocked wildlife workers in the north and left stockmen a thousand miles to the south, with a feeling of anxiety.

The magnitude of the biologist's problem during the epidemic was indicated when N.S. Novakowski, a long-time worker with the Canadian Wildlife Service, wrote that "approximately 10,000 square miles of bison range is now infected and there can be little doubt that positive control measures are necessary. Burial of carcasses has in itself proved to be an ineffective and expensive method. Although this process must be continued as long as the bison are dying from the disease, other measures should be adopted as soon as possible to control the disease."[157]

Northern federal workers responded to the call like a fire department answering an alarm. They buried and lymed dead carcasses, halted and rerouted all traffic in the emergency zone and attempted to round up and drive out of the area all healthy animals in the hope of preventing further infection. The remoteness of the area made the tasks additionally difficult. Given anthrax is such an unsatisfactory working subject — invisible, unpredictable, durable and destructive — it was almost impossible to know when disease control measures were really effective.

For a glimpse of how the anthrax battle was fought in the chilly and silent north, reader attention is directed to extracts from a letter of instructions sent by A.E. Lewis, district veterinarian at Calgary to a junior colleague on August 17, 1962.

"Anthrax," wrote the senior officer, "has been diagnosed in buffalo north of Fort Smith, NWT, in an area between the Slave and Taltson Rivers. The evidence indicates there are 200 carcasses and these must be disposed of by deep burial or burning. You are to proceed to Fort Smith via Pacific Western Airlines. . .

"The infected area is about 60 miles north of Fort Smith. The wildlife people will take you to the infected area where arrangements are being made to house and feed about 50 men (at) an abandoned sawmill. You will be given quarters that have been removed from a one-half ton truck. . . You will direct and supervise the burials. It is imperative that a grave be dug beside each carcass. You must not permit the transporting of dead animals because this would contaminate all the area over which the animal had (been) moved.

"When the hole is dug and the carcass put into it, the ground around the carcass is to be covered with a lye solution. The carcass is to be covered with lyme and the earth where the carcass was lying is to be pushed into the hole. This will be a long pit and after the carcass is in the hole, the bulldozer will push the earth close to the carcass and this will permit a better coverage of the carcass with lyme... As you are aware, it is imperative that nobody touches these carcasses. The labourers may be tempted to take horns but this must not happen.

"No one must be permitted to take a trophy. It is also important that Indians do not take carcasses for dog meat... It is possible that a few carcasses are in areas that are swampy and it may be impossible to dig a hole. In such cases, the carcasses must be burned completely and the forestry people will assist in this work. This will require fuel oil, old hay, trees and the forestry people will have flame torches.

"After each burial the bulldozer is to be cleaned as well as possible and sprayed with lye solution... Arrangements are being made to drive the buffalo in the infected area north and we want to know how this project gets along, also about any more deaths... There is some indication that, after the burial is completed, the forestry people will burn off the infected area but this will not be under our supervision. From our point of view it is not necessary to burn the abandoned sawmills or other camps."[158]

A few minor outbreaks of anthrax occurred in the north following the 1962 epidemic, thus pointing to the high quality of the work performed by Canada's teams of scientists and technicians. But Canadians hadn't yet heard the last of the complaints about the federal government's failure to come to grips with certain of the perils of the north, tuberculosis, brucellosis and now anthrax. Agriculturalists became the most vociferous, especially since anthrax threatened to become entrenched in the area of Wood Buffalo National Park.

The fears of Western cattlemen were growing. More and more farmers and ranchers were trucking cattle into the Ft. Vermilion area in Alberta for summer grazing, and encroachment upon Wood Buffalo Park raised the possibilities of interbreeding and accompanying disease risks. "Sooner or later," said observers, "the Park's treasured isolation will be breached and the work of years in recovering a strain of pure wood buffalo (1925-28 reintroduced plains bison) will be lost, to say nothing of the new danger of disease transmission, southward."

Southern stockmen, fearful of anthrax infection being transmitted to their ranges by predators, carrion feeders and even human travellers, braced themselves to demand nothing less than the complete destruction of diseased herds. Northern Indians, Métis, hunters and naturalists argued for increased testing for disease, additional segregation of northern buffalo after testing, added use of fencing, improved isolation and buffer zones. It was generally agreed that animals known by test to be diseased should be slaughtered but beyond that there should be compromise.

Northern citizens were far from agreement about the best policies. One of the clearest voices belonged to Ken east, superintendent of the National Park from 1980 to 1990, but he didn't always echo the sentiment expressed by most northerners. He sounded more like a philosopher than a public servant when he said: "You must not consider the Armageddon solution unless you've exhausted every other alternative." east believed that the large scale slaughter of the big park herd should be made "as the very last resort." Superintendent east, as a member of the federal task force appointed to find answers to the buffalo questions of the day, warned that the panel "will have to weigh commercial and scientific priorities against Canadian historic obligations to one of its most majestic and ill-treated wild animals."[159]

One year later, Ken east spoke to the Saskatchewan Stock Growers' at Saskatoon about the agency's resolution for total destruction of these animals. "My point of view is that it seems to be naively optimistic. The suggestion has been made without sound knowledge of the area and the logistics. The bison herd is not just in the park, this is 44,000 square kilometres of rugged mountainous countryside."[160] To make his point more convincing, east could have told the audience about the wood buffalo that were "discovered" in the northwest corner of Wood Buffalo Park in 1957 after being lost for 17 years.

The task force reporting in 1988 offered various solutions to the dilemma. Members of the force might have yawned and said: "We've considered them all before." One was the construction of a fence of unusual strength around the park perimeter of 1,160 kilometres or 696 miles. The estimated price was $28 million, and the cost to patrol and service it was staggering. A fence with ample buffer zones in which almost unlimited hunting would be allowed was also suggested as was a partial fence, built only where the need was considered most important. The latter fence would give the appearance of always being in disrepair. The two remaining proposals were likely to receive the most support. One, more of the same or "status quo" and, finally, the destruction of all the buffalo of mixed strains. The slaughter of the main park herd — half of which are believed to be infected with tuberculosis or brucellosis or both — is the decision which the federal government has successfully avoided for the better half of this century.

While the report was acknowledged as a good effort, it didn't really settle anything and a year or two later it was routinely referred to the Federal Environmental Assessment and Review panel. When the action to destroy the free ranging buffalo on and around the Park was favoured, more public hearings and more consultations with prescribe authorities followed. Finally, it was made clear that there could be no action until the Government of Canada, in consultation with the Governments of Alberta and the Northwest Territories, gave approval.

There could be no better guarantee of further delay and the 4800 buffalo in the free-ranging northern herd — neither seriously disturbed about their incurable infirmities nor greatly worried about their proximity to anthrax — were granted a further reprieve.

As we near the end of this chapter, there must be moral principles and lessons waiting to be sounded. One century ago there was grave fear that the bison species was heading straight for extinction. As it turned out, the race missed oblivion by a small margin. Nevertheless, Canadians should be thankful that bison numbers have grown to the point of offering perfect security in each of three distinct forms of useful service:

Park herds, big or small.

Free ranging wild herds in carefully chosen regions, mainly in the north.

The new and expanding role of buffalo in Canadian agriculture

156   Childs, T., Tuberculosis Widespread Among Our Northern Bison, Western Producer, Saskatoon, Date missing.
157   Novakowski, N.S., Report and Recommendations Concerning the Occurrence and Control of Anthrax in Bison in Wood Buffalo Park and Vicinity, Canadian Wildlife Service, Edmonton, 1964.
158   Lewis, A.E., District Veterinarian Calgary (Federal) Letter to W.M. Norton, Veterinarian in charge, Camrose, Aug. 17, 1962.
159   Bergman, Brian, Disease May Force Slaughter Of The Bison, (Reference to east) Edmonton Journal, Dec. 4, 1988.
160   Calgary Herald, Cattlemen Call For Destruction Of Bison, Sept. 2, 1989.

Epilogue

Will Canada Contribute to Conservation?

Gordon R. Kerr

North American bison played an important role in the evolution of the Great Plains region of the continent. The ecological balance of the Prairies, directly reflected in its vegetation and animal communities, was greatly influenced by the dominant herbivore whose primary range within Canada comprised major portions of present-day Alberta, Saskatchewan, Manitoba and the southwestern reaches of the Northwest Territories. Once viewed as in unlimited supply both the plains bison and the wood bison declined to perilous levels by 1885. With the disappearance of the bison, so vanished the buffalo wolf, the swift fox and the grizzly bear from the plains.

Long after the bison's decline, Canada implemented protection and recovery efforts. Bison protection and recovery rested with the Government of Canada until 1930 when through The Natural Resources Transfer Act jurisdiction for land and resources was transferred to the prairie provinces. By this date there were no free roaming bison on provincial lands and so research and conservation of bison remained primarily a federal effort.

However, during the 1960s governments faced heightened public sensitivities to environmental issues and found it necessary to form environment departments. By 1977, federal and provincial agencies formed the Committee On Status of Endangered Wildlife In Canada (COSEWIC) to identify threatened and endangered species, and to formulate recovery recommendations. Similar public concern in the United States resulted in the Endangered Species Act and related recovery efforts. The wood bison, first classified as an 'endangered' in 1978 was down-listed to 'threatened' in 1988 as herd numbers increased.

Meanwhile the smaller subspecies, the plains bison, benefited from captive husbandry. Canada's first major bison conservation effort occurred between 1906 and 1910 with plains bison in Buffalo Park at Wainwright and Elk Island National Park near Edmonton, Alberta. This commitment plus other public and private herd developments elsewhere on the continent secured the future of plains bison as a subspecies. By 1992, because of limited land area, the total number of animals under the federal government's care was not markedly greater than originally purchased from Michel Pablo in 1906. Current opportunities to expand that number on specifically dedicated lands appear remote with the possible exception of the recently formed Grasslands National Park in southern Saskatchewan. Interestingly, author MacEwan served, during the 70s, as chairman of the joint federal-provincial committee to conduct public hearings for this 360-square-mile park. The greatest growth of plains bison has been in private herds.

In 1922, Wood Buffalo National Park was created to save the estimated 1,500 to 2,000 wood bison from extinction, but the security of the subspecies was placed in peril when plains bison from Wainwright were relocated to the new park between 1925 and 1928. The Wainwright bison were known to be infected with both bovine tuberculosis and brucellosis. Although scientific opinion then indicated that the Wainwright bison should have been slaughtered to control the diseases, public objection and political procrastination prevented it.

With the mistaken belief that primarily older animals were infected — because they more commonly showed the symptoms — only younger animals were relocated. This decision resulted in two serious biological errors: the introduction of diseases into an otherwise healthy wood bison herd and the introduction of plains bison features into the wood bison gene pool. Initially, bison numbers increased rapidly in the new park and by 1934, there were approximately 12,000 animals. However, the only known wood buffalo herd had become diseased and the gene pool hybridized.

Fortunately, Dr. Nick Novakowski of the Canadian Wildlife Service discovered, in 1957, a "lost" herd of what he suspected were wood bison near Nyarling River and Buffalo Lake. Collection of three specimens proved his suspicions to be correct. In February 1963, some 77 wood bison were captured near Needle Lake. Subsequent disease tests showed one animal positive for tuberculosis and 52 per cent infected with brucellosis. The remaining 21 animals were selected for a future recovery herd and all but two were successfully corralled west of Fort Smith, Northwest Territories.

Unfortunately, an outbreak of anthrax struck the park in 1962, forcing officials to remove the healthy animals to a distant but suitable range north of Fort Providence, Northwest Territories. Eighteen wood bison were shipped to what is now the Mackenzie Bison Sanctuary, resulting in the establishment of the present day herd of over 2,000 animals. In February 1965, a second roundup in the Needle Lake area resulted in 40 wood bison being transported to corrals at Fort Smith. It was decided to relocate 23 animals to holding pens in Elk Island

National Park given the ongoing threat of anthrax. By 1991, the sum of these efforts produced about 2,500 wood bison, mostly in small, free-roaming herds from Manitoba to the Yukon. Another 540 animals existed in captivity beyond their natural range.

Despite decades of effort, the future of the wood bison remains as tenuous today as it did in 1925. Disease and genetic management in and around Wood Buffalo National Park remains a subject of concern for both the Wood Bison Recovery Team and more recently, Canada's extensive cattle industry. Increasingly, it has become a practice to truck livestock north for summer grazing and back south for the winter. Some of the grazing areas are close enough to the park to present a definite risk of spread of the diseases.

Livestock industry interests proposed the eradication of the Wood Buffalo Park area bison herd and its replacement with healthy wood bison. Wildlife agencies recognized this as an opportunity to correct both the disease problem and the genetics which had plagued wood bison recovery. They lent their support to the livestock industry proposal. However, controversy over this proposed eradication of the diseased herd, escalated to involve the jurisdictions of federal, provincial and territorial governments among others, and the issue became the subject of the Environmental Impact Assessment and Review Panel (EARP) hearings in 1990. The main conclusion of the panel was: "Eradication of the existing bison population is the only method of eliminating the risk of transmission of bovine brucellosis and tuberculosis from bison in and around Wood Buffalo National Park to domestic cattle, wood bison and humans." The Government of Canada received the report and proceeded to form the Northern Buffalo Management Board in June of 1991. This board deliberated at length and delivered to the federal government yet another report on March 31, 1993.

On April 21, 1995, the Government of Canada announced that it would spend $5 million to "fund research on bison ecology to learn more about the dynamics of predators, disease and habitat change on the population of park bison." Money, a buffer zone and a surveillance effort are being offered in the hope of containing the sick animals within the park. The probability of disease contamination of the world's largest herd of wood bison, resident in Canada's Mackenzie Bison Sanctuary and once before brought back from the brink of extinction, threatens to negate all conservation efforts to date in the heart of the wood bison historic range. Given the mobility of these wonders of the wild, the virulent spread of disease throughout all free populations of wood bison existent on the continent looms in the shadows, ready to spring into reality at any moment.

When this happens — given history and circumstances it is hard to be reassured that it will not — the ensuing loss of opportunities, both economic and biological, may well terminate the wood bison as a subspecies, forever. Have we learned nothing in these past 70 years? Do we have to make the same ill-advised mistake as made at Wainwright Buffalo Park when the diseased herd was "saved" only to threaten the existence of viable healthy populations?

Scientifically-based speculations of climate change most commonly predict global warming; if true, it is not unreasonable to speculate that prairie climate and, thus, lowland meadows will become more common throughout the Mackenzie River Valley as it stretches north to the Beaufort Sea. What are the future prospects for a bison-based industry should even a fraction of those speculations be realized? Could bison become a major northern industry? What will be the opportunities foregone for northern Canadians if the diseases in and around Wood Buffalo National Park spread beyond the present-day range and become, in all practicality, out of control and beyond correction? Of what value is Wood Buffalo National Park without healthy wood bison? Will we continue to ignore the opportunity to eradicate the diseases as these spread and render the wood bison as a species sacrificed for all time? If we do — it will not be the scientists, the Environmental Assessment and Review Panel, or the Northern Buffalo Management Board who have failed in their task of preservation — rather, the bungled rescue will rest on the shoulders of governments who, once again, have failed to follow scientific advice. Will the sacred spirit of the buffalo — with its great gift to all — be sacrificed yet again through human-kind's self-serving values and political procrastination?

A Ray of Hope for the Bison

Ronald W. Pauls

There are an estimated 200,000 bison in North America, up to 18,000 of them in Alberta alone. But today's bison are generally not free-ranging; most animals live inside fences as managed herds. Once an endangered species, bison are now highly prized by an industry that is seeking profitable alternatives to traditional cattle ranching. Bison ranches now number over 400 in Canada and many more operate in the United States. Few bison females with any chance of producing calves are being slaughtered today. Herd size has been increasing approximately 25 per cent per year since the early 1980s, and this growth rate is expected to continue.

What makes bison an attractive alternative to traditional livestock is its gift for self-sufficiency. If a producer provides access to adequate feed and water, bison will largely look after themselves. Bison rarely have difficulty calving. Tolerance of extreme cold is another attribute.

Bison can survive blizzards because they can use their large muzzles and beards to sweep snow aside and expose forage. Their ability to endure winter conditions results from the efficient digestion of the low-protein, high-fibre forage. This enables the species to survive where cattle would starve, and to thrive where cattle would not. Due to an adaptation known as nitrogen recycling and the fact that food passes more slowly through the digestive tract, bison obtain a substantial proportion of their nutrition from the digestion of microorganisms in the gut which live on the forage they consume. The slow passage of food through the digestive tract allows more time for the microorganisms in the gut to digest low quality forage. Moreover, most mammals excrete urea, a nitrogen-based product of protein metabolism, through the kidneys. Bison recycle a substantial proportion of their urea back to the gut, where it is used by microorganisms to synthesize additional protein. This reduces the need for protein in feed. For the bison producer, the ability of the bison to gain weight on lower quality and less costly feed translates into lower costs.

Dr. Ken Throlson, a well-known North Dakota bison rancher and veterinarian, believes bison have the strongest immune system of any large mammals in North America: they rarely need antibiotics or other medication. However, captive bison are susceptible to intestinal parasites which may reduce their growth and calving rates. Most bison producers control parasites with some form of medication added to feed or water, or with an annual injection. In boreal regions, black flies and other biting insects are merciless during the summer months. Unless insect control is provided, cattle will lose weight but bison tolerate insects better and, thus, continue to thrive during the fly season.

Bison are well adapted to extensive rangelands and widely dispersed water sources as they will travel much further from water sources to feed than cattle. The same change in the pelvic girdle which causes calving difficulty in cattle also makes walking more difficult. As a result, cattle tend to overgraze the range near water sources and to undergraze the range further away.

Bison live longer than cattle. This means female bison typically produce many more calves than female cattle. Although bison were once thought to be less fertile than cattle, today more than 90 per cent of mature cows will calve in a well-managed herd. Ranchers have found that the key to high calving rates is high quality pasture during the month or two preceding the August mating season. On poor quality range, bison cows forego reproduction in favour of survival.

Even with all these advantages, bison may sometimes cost more to produce than domestic cattle. They require a year longer to reach slaughter weight and reproductive maturity. They also require a higher proportion of breeding bulls to cows: in bison the ratio is typically 10 cows per bull compared to 40 cows per bull in cattle. The reason for this difference is the large amount of time and effort a bison bull puts into courtship. A bull will typically court a cow for one to two days before breeding her and moving on to another cow. During this time he tends the cow continuously, moving whenever she moves and keeping rival males away.

The extra-strong fences and heavy-duty handling facilities required for bison are another add-on to the cost of production. Some bison producers use lighter cattle fences with varying degrees of success. But effective bison fences are higher, stronger and often constructed of woven wire. Small holding corrals and handling chutes for bison usually are solidly closed in at the sides with a minimum height of seven feet, or they are closed in at the top. If a bison which feels threatened can see even a small opening, it will charge repeatedly in a bid for freedom and may injure itself or other animals.

Environmentalists are enthusiastic about replacing cattle with bison on native rangelands. Bison feed primarily on grasses, but cattle eat both grasses and forbs, non-grass vegetation which doesn't regenerate well on prairie land. This means that forbs have a greater chance of survival and, therefore, native rangelands retain greater botanical diversity. Also, because they are more mobile than cattle, bison concentrate less of their activity around water and are less destructive of nesting waterfowl and riparian habitat.

The bison industry is still small compared to the beef industry. Until recently, most producers personally sold to the consumer. While some of the industry has already grown too large to continue marketing in this manner, it still remains too small to provide the consistent, year-round supply required by the large food distribution chains. The "middlemen" typical of the cattle industry — auction marts, feedlot operators and wholesale meat distributors — are entering the bison industry in greater numbers. For example, Moore's Auctioneering in Alberta is an active auction mart for bison and the Canada North Marketing Corporation, formed in 1991, promotes bison products to global markets. Currently, Alberta bison are sold in the United States, Japan, France and Belgium and the meat is a specialty item in fine diners worldwide.

One of the issues producers are debating is the question of selection criteria for breeding stock. Many in the industry feel that natural selection has resulted in an animal with optimal growth rate, size, and other characteristics and argue that producers should select average rather than "superior" animals for breeding. Others suggest that the near extermination of the bison in the late 1880s resulted in a loss of genetic diversity. This was aggravated, they say, by extensive inbreeding among the small numbers of remaining bison from which present herds developed and, thus, today's bison are smaller and have a slower growth rate than bison before the slaughter. Selective breeding, therefore, is thought to restore the original size and growth rate. The debate continues.

Whether selective breeding is deliberate or inadvertent, it appears likely that the characteristics of ranched bison will be altered over time. To guard against the loss of characteristics now valued by the bison industry, large, unmanaged public herds may be necessary. Such a safeguard is currently provided by large herds of plains bison in their native habitats in various parks and sanctuaries across North America. However, the status of the wood bison is less secure. Only one large herd of free-ranging wood bison exists in its native habitat, the Mackenzie Bison Sanctuary in Canada's Northwest Territories. But this herd is under constant threat of genetic contamination and disease from the nearby herd of hybrid and diseased bison in Wood Buffalo National Park.

That the wood bison's survival is so tenuous has come to the attention of industry. In early 1993, Syncrude Canada Ltd. of Fort McMurray, Alberta, in partnership with the nearby aboriginal community of Fort MacKay, brought 30 wood bison from Elk Island National Park to land reclaimed from the company's Athabasca oil sands extraction activity. This marked the beginning of a five-year project to examine the productivity of reclaimed grasslands and their suitability for bison. By early 1995, eleven bison born on the Syncrude site and additional animals brought in from Elk Island and Banff National Parks had increased this herd to 58 animals.

The Athabasca oil sands deposit lies in the boreal forest zone of northeastern Alberta and is so immense that it reaches to a point 80 kilometres south of Wood Buffalo National Park, and entirely within the wood bison's original range. Two giant oil sands extraction and upgrading plants in the area, Syncrude Canada Ltd. and its smaller counterpart, Suncor Ltd., together provide some 18 per cent of Canada's crude oil production. The surface mines, tailing ponds, and other features associated with these developments have resulted in approximately 130 square kilometres of disturbance to date. The surface already mined represents only a small proportion of mineable oil sands in the area, and additional future developments are certain to occur. As a result, land disturbance is expected to more than double over the next 30 years.

There were initial concerns that bison traffic would compact the newly rebuilt soil which had not had time to develop internal structure. This would reduce water absorption and aeration, and ultimately affect productivity. The Alberta Research Council has conducted soil studies within the bison enclosure and has found no significant changes in the chemical and physical structure of soils over the first two growing seasons. Preliminary results suggest the land can support one bison per two hectares with rotational grazing, annual fertilization and feeding during the winter months. Further studies will be done.

In 1995, Syncrude submitted an updated Land Conservation and Reclamation Plan to Alberta Environmental Protection. On the 250 square kilometres of land that will be disturbed, the company proposes to create a mosaic of grassland, forest, wetland and lakes capable of supporting between 1,000 and 2,500 bison, depending on the nature and intensity of management. If future oil sands projects choose a similar reclamation strategy, the area could one day support the largest wood bison herd in the world.

The wisdom of converting boreal forest to grassland has been the subject of considerable debate, both in public hearings concerning an increase in Syncrude's production limit and in informal discussions. Those in favour suggest that introducing a small area of grassland relative to the huge expanse of boreal forest in northeastern Alberta will bring about desirable regional diversity in landform without significantly reducing habitat for boreal wildlife. Nor will it reduce production of timber and pulp. From a local and regional perspective, a large bison herd can be a significant renewable resource and the basis for a new and profitable tourism or ranching industry. From a larger perspective, it is not clear whether these lands are more valuable as forest lands or grasslands. Further economic studies will help to clarify this question but will not definitively answer it. Value judgments are involved.

Opponents of conversion suggest that constraints of climate and soil quality in the area will make grassland unproductive without major ongoing management. Furthermore, they argue that the same climatic factors that led to the development of boreal forest in this area during the 10,000 years since the glaciers retreated will ultimately lead back to boreal forest. Without bison, there is little doubt that this will happen unless global warming moves the limit of naturally occurring grassland northwards. With bison, the encroachment of forest on grassland will be slowed. In fact, it may not occur for centuries, if at all.

A free-ranging herd in the Athabasca oil sands area would face the same risks of disease and hybridization with bison from Wood Buffalo National Park as the herd in the Mackenzie Bison Sanctuary north of the park now faces. This may require that the area be fenced like Elk Island National Park. However, the declining numbers of the diseased park herd, the existence of the Mackenzie herd north of the park, and the development of a larger healthy herd in the oil sands area south of the park may make removal of the diseased park herd more palatable to those currently opposed to this action. The presence of the diseased herd is the major constraint to the return of free-ranging wood bison to much of their former range.

Local communities may find the commercial potential of a bison industry based on land reclaimed from oil sands mining an irresistible opportunity. These lands have the potential to support a multi-million-dollar sustainable industry and provide much needed economic diversification in the area. Regardless of the management option chosen, bison could be a valuable legacy of the oil sands industry to this region, either as the largest free-roaming herd of wood bison in the world or as the basis of a sustainable economy for the region after the oil sands have been exhausted. Time will tell.

Olson '93

208